THE GREEN QUOTIENT
Insights from Leading Experts on Sustainability

Charles Lockwood

Urban Land Institute

Project Staff

RACHELLE L. LEVITT
Executive Vice President, Global Information Group
Publisher

DEAN SCHWANKE
Senior Vice President, Publications and Awards

JAMES A. MULLIGAN
Managing Editor/Manuscript Editor

BETSY VANBUSKIRK
Creative Director

ANNE MORGAN
Graphic Design

CRAIG CHAPMAN
Director, Publishing Operations

RECOMMENDED BIBLIOGRAPHIC LISTING:
Lockwood, Charles. *The Green Quotient: Insights from Leading Experts on Sustainability.*
Washington, D.C.: Urban Land Institute, 2009.

Urban Land Institute
1025 Thomas Jefferson Street, N.W.
Suite 500 West
Washington, D.C. 20007-5201

ULI Catalog Number: G19
ISBN: 978-0-87420-121-5

10 9 8 7 6 5 4 3 2 1
Printed in the United States of America.

Library of Congress Cataloging-in-Publication Data

Lockwood, Charles.
   The green quotient : insights from leading experts on sustainability /
Charles Lockwood.
      p. cm.
   ISBN 978-0-87420-121-5
   1. Sustainability--Social aspects. 2. Sustainable development--Social
aspects. 3. Sustainable development—Political aspects. 4. Consumption
(Economics)—Environmental aspects. 5. Interviews. I. Title.
   HC79.E5L637 2009
   338.9'27—dc22

2009015524

About the Urban Land Institute

The mission of the Urban Land Institute is to provide leadership in the responsible use of land and in creating and sustaining thriving communities worldwide. ULI is committed to

- Bringing together leaders from across the fields of real estate and land use policy to exchange best practices and serve community needs;

- Fostering collaboration within and beyond ULI's membership through mentoring, dialogue, and problem solving;

- Exploring issues of urbanization, conservation, regeneration, land use, capital formation, and sustainable development;

- Advancing land use policies and design practices that respect the uniqueness of both built and natural environments;

- Sharing knowledge through education, applied research, publishing, and electronic media; and

- Sustaining a diverse global network of local practice and advisory efforts that address current and future challenges.

Established in 1936, the Institute today has more than 38,000 members worldwide, representing the entire spectrum of the land use and development disciplines. ULI relies heavily on the experience of its members. It is through member involvement and information resources that ULI has been able to set standards of excellence in development practice. The Institute has long been recognized as one of the world's most respected and widely quoted sources of objective information on urban planning, growth, and development.

Foreword

SINCE ITS FOUNDING IN 1936, THE URBAN LAND INSTITUTE HAS SUPPORTED high-quality planning and architectural design to ensure the best use of land, create better commercial districts and residential neighborhoods, and generate long-term value for investors and owners, as well as the surrounding communities.

Famed developer J.C. Nichols, one of the founders of ULI, was the master planner and developer of the Country Club District in Kansas City, Missouri, the largest contiguous master-planned community in the United States, which he began building in 1906 and completed in 1950. Nichols created a development process he called "planning for permanence." He wanted to "develop whole residential neighborhoods that would attract . . . people who desired a better way of life," and that is what he did.

At the turn of the 20th century, Nichols was one of a handful of developers who espoused and carried out such advanced planning theories. Other well-planned communities have remained attractive and desirable decade after decade, from Forest Hills in Queens, New York, and Chestnut Hill in Philadelphia, to Shaker Heights, Ohio, and Beverly Hills, California.

While Nichols's principles were ignored by too many city and urban planners and developers in the second half of the 20th century—during which the United States shifted to an automobile-dependent culture and built environment epitomized by widespread metropolitan areas and single-use suburban sprawl—his basic community development principles remain valid. The new urbanist movement that began in the 1990s, for example, drew much of its inspiration from Nichols and the Country Club District.

In the 1990s, ULI emphasized and promoted smart growth, the precursor to sustainability, which continues to be a focus of the Institute. Since the dawn of the 21st century, sustainable—or green—buildings have become an increasingly vital component of successful community development. Green buildings incorporate design, technology, and construction practices that significantly reduce the negative impact those buildings have on the environment and on human health. All green buildings—from homes to workplaces to schools—have the following attributes:

■ lower operating costs—including for energy, water, and waste;

■ a healthier indoor environment, thanks to more filtered fresh air, natural daylighting and outdoor views, and nontoxic, low-volatile-organic-compound (VOC) building materials; and

■ reduced greenhouse gas emissions.

In the United States, green is becoming the accepted standard for Class A workplaces, schools, and colleges, and it is gaining wider acceptance in housing, retail space, factories, and warehouses. Now, green is spreading far beyond individual buildings and business campuses to entire neighborhoods and communities.

In the near future, environmental priorities will play a greater and greater role in real estate development. Even in the midst of economic turmoil, a boom in the greening of existing buildings, from high-rise office towers to suburban single-family homes, can be expected. Metropolitan districts will be transformed with the adoption of compact, pedestrian- and transit-oriented mixed-use districts, and communities enabling walkability.

The greening of buildings and development also will be embraced as a pivotal weapon in the war against global climate change.

ULI is particularly interested in new policies and solutions to address global climate change that are at the nexus of energy, land use, infrastructure, and real estate.

Charles Lockwood's conversations with cutting-edge green thinkers from around the world identify not only the challenges of creating a more sustainable built environment, but also of formulating a wide variety of solutions—from tools to policies—that can further advance green development as a fundamental real estate, social, and even political practice.

Rachelle L. Levitt
Executive Vice President, Global Information Group
Publisher
Urban Land Institute

About the Author

CHARLES LOCKWOOD, RECOGNIZED AS A "GREEN REAL ESTATE AUTHORITY" by the *Wall Street Journal*, works with companies and investors on maximizing the value of their properties and on their broader corporate sustainability strategies. He is a keynote speaker at U.S. and international conferences.

His insights and research have been published in leading media worldwide, including the *Harvard Business Review, Wall Street Journal, New York Times, Barron's, International Herald Tribune,* and *South China Morning Post,* and he has appeared on PBS, National Public Radio, and Jim Cramer's TheStreet.com Web site.

He contributed the first chapter to the book *Harvard Business Revie*w on Green Business Strategy (2007).

He has been a frequent contributor to *Urban Land* for 20 years, and began his Green Quotient column for that magazine in June 2006. See www.charleslockwood.com.

Preface

MOST REAL ESTATE PROFESSIONALS AND INVESTORS KNOW THAT SUCCESSFUL development and redevelopment requires more than selecting a well-located site and constructing a building for the fastest payback. Green principles are having a direct impact on what gets built and where, and how well it does in the marketplace now and in the future. Because of the Urban Land Institute's commitment to a sustainable built environment and the growing importance of green development, its *Urban Land* magazine asked me to contribute my conversations with cutting-edge green thinkers in a monthly Green Quotient column, starting in June 2006.

My column was meant to offer a fresh perspective for ULI members. I chose *not* to speak with talented but familiar real estate experts. Instead, I discussed a wide variety of green issues with men and women around the world with expertise in sustainability who could provide their valuable insights about its impact on real estate.

Over the past three years, we have experienced the advance of the green building movement in many sectors, a roller-coaster ride in the energy industry, significant political changes, and a profound economic crisis. Each column is a snapshot of a moment in time, reflecting the issues of importance in that moment and the realities of the country and the world at that time.

But this book is no time capsule. It shows the clear progression of thinking and green actions in the United States and abroad over the past three years. In reading these conversations, reproduced in the order they were published in *Urban Land*, you will find that the issues, challenges, and trends discussed with these opinionated and insightful green experts are as relevant today to the real estate industry and the country as a whole as when I first spoke with them.

My inquiry began with Thomas L. Friedman, the Pulitzer Prize–winning *New York Times* columnist and best-selling author of *The World Is Flat* and, at the time, yet-unpublished *Hot, Flat, and Crowded*, who generously agreed to a lengthy conversation for my first column. He held nothing back when giving his forthright opinions on everything from the real estate industry to the benefits of high gasoline prices, and he has continued to share his thoughts and insights with me in the intervening three years.

But my Green Quotient interviews were *not* conducted with a who's who of well-known people. Many of my conversations were with people unfamiliar to most readers. Ron King, chief executive of King County, Washington, for example, is little known outside Greater Seattle, but he has been creating and enacting trendsetting sustainability policies for his county for more than ten years. Most people probably do not know of Michael Gainer, the executive director of Buffalo ReUse Inc., which carries out the green deconstruction of abandoned homes, but his company and his insights are critical in addressing our current built environment. Before Van Jones's new book *The Green Collar Economy* became a bestseller, I discussed with him his practical solutions to boost the economy, raise many Americans out of poverty, and protect the environment, as well as the potential impact of a green economy on land use and the real estate industry.

My original conversations with each person in this book were much longer than the final columns published in *Urban Land*, which had to be edited for length to meet space requirements. For this book, however, I have had the freedom to publish my longer conversations and to fully capture the unique perspectives of each person with whom I have spoken. I am grateful to each and every one of them for giving me their time, their honesty, and their insights, and for greatly expanding my own knowledge and understanding of sustainability.

Charles Lockwood
Los Angeles, 2009

CONTENTS

THOMAS L. FRIEDMAN

The first Green Quotient interview was conducted in early 2006 in the Washington, D.C., office of Thomas L. Friedman, the three-time Pulitzer Prize–winning *New York Times* columnist and best-selling author of several books, including *The World Is Flat: A Brief History of the 21st Century*. He is a visiting professor at Harvard University.

"I want to redefine green as geostrategic, geoeconomic, capitalist, and the most patriotic thing you can do. My mantra is that green is the new red, white, and blue."

Friedman has traveled hundreds of thousands of miles reporting on the Middle East, the end of the cold war, U.S. domestic politics and foreign policy, international economics, and the worldwide impact of the terrorist threat. Knowledgeable, outspoken, and occasionally controversial, he offers keen insights into today's world, provides his unique and global perspectives on green development, and gives specific recommendations on how to create a more sustainable, prosperous, and satisfying future.

>> **What do you think is the biggest environmental problem in the world? Is it our own practices in the United States, or is it the more rapidly growing and industrializing countries like China and India?**

Well, it's all of the above. My argument, very simply, is this is not your grandfather's energy crisis. It's not 1973. It's not 1979.

Reason number one: We're in a war on terrorism that the American people have fueled and financed by our energy purchases. We are doing the craziest thing in the world: we're funding both sides in the war on terrorism. We finance the U.S. Army, Navy, and Marine Corps with our tax dollars, and we fund Al Qaeda, Iran, Venezuela, and various hostile Islamist charities with our energy purchases.

Reason number two: The world is flat and 3 billion new players just walked onto the playing field, all with their own version of the American dream—a house, a car, a toaster, a microwave, and a refrigerator. Three billion people moving from energy life-styles that have a low impact on the environment to energy lifestyles that have a high impact on the environment. If we don't find an alternative source to fossil fuels, we're going to burn up, choke up, heat up, and smoke up this planet far faster than anybody realizes. We're going to approach that tipping point—if we're not already past it—just that much quicker.

Reason number three: Because of number two, green technology is going to be the industry of the 21st century. Now, China's going to go green. Not because they've got me, or you, or Rachel Carson [looking over their shoulder]. China's going to go green because China can't breathe. They're growing at 10 percent and they're giving 3 percent back in the form of lost work days, health care issues, and brownouts and blackouts. So, China's going to go green and, as it does, it will design low-cost scalable solutions. If that happens, they will really become green innovators. As they do, they'll come our way, and they'll clean our clock on the industry of the 21st century.

Reason number four: People don't see that we're in a new strategic environment. We've had a $60 barrel of oil; we've had a $70 of barrel oil; we've had spikes in the past. But we've never had a $60 barrel of oil structurally as far as the eye can see. What that is going to involve is the massive transfer of wealth to the worst regimes in the world to do the worst things. Therefore, what we're actually seeing at the meta-strategic level is that the tie to free markets and democratization that we thought was unleashed by the fall of the Berlin Wall is now running into a countertide, a black wave of what I call petro-authoritarianism that is fueling and funding Russia, Venezuela, Burma, Nigeria, Iran, Saudi Arabia—you name it. That counterwave is making what we thought was the unstoppable wave of democracy and free markets actually quite stop-pable. This, to me, is the meta-geostrategic environment we're in right now. We need to wake up to that. But what I find is that a lot of people in government, a lot of people in industry, haven't really come to it yet.

>> **Green buildings are one solution for reducing U.S. energy consumption. Buildings account for 36 percent of total U.S. energy consumption, including 65 percent of its electricity use. What can we do to make green building development the rule and not the exception in the United States?**
The first change agent I'm rooting for is a gasoline tax that fixes gasoline prices some-where between $3.50 and $4 a gallon, with rebates for people who have to drive long distances and for people with low incomes. When you put gasoline in the $3.50-to-$4-a-gallon range, then you change consumer behavior. Change consumer behavior and you force Detroit to massively transform its fleets, and then you're headed down the innova-

tion curve. When we do it, the whole world does it. I hope that will be the change agent because with that tax we capture the benefits for our deficit, for our schools, for our roads, for our transport system, for our health care.

If we don't do it, then I'm rooting for the president of Iran. What I say to Mahmoud Ahmadinejad is "You go, girl! The crazier you get, the happier I am because the crazier you get, the sooner we get oil priced at $100 a barrel." If we can keep the price that high for about six months, then the shift to sustainable, scalable alternatives will be unstoppable.

Secondly, if I could wave my magic wand, I'd have every single architecture student at every single architecture school attend at least a year's worth of courses on sustainable design and energy-conserving design so that it is imbedded in every architect. Then the first question they ask is, how do I design energy and mass out of whatever you're asking me to build: a garage, a house, a high-rise, an apartment block? If every architect thought that way, then I think you'd have a really scalable energy-saving solution. And every building should have a garden on the roof. Every single building. I believe that when you design energy and mass out of a building from day one, then you are doing the greatest thing you can do for the environment.

For me, it's always one simple question: scale. When you get massive numbers of architects designing only green designs, and then their clients demanding only green building designs, and then corporations and their employees demanding to work only in green buildings, and consumers demanding only green cars, then it scales. Then the best of our system—which is all of this experimentation, free market—will just take over.

>> **Suburban sprawl is another reason for our wasteful energy consumption and environmental problems. Can we realistically contemplate a new life/work model—including more compact development—to reduce these problems?**

If I could wave my magic wand again, I'd have every real estate developer and local regulatory agency take a course called "Up, Not Out" so that when they look at every question of land use and regulation, they approach it with the mindset of building up and not out. Then, we'd stop the sprawl that means more energy use, more highways, more driving.

>> **Many cities in the United States—not just places like Portland, Oregon, and Seattle, Washington, but also cities like Scottsdale, Arizona, and Salt Lake City— are already mandating that their new public buildings be constructed according to green criteria.**

Interesting. So, actually, we not only need every architect to go to green school, we also need every public official and regulator to go as well so that they bring the hammer of a public policy to this.

A lot of cities and towns don't want more urban sprawl. They're actually coming back to the developers now and telling them to build up and not out. Therefore, you get much more efficient energy usage out of the same footprint rather than starting ten new footprints out there. We're really close. But we've got to change the market conditions so that all of these alternatives start to really scale in people's minds because if they don't scale, they don't have an impact.

>> Will the real impetus for the mainstreaming of green buildings and more compact, energy-efficient development in the United States only come from government? What about corporations?

I would say the business community is poised—for its own reasons right now—to really go down this road of green building, green appliances, green technologies, green building materials. Some of the most farsighted are already there.

I'm a big believer that you get real change in the world when the big players do the right thing for the wrong reasons. If you wait for all the big players to do the right thing for the right reasons, you wait forever. So, if every shopping center or office building developer will go green because they think it's a great way to attract customers and lease their space, God bless them. I don't need them to do the right thing for the right reasons. I just need them to do the right thing.

Often, the scalable solution is when the big players do the right thing for the wrong reasons. Wal-Mart now is really moving down this path of looking at much more sustainable criteria in how they source their products. When Wal-Mart makes a change like that, you've got to sit up and take notice. I think it's very important.

>> The shopping center industry can actually be a change agent for more compact development.

Absolutely. The most exciting thing going on there is that, basically, department stores are leaving. There's consolidation in that industry. So, the industry is taking that empty space and building condos and office buildings.

>> Creating compact town centers with a broad mix of uses.

Right. I think that is the future of the shopping center industry both in terms of where the whole energy question will mandate it to go, but also where it could find a whole new lease on life by converting every shopping center into a town center with banks, a dry cleaner, government offices, and residential and office buildings. The infrastructure is already there: the grid, the pipes, the wires, the sewers are connected. If I were an investor and I was looking at the shopping center industry, I'd be drooling right now, because if you approach it with this mindset, what it basically means is every failing shopping center is a whole new opportunity—a land bank.

>> How would you convince the real estate industry to go green?

You have some farsighted developers who are listening to their tenants, who understand that being able to offer people a green building is an incredible branding opportunity that attracts younger workers in particular. But it has got to scale.

So, for the rest, I want to appeal to their profit motive. What would you rather do— compete with one another over the last scraps of open land around major cities, bid up the prices for those green spaces, or suddenly be able to look at a city and see it as a much richer supply to go up almost anywhere that your imagination will take you and where your bankers will finance you? You know, when you go up, the risks are so much less because the neighborhood's already there. It's a much more efficient opportunity. When you go out, you never know whether people are really going to follow you. So, you're competing for a much scarcer resource, having to pay a higher price for a much more risky return, and you don't know when the last "out" is going to be.

>> What are some of the challenges you see to green going fully mainstream?

The environmental movement. They got wrapped up in green as a personal virtue—"We are better because we are green"—and they've put off a lot of people, I think. That's why my whole goal for this year is to redefine green—to redefine it as not liberal, tree-hugging, sissy, girly-man, and kind of French, slightly unpatriotic. I want to redefine green as geo-strategic, geoeconomic, capitalist, and the most patriotic thing you can do. My mantra is that green is the new red, white, and blue. To name something is to own it. Right now the opponents have owned the word *green*. I want to retake it from them and redefine it in geopolitical, geostrategic, patriotic terms. Then it scales.

I'm less pessimistic than I was even a year ago, because what I've seen is enormous amounts of experimentation going on now. Every time I meet with someone who's knowledgeable about what's going on, they tell me a story I didn't know about. Just as you have today. But if we really want it to scale, we have got to make fossil fuels more expensive than they are right now. We have to price the real price.

CHÉ WALL

Ché Wall is chair of the World Green Building Council (WGBC), cofounder and director of the Green Building Council of Australia, and joint managing director of the Asia/Australia-based Lincolne Scott engineering consulting group. He established the company's Advanced Environmental specialist service, Australia's first professional practice dedicated to the design of passive and integrated environmental systems.

"It is a very brave investor today who doesn't think that sustainability will be in much greater demand ten years from now."

Green buildings are rising around the world, but the catalysts for this significant change and the challenges the buildings face are as different as the countries in which these structures are being built. Wall discusses his global perspectives on the current state of green development and shares some thought-provoking ideas about the disconnect between media and cultural values, the Asian green movement, residential development, and the green asset valuation process.

>> Has green reached the tipping point? Has it reached the brink of becoming part of the mainstream built environment?

Yes. At least it has in Australia, and it is coming close in several European countries and the U.S. The model for market transformation is well-known. If you can get people in the market to see the value of innovating in terms of product or outcome, the rest of the market picks up quite quickly.

When you develop commercial buildings, for example, you must think of rentability and value in the future. The largest commercial building projects in the Australian marketplace today require high green environmental ratings. The major tenants are driving this demand. It is a very brave investor today who doesn't think that sustainability will be in much greater demand ten years from now. With the market essentially asking for LEED [Leadership in Energy and Environmental Design] Silver buildings now, it will certainly be asking for LEED Gold in the next decade.

Obviously, the market for green buildings differs from country to country. When the market can set a value on a green building, you will see a major shift. The United States, like Australia, has a REIT [real estate investment trust] structure. Assets are quite astutely valued, which supports the shift to green buildings. The U.K. is moving toward a REIT structure in which asset values are decided quite aggressively.

>> Why has green reached the tipping point?

Green has become common sense. The nature of a building is decided by the people who finance, develop, occupy, and own it, not the architects, or engineers, or environmentalists. That's one reason why we are going green now. The financiers, developers, tenants, and building owners are finally getting the message of green's multiple benefits, a green measuring system, and reasonable construction budgets.

Market transformation in the commercial sector has been successful. Corporations understand that green is good news for employees, their shareholders, and their image. When a company wants a new building, three things are paramount: the CFO is concerned about the rent and the occupancy cost over ten years; the HR manager cares about keeping the staff; the CEO needs to make the shareholders happy. In comparing a green building to a standard building, the green building will have the greater desirability and greater value because it gives all three executives, and the company, what they need at market rates, with lower overhead, greater productivity, and stronger employee attraction and retention compared to a standard building.

Green also increases a company's standing. Tenants in Australia, for example, are paying a 15 percent premium for rents in green buildings. They are putting their money where their mouth is. They are paying the premium to get actual value by fulfilling their corporate social responsibility, being good corporate citizens, looking after their workers, and improving their productivity. Those are fundamental business drivers.

Therefore, if I am a developer, can I afford *not* to build green any more?

>> What is driving the growth of the green building movement in countries like China and India?

Their motivation is very different from ours. We are basically motivated by guilt because of the environmental damage done by past generations. We feel we have a duty to look after and remediate what we have left in a state of disrepair, like our air quality and fouled rivers. But China and India don't have a sense of guilt because they didn't go through the large-scale, 19th-century industrialization or the massive development in the 1950s and onward. They are only now reaching that point of rapid development.

China and India have a sense of obligation toward the future, not the past. They are also confronting a resource-constrained environment. They understand that if they don't get the environmental part right, they cannot develop successfully. Their economic future is intrinsically linked to their ability to tackle sustainable development. They cannot de-laminate their economic agenda from the environmental agenda. They say quite openly that they are facing a challenge that has never been faced in human history.

>> What are the remaining challenges to green going mainstream?

First is the continuing notion that we must pay more for a green building. That just isn't true, as the Lend Lease headquarters in Sydney and other buildings around the world have proved. But the notion remains.

Second, we are struggling with light industrial going green because light-industrial delivery is based almost entirely on a really low price, rather than on criteria like worker attraction, retention, and productivity.

Third, systems such as the USGBC's [U.S. Green Building Council's] LEED and the U.K.'s BREEAM [Building Research Establishment's Environmental Assessment Method] rating programs, while both valuable and successful, are being imported into other countries. Unfortunately, LEED is a compendium of U.S.-based regulations, which is totally appropriate for the U.S. markets, but won't work well in other countries. LEED, for example, gives points for sustainable carpeting, but offices in India don't have carpets, so that credit lacks reference to their market.

We cannot roll out the same buildings from the U.S., the United Kingdom, and Australia into other countries. We cannot judge their sustainability efforts by our standards. We must judge them against their own standards. Every building must be a response to the local market, culture, products, and skills.

The best thing we can do is export the *discipline* of sustainable design decision making— is it green? how do we quantify that? how do we communicate that to help inform the market of the value of green buildings?—and let the local market develop the appropriate technical solutions. Systems such as LEED must become flexible enough and evolve enough to encompass the differences of place and culture.

Fourth, a major challenge to pushing green fully into the mainstream is the existing building stock. Reality check time: new buildings represent just 2 percent of the footprint per annum in the U.S. and Australia. So, if you reduce the environmental impact of new buildings by 50 percent, that only makes a 1 percent dent in the overall negative impact of our buildings on the environment.

WILLIAM D. BROWNING

William D. Browning, a principal at Browning Partners LLC and a senior fellow at the Rocky Mountain Institute, has been active in the environmental movement for more than two decades as a leading researcher and writer, and as a consultant on projects ranging from the 2000 Summer Olympics in Sydney, Australia, to the greening of the White House, to LucasFilm's Letterman Digital Arts Center at the Presidio in San Francisco.

"We have gotten very good at techno-fixes for indoor air quality and energy use, but we really need to focus now on the building environment and how it affects the people within it."

When most people talk about green buildings, the topics are energy efficiency; reduced water consumption; natural daylighting and outdoor views; green building materials and furnishings that do not off-gas toxins; energy-efficient heating, venting, and air-conditioning systems; and more fresh air. They usually do not talk about the importance of biophilia *and how it should be incorporated into building design. But Browning does. He also provides a fresh take on this country's infrastructure issues.*

>> **What are some of the newest green trends that will affect the real estate industry, the country, and the planet?**

We're looking at how green buildings can maximize people's physical well-being beyond air quality and thermal comfort, how people respond to places, and how spaces affect people psychologically. What makes a space feel secure? What make people feel comforted and nurtured and even challenged in a place?

I'm particularly excited about and active in the field of *biophilia*—studying and using the deep-seated human need to be connected to nature. Human genetic memory is conditioned to a specific landscape, the savannah [a grassy plain with scattered trees adjacent to woodland]—a finding that fits with all the archeological and anthropological research.

So, a savannah is the preferred human ecosystem. It's where we function best. Prior to the European colonization of North America, for example, Native Americans managed big chunks of the continent as savannah ecosystems through the use of annual fires. Closed-canopy forests were considered unsafe, as places of fear.

This relates directly to green buildings and development because human beings still react to their landscape, to their habitat, and evaluate it according to its survival value. Shade, shelter, clean water, flowers, and fruits—indicating things to eat—all of these things have survival value. Think about how much money we spend today on buying flowers or maintaining lawns. Look at how real estate prices play out. What's more expensive, an apartment with a view into Central Park or a view of Lexington Avenue? What do you pay more for in hotels, a city view or a water view?

When people are in an environment that has the savannah elements, they are healthier and happier, and they have a greater sense of well-being. There's lots of research by Dr. Roger S. Ulrich [professor in the Department of Landscape Architecture and Urban Planning at Texas A&M University] and others, for example, about hospital healing rates and stress indicators. They've found that things like healing gardens and views of trees have a positive impact on recovery time, reduced drug use, lower blood pressure, and other indicators.

Research has been done on how green buildings generate better sales, better test scores, and better productivity. While all of that has huge financial implications, it has really just served as a placeholder for the well-being of humans in buildings.

We have gotten very good at techno-fixes for indoor air quality and energy use, but we really need to focus now on the building environment and how it affects the people within it. So, those of us who are working with biophilia are now identifying how we can connect people in a building with nature. We are literally taking the genetic tendency for preferred landscapes and elements from those preferred landscapes and incorporating them into buildings. Biophilia may dramatically change the nature of what we put into a building and how we put it together. That's the next step in green buildings.

>> What does biophilia look like in a real workplace?

Genzyme's headquarters building [the 12-story, 350,000-square-foot (32,500-square-meter) Genzyme Center in Cambridge, Massachusetts, certified Platinum under the Leadership in Energy and Environmental Design (LEED) program] has elements of biophilic design as part of its overall green design. First, daylight is used extensively in the core of the building.

Second is the use of a water feature in the atrium. People are strongly attracted to places with clean, clear, running water and the sound of the water. It is a preferred landscape. Third is the extensive use of gardens throughout the building, which gives people a direct connection to nature within the building. Having plants is good. Having small gardens—Genzyme has 18—is the next step.

Fourth, the building has powerful spatial configurations—known as prospects—that give people great views from offices or balconies through the building space into the light well and central atrium. You don't see everything at once, but you are drawn into it, which creates enticement and mystery. Fifth, the building generates a sense of refuge through the use of overhangs, which make people feel protected and sheltered by the building. Sixth, you can get up on the balcony railing and look down—and it's a little scary looking down. That's called peril. The building has a layer of thrill.

You put all of those elements together and you have a building that keeps people's interest and elevates their well-being while also providing the company with all the other benefits of green design and technologies.

>> Those actually sound like very familiar elements.

Of course they are. Long before all the biophilia studies started coming out, developers intuitively incorporated many of those elements into their projects. The designers of shopping center malls, for example, created spaces that generate excitement, they put in plants and water features, and they added natural light.

>> With rising oil and gasoline prices, America is in the midst of another energy crisis. Green buildings are noted for their reduced energy consumption, but are current green design and technologies doing enough?

The combination of Energy Star and LEED is creating projects that are averaging 30 percent less energy use than comparable standard buildings. That is a significant cost savings and it helps with environmental impacts, but ultimately it's not enough. We have to do dramatically better.

The direction we need to go is buildings as net energy producers. You've heard of the net-zero energy movement, but it's really about net energy production.

Bill Sisson, director of sustainability at the United Technologies Research Center, is looking at what we need to do to impact global warming. [The research center] estimate[s] that to stabilize the carbon dioxide output of U.S. buildings by the year 2050, all new buildings must be 94 percent energy efficient or better. Actually, their take is that 94 percent is not enough. Buildings must have no net energy draw [from grids].

>> Green infrastructure is a field that has been growing in recent years. What direction should this field take?

When we look at development patterns and the infrastructure that supports it, we need to go beyond individual buildings, the neighborhood, even the metropolitan area to include the systems *beneath* the built environment, like energy, water, and sewers. Once again, biophilia can help us radically rethink our development and infrastructure systems, particularly stormwater.

Rain is an incredible resource that we should be using to, among other things, restore our groundwater. But we treat rainwater as an engineering problem. We try to get rid of it as quickly as possible. We treat it like a waste product. Many cities in the United States, for example, have combined sewer systems that serve both building waste and rainwater. During large storms, the treatment plant gets overloaded and dumps the mixture of sewage and rainwater into natural water systems—rivers, lakes, and oceans. At least 1,500 U.S. municipal sewer systems are out of compliance, and the EPA [U.S. Environmental Protection Agency] is threatening to drop the hammer on them.

The solution is to treat rainwater as a precious commodity—as life. Rather than spend billions of dollars to dig up a city and install a second sewer system designated solely for handling rainwater—a stunning misallocation of money—we should be planting street trees, using water-capturing landscape features like bioswales and even tree wells along sidewalks, engineering soils, insisting on green roofs, and capturing stormwater for use in mechanical systems like air-conditioning and plumbing systems like toilet fixtures.

Buildings should be designed to capture all the rainwater that falls on them throughout the year, like the healthy ecosystem that was on those sites before they were developed, so there is no net runoff. The older neighborhoods in New Orleans, for example, had cisterns. The LEED Platinum Bank of America Tower in Manhattan captures, stores, and uses all the rainwater that falls on it to run mechanical systems, flush toilets, and irrigate its one-acre [0.4-hectare] green roof during dry periods.

But, of course, dealing with water goes far beyond individual buildings. Mithun Architects+Designers+Planners [of Seattle] has done great work with the city of Portland, Oregon, in planning an area called Lloyd Crossing [a 35-block inner-city commercial district] near the Portland Convention Center. One of the things they've done is to use the urban fabric—the public realm, the air, the alleyways, the spaces between the buildings—to provide stormwater management so that the district has no more rainwater runoff than occurred before European settlement when the site was primary forest.

>> Wetlands have been a popular stormwater management strategy for many green projects.

That's because we've bought into the big lie about natural wetlands. They are not sponges. Yes, they may help serve as a stormwater and storm-surge buffer mechanism, but how much help they really are is uncertain. Only one study was done in the 1960s of the impact on the reuse of storm surge, and we rely on it today, but the results in that study are not proven now.

If you use manmade wetlands for stormwater retention and dump stormwater into it, that makes sense because those wetlands are designed to handle both stormwater retention and the cleansing of pollutants from the water.

But natural wetlands aren't. They get their water from underground water recharge. If you dump water and pollutants from the built environment on *top* of them, you affect the pH and the chemistry. You end up degrading that land, you negatively affect the native plant and animal species, and you encourage the growth of invasive species like cattails and reed canary grass, which *can* tolerate pollutants.

The water conversation and the energy conversation are similar conversations about changing how we think about these issues. Rather than building by building, we should be looking at entire districts.

>> Have any large projects actually been constructed using that philosophy?

In the U.K., there's a project called BedZED—the Beddington Zero Energy Development [a Peabody Trust project in the town of Beddington]—south of downtown London that's a brownfield redevelopment with housing and workplaces. BedZED only uses energy generated on site from renewable sources, it is the first community that does not add to the amount of carbon dioxide in the atmosphere, and it values and makes the most of rainwater rather than getting rid of it.

The same development team is now working on a much larger project called Z-Squared in the Thames Gateway London area, which incorporates zero energy use, captures and reuses water and wastewater, and they are looking at local food production, greater native biodiversity on the site, connecting to mass transit, the delivery of goods and services, dealing with municipal trash and recyclables, materials issues, and cultural and heritage issues.

>> The U.K. got into the green building movement long before the United States. Is it still cutting-edge?

The U.K. is doing innovative work on natural ventilation and advanced energy engineering. There's a lot going on all around the world. Germany is a leader in stormwater management, green roofs, and biological systems. Australia is working with natural and passive ventilation, and it is doing some very interesting residential projects. The first one was the 2000 Olympic Village [in Sydney]. Half the houses had integral photovoltaic systems. The United States, meanwhile, is making strong advances in integrated design, which addresses several green issues in a single building plan.

>> Where are we going from here? What's beyond LEED Platinum?

We'll move beyond net-energy-producer buildings and districts to look at the original ecological context of a site and figure out how we get a building to behave as the ecology of that place once did.

Buildings will maximize people's physical and psychological well-being because we'll ask questions like: How do spatial considerations influence how we think about and experience life? What makes us feel comforted and nurtured and excited in a place? Those issues are important for companies like Bank of America, Genzyme, and LucasFilms, which look at their green buildings as a tool to capture and retain the best possible employees.

Then there are companies like Wal-Mart, which is thinking well beyond green buildings and vehicle efficiency. It is trying to green up its entire supply chain, and that will have impacts all the way to the shop floors in China.

The classic example of a truly green company is, of course, Interface [based in Atlanta, the world's largest manufacturer of commercial carpet, modular carpet, carpet tiles, and carpet squares], which completely transformed its corporate culture. They are pretty clear that their company survived the roughest part of the economy because of their greenness, which generated operational savings and opened up new markets and new product lines.

>> Has green come in time? Are we making enough advances and institutionalizing green fast enough to have a real, beneficial, and lasting impact on the environment and on the global climate?

We must always have hope, you know. This has been one of our experiences in New Orleans. The green building message has been one of the true hopeful visions there. Rather than a conversation about putting the city back the way it was, we are having a conversation about putting it back better.

Green building councils and efforts are springing up all over the world—India, China, Mexico.

But in the end, we just don't know if all of these efforts are in time. We are already seeing the impacts of global warming. What happens on that front really depends on how well we succeed now. This is a race and we won't know the outcome for a while.

CHRISTOPHER B. LEINBERGER

Christopher B. Leinberger is a land use strategist, the author of award-winning real estate articles, a former professor of practice and director of the Graduate Real Estate Program at the University of Michigan, a fellow at the Brookings Institution in Washington, D.C., and a founding partner of Arcadia Land Company.

"The pent-up market demand in the United States for walkable urbanity represents trillions of dollars of development over the next 20 years. It's my experience that you don't mess with Mother Market or Mother Nature."

In his book The Option of Urbanism: Investing in a New American Dream *(2007), Leinberger describes how the American dream is expanding to include urban as well as suburban lifestyles and explains how the real estate industry, investors, and lenders must respond by building the higher-density, mixed-use, walkable communities that more and more Americans want for social, economic, and environmental reasons*

>> **As volatile oil and gasoline prices, air pollution, and climate change prove, we can no longer afford the post–World War II development patterns created 50 years ago that are dependent on cheap gas. We need to rethink suburbia and other conventional—and wasteful—development. What alternative development patterns do you recommend, and why?**

The current development pattern of low-density, car-dependent sprawl is basically modular, focused on single products, relatively simple to develop, and commoditized with floor/area ratios [FAR] of under 0.3.

The alternative development pattern that many people want but have a hard time finding is high-density, multiple-transportation, "walkable urbanity," which is integrated, mixed use, quite complex to develop, not yet commoditized, with everyday basic services and maybe even jobs all within walking distance. Walkable urbanity has a FAR ranging from over 1.0 to 10.0 and higher. That means that walkable urbanity has a density that is five to 50 times higher than conventional sprawl development. It is a completely different animal—as different as night from day.

>> Will the general public—particularly SUV-addicted Americans with large exurban homes—accept and support walkable urbanity? Isn't many people's environmental support just a mile wide and an inch deep?

Recent studies show that a third to maybe even half of the households in this country *want* walkable urbanity, and not always for environmental reasons. First, they have realized the built-in flaw of conventional development—*more is less*. As more suburban development takes place, the very reasons people were drawn to the suburbs in the first place—open space, ease of commuting, safety—are degraded.

Second, the market has fundamentally changed. Over 75 percent of U.S. households have no school-age children, so yards and schools have become less important.

Third, many empty nester baby boomers and young gen-Xers find the suburbs sterile. They want the hustle and options of walkable urbanism. As empty nester baby boomers, my wife and I live within blocks of all our basic needs and our workplaces. None of our kids, who are in their 20s and 30s, has yet to even consider a suburban home. They all live and work in cities.

Fourth, there is the commute. Contrary to the car company commercials showing a carefree motorist driving up the *only* road in California that has absolutely no traffic, driving is now a grinding chore. And it's now an increasingly expensive chore because the era of cheap energy is over.

Finally, people are just beginning to realize that removing one car from the household budget frees up as much as $125,000 that can be applied instead to additional mortgage. The AAA [American Automobile Association] reports that the average annual cost for the care and feeding of a car is $7,800 after taxes. Drop a car out of the household and, with a 6 percent mortgage, you can buy quite a bit more house. We in the real estate industry should be fighting harder for our customers to switch their household spending from a depreciable asset—the automobile—to the appreciable asset that we sell: real estate.

>> What is the connection between walkable urbanity and environmental and government fiscal sustainability?

Preliminary research shows that reducing the number of car trips, increasing the number of activities that are within walking distance or are transit accessible, using infrastructure more intensely, and building at a much higher density—all of which are components of walkable urbanity—significantly reduce greenhouse gas emissions. If you construct green buildings within that walkable urbane environment, you reduce greenhouse gas emissions even further. Building walkable places is not the single solution to climate change, but it addresses one of the four major sources of greenhouse gas emissions and it is a necessary component in an overall strategy.

As for government financial sustainability, about 20 years ago, fiscal impact analysis was invented to study the effect of development on local and state finances. A picture is emerging from that research showing that nearly all ten major categories of infrastructure—both publicly provided infrastructure like education, roads, and sewers, as well as privately provided infrastructure like electricity and telecommunications—are being mispriced. The research shows that low-density sprawl has been and continues to be massively subsidized by high-density development and the general taxpayer. This is not a conspiracy; it's just the unintended consequence of countless small decisions made at the federal, state, and local levels. Subsidizing sprawl has been and continues to be *the* major domestic policy of our country.

Getting those subsidies out of the government fiscal system and leveling the playing field is essential. The market must be able to freely express itself. Putting a heavy thumb on the scale in favor of low-density sprawl is not what a capitalist society should be doing.

>> What can be done to overcome Wall Street's and the real estate industry's resistance to sustainable development patterns and building products?

About 15 years ago, Wall Street became the guardian of real estate finance due to the excesses of the 1980s. We borrowed hundreds of billions of dollars—and we forgot to pay much of it back. Following the worst real estate depression since the 1930s, the Federal Reserve only agreed to turn the tap back on for real estate after new watchdogs were in place: the investment banking houses.

Wall Street and commercial banks must trade like for like, so they commoditized real estate into what I refer to as the 19 standard product types. Nearly every one of those product types builds low-density sprawl. If you wanted to build anything other than one of those 19 product types—anything mixed use or higher density—you had to arrange unusual and generally much more expensive financing, if you could do it at all.

Two factors, however, are finally helping to overcome Wall Street's resistance to anything different. First, is the demonstrable financial success of new urbanist development in the suburbs. Second—and probably more important over time—is the turnaround of our downtowns and the rise and success of higher-density mixed-use suburban town centers and lifestyle centers.

Wall Street is loosening the reins a little, especially since real estate has become a proven asset class over the last 15 years. I have always found it ironic that Wall Street investment bankers would not invest in mixed-use walkable product, but then they'd leave their offices and go home to Greenwich Village or the Upper West Side, which are some of the best examples of walkable urbanity in the country.

>> **In working on projects throughout the country as a consultant and developer, what resistance have you found on a government level to green development, and how have you overcome that resistance?**

The greatest resistance has come not from government, but from NIMBY [not in my backyard] opposition to high-density development. And the battles are getting even nastier. My development company's associates now go to public meetings with bodyguards. Another developer working on a mixed-use project outside Philadelphia is regularly getting death threats.

Our company has overcome even this level of resistance by working with the community upfront and educating people about the many benefits of walkable urbanity, from an improved quality of life to increased real estate values and tax revenues. And the low-density housing owners adjacent to a walkable place actually get a double benefit: they continue to live in low-density suburban splendor, but within walking distance of urban amenities and services, assuming that measures are taken to curb spillover parking, noise, and cut-through traffic. We also take neighbors on bus tours of comparable new urbanist communities so they can see the benefits of walkable urbanity firsthand.

I believe, however, that the environmental community needs to become an ally in our battle for mixed-use, high-density, walkable urbanity. From an environmental and social perspective, we have a moral imperative to concentrate human settlement patterns, stop car-fueled sprawl, rezone existing transit stations, build greenfield lifestyle centers like Reston Town Center [in northern Virginia], and continue the crucial redevelopment of existing downtowns and suburban town centers. Given the fact that developers are viewed as being only somewhat better than slugs, however, we just aren't very credible in making those arguments. So, the environmental community needs to be on the barricades fighting for walkable urbanity.

>> **Do you believe that government mandates on a local, regional, state, and federal level are the only way to bring green development into the mainstream, or can market forces really turn our built environment green?**

I don't like government mandates. I do like leveling the playing field by not subsidizing low-density sprawl.

I think the market should be encouraged to satisfy the significant pent-up demand for walkable urbanity. Arthur Nelson of Virginia Tech, one of the country's most highly regarded land use analysts, reports in a recently published paper that if the market is given what it wants, the vast majority of all housing permits over the next 20 years will be for attached or small-lot walkable product. For example, in the Washington, D.C., market—which is a bellwether for the future because of the significant impact of its subway system—*70 percent* of building permits over the past two years have been for attached product. In 2003, the national average selling price per square foot for attached product was higher than for detached product—for the first time ever.

I think the market needs to be unleashed and let the development community satisfy the pent-up demand for walkable urbanity.

Nelson's report also mentions that half of the *existing* large-lot single-family homes, particularly on the fringe of our metropolitan areas, will have a hard time finding buyers.

>> **What lessons do other countries offer us for developing environmentally and financially sustainable places? Didn't Prince Charles, for example, give you a walking tour of Poundbury, his experimental village on the outskirts of Dorchester in the county of Dorset, England?**

Prince Charles has been a beacon of alternative ways of developing. He asked me to come to England last year to explain the need for "patient equity"—the old-fashioned way we used to finance real estate where a portion of the equity did not expect short-term returns in exchange for the lion's share of the mid- to long-term returns—in the development of walkable urbane places. While I was there, he showed me Poundbury, which is his mixed-use, mixed-income, walkable, and financially very successful development. It was modeled after the project my development partner, Robert Davis, is best known for: Seaside, Florida.

During the tour, Prince Charles asked one of the residents who was walking toward the local pub why he lived in Poundbury. The fellow turned out to be a Yank, and he replied that he loved the intimate, walkable nature of the place, though he only spent half his time there. The other half of the year, he lived in Seaside.

Americans have always gone to European cities for their architectural and development inspirations, but lately the reverse has been true. Most European developers over recent generations have actually followed *us*—to the fringe of their metropolitan areas. The really depressing thing about European fringe development is that it often combines high-density housing with surface parking around the base of the building and big-box retail or suburban office parks that can only be reached by car. It's the worst of all worlds.

Today, most middle-class Europeans aren't able to enjoy daily walks down their own boulevards or avenues because they aren't being built anymore. The traditional European public realm usually can only be found in the expensive historic downtowns that are now reserved for the upper-middle- and upper-income families—and tourists. Europe also has a pent-up demand for walkable urbanity, but Europe's developers have not yet discovered it outside the historic city.

>> Is it going to be "business as usual" for the real estate industry—particularly long-term investors like REITs [real estate investment trusts]—over the next 20 years? Or should farsighted developers and investors change their plans and activities now?

Obviously, there is a market change taking place, because consumer demand has fundamentally changed. To succeed, I think that farsighted developers and REITs would be wise to recognize some fundamental truths—that great real estate development must employ patient equity, and that we should invest for the long term. That means building higher-quality projects that make places walkable and special.

With conventional development, we drive at 45 miles [72 kilometers] an hour past "billboard architecture" set back 100 feet [30 meters] from the street. With walkable urbanity, however, we stroll right next to the buildings on the sidewalk. So, we have to use real brick, stone, and concrete, not some spray-on synthetic material, if we are going to give the market the quality it demands. Yes, that will cost more money, but the return on investment will more than make up for it, and we can be proud of what we build.

I believe that over the past several decades we have cheapened the built environment—turned it into a seven- to ten-year asset class, rather than the 40-year asset that our grandfathers and all who came before them built—thanks in large part to our exclusive use of net-present-value [NPV] underwriting methodologies introduced by our business schools 50 years ago this year. While it works well for short-term investments, NPV does not measure returns beyond seven to ten years very well. A dollar in year 10 doesn't discount back to anything meaningful in present value terms. So, developers cut construction costs to increase their front-end returns, not caring about mid- to long-term returns.

We have ended up constructing a throwaway built environment that reflects our measurement tools, not our long-term financial interests or our deeper values. Considering that real estate represents about 33 to 40 percent of our nation's wealth, we have not invested that wealth as well as we should have.

>> Where are urban and suburban development going in the next 20 years? Will sustainable development creep forward slowly, or do you see any leaps and bounds coming?

Most medium-sized to large metropolitan areas have a pent-up demand for 15 to 30 region-serving, walkable urbane places right now. Currently, metropolitan Detroit only has three walkable urbane places—Ann Arbor, Birmingham, and Royal Oak. Philadelphia only has four—Society Hill in the Center City, Rittenhouse Square in the Center City,

Manayunk, and University City. Greater Los Angeles only has five region-serving walkable urbane places—Pasadena, Santa Monica, West Hollywood, Farmer's Market, and Beverly Hills—assuming you don't count Main Street Disneyland.

Washington, D.C., however, has 16 walkable places right now, up from two just 20 years ago. Of those 16 places, 15 of them are served by the subway, and the one that isn't, Reston Town Center—the best example of a greenfield walkable urbane place in the country—will be linked to the system soon. Tysons Corner may become walkable someday! Metropolitan D.C. offers residents and business owners an incredible range of choices, from its revived downtown to Dupont Circle, Bethesda, Adams Morgan, Silver Spring, as well as a great variety of suburban and semirural areas.

The pent-up market demand in the United States for walkable urbanity represents trillions of dollars of development over the next 20 years. It's my experience that you don't mess with Mother Market *or* Mother Nature. The market will get what it wants—in spite of the massive subsidies that support sprawl, the zoning that makes mixed-use development illegal, and the NIMBYs—and we will have little choice but to mess less with Mother Nature.

So, I see leaps and bounds coming for sustainable development. This is the most exciting time in my career to be in real estate.

JAMES H. KUNSTLER

James H. Kunstler is the outspoken author of three books on what he calls America's "mutilated" cities: *Geography of Nowhere: The Rise and Decline of America's Man-Made Landscape* (1994), *Home from Nowhere: Remaking Our Everyday World for the Twenty-First Century* (1998), and *The City in Mind: Notes on the Urban Condition* (2003). He is a regular contributor to leading media and has lectured around the world on environmental, economic, and urban development issues.

"In my view, there will be little to zero development of any kind in the decades ahead. We will be faced mainly with an oversupply of severely devalued properties, terrible problems in the finance sector resulting in sharply curtailed investment capital, and a bankrupted middle class."

It is a truism that the real estate industry is tradition bound and often reluctant to change. The industry, however, may soon have change forced upon it. Kunstler's *The Long Emergency: Surviving the End of Oil, Climate Change, and Other Converging Catastrophes of the Twenty-First Century (2005) predicts an imminent socioeconomic crisis that will profoundly affect our way of life, our way of doing business, and where we live and do business.*

>> **The *Washington Post* wrote that *The Long Emergency* is "As brilliant as it is baleful . . . and we disregard it at our peril." Business people, environmentalists, and bloggers have praised—or disputed—your book's assertions, and many of your predictions. Why has your book been so controversial?**

The American public, at all levels, is gripped by a powerful psychology of previous investment, meaning we have put so much of our post–World War II wealth in the infrastructure of a particular way of life that we can't entertain the necessity to change it. It makes our heads hurt to think about it. I refer here to the suburban development pattern and all its furnishings, which I describe as "the greatest misallocation of resources in the history of the world." I say that because it has no future as a practical living arrangement as we move into an era of permanent and severe fossil fuel scarcity.

This psychology has spawned a lot of wishful and delusional thinking. The main wish these days is that we will be able to run all our stuff by some other means than oil and gas. The truth, I believe, is that no combination of alternative fuels or systems for running them will allow us to keep enjoying Walt Disney World, Wal-Mart, the interstate highways, and the rest of the kit. We'll try everything we possibly can, but we're going to be disappointed, and in the long run we will discover painfully that we have to make a lot of other arrangements for daily life. This is a rather harsh message and hard for people to take, so they resort to slogans, dogmas, and wishes.

>> How, in general, will your predicted scarcity of fossil fuels affect the U.S. real estate industry, including development and investment?

I'd go as far to say that it will be the end of real estate as an industry in the sense that you mean—a set of business activities organized on the gigantic scale. In particular, I think we will say goodbye to the big production homebuilders, the commercial developers of suburban retail venues, the mortgage financing rackets based on grossly irresponsible lending practices that have tragically become routine, and the real estate investment trusts based on the hoped-for appreciation of suburban or tourism assets and cash flows which will, in reality, crater.

In my view, there will be little to zero development of any kind in the decades ahead. We will be faced mainly with an oversupply of severely devalued properties, terrible problems in the finance sector resulting in sharply curtailed investment capital, and a bankrupted middle class. You could throw in some wild cards, too, like either possible hyperinflation of the U.S. dollar due to government debt policy, or deflationary depression, or both in some kind of sequence, not to mention the potential for social and political turmoil that usually accompanies these disorders.

Behind all these things, of course, lurks the additional case of climate change, which will only aggravate matters. Finally, don't forget international military mischief over energy resources and religion. Not a nice combo.

>> How, in particular, will these trends affect U.S. commercial properties—office, industrial/warehouse, retail, hotels? Are some types of commercial properties— and their developers and owners—going to be affected profoundly more than others by the fossil fuel scarcity?

Anything based on car dependency is going to lose value, whether it is a McHouse 30 miles [48 kilometers] outside Denver or a Jiffy Lube. Anything based on national chain retail will probably falter and fail—namely Wal-Mart and its imitators—since economic relations such as 12,000-mile [19,300-kilometer] merchandise supply chains to China and the vaunted "warehouse on wheels" will not work in a world of declining energy supplies and resource wars. You can forget about the investments related to motor tourism—the chain hotels, chain restaurants, resorts, theme parks, time shares, etc. I would also include all skyscrapers and megastructures, which are apt to lose their value as we run into trouble with the natural gas supply and the electric grid.

>> How will these trends affect U.S. residential properties, particularly standard suburban development?

Standard suburban development will no longer exist because suburbia will be self-evidently obsolete. The case of our cities is another matter. They are going to contract, too, I believe, even while they densify at their cores and around their waterfronts. We will see a reversal of the 200-year-long trend of people leaving the farms and small towns for the big cities because industrial farming of the kind that produces Corn Flakes and Pepsi-Cola will have to be replaced by more intensive local agriculture wherever that is still possible, and it will come much closer to the center of economic life than it has been within memory. Meanwhile, whole urban precincts will wither away.

Again, I would caution against expecting to use large or tall buildings. Scale will be crucial. We have made some mistakes with our waterfronts, too, thinking that their highest and best uses are condo sites and parks. In reality, we will have to get serious about maritime activities again at a smaller scale than the giant container ship. We will probably need our waterfronts for the infrastructure associated with that—wharves, warehouses, and flophouses for sailors. This will be inconsistent with luxury housing.

>> How will government on various levels be affected in the United States? How will these trends affect government's ability to provide the basic services that we take for granted?

I maintain that anything organized on the giant scale, whether it's a government, a retail trade corporation, or a state university, will tend to not do well under the conditions I have described. Bigness has strictly been a luxury of cheap energy.

The response to the hurricanes of 2005 was probably a preview of what we may expect generally from the federal government—impotence and poor performance.

At the local level, I believe that our planning and zoning legislation will no longer be enforced—or enforceable—since it mandates a suburban outcome nearly everywhere in our country, and we won't be doing that anymore. I think we'll have to ignore many of the building codes, too, which make it onerously difficult to reuse or retrofit older buildings.

>> What will happen in other nations if your predicted "long emergency" occurs—in Europe, Asia, Latin America?

Europe has plenty of problems and will no doubt suffer its share of hardship, but at least they did three things that we didn't do. First, they retained healthy central cities at the scale that will work in an energy-scarcer future—seven stories and under. Second, they supported robust passenger rail systems along with public transit links that make U.S.-style incessant motoring unnecessary. Finally, they propped up local agriculture and the value-added activities associated with it on the regional level.

China will implode politically, I believe, since it faces horrific problems with overpopulation, pollution, reckless finance, energy scarcity, and lack of government legitimacy much worse than anything we have in the United States. God knows what will happen to Japan, which imports 95 percent of its energy, or India, ditto—plus problems similar to China's.

Latin America will become a backwater, with a mix of a few relatively pleasant places (Argentina, Chile), chaotic bandit nations (Colombia, Mexico), and tinhorn tyrannies (Venezuela).

Australia and New Zealand might be okay if they can escape the wrath of refugees fleeing failing states like Indonesia and the Philippines.

>> What U.S. regions are best positioned in what you see as the long emergency, and which areas might face real problems?

The Southwest is basically out of business. Phoenix, Las Vegas, Tucson—these places are toast. The people who live there now think the opposite. They're merrily issuing permits for a zillion acres of new housing subdivisions. Let's say their disappointment will be keen. On top of an unresilient hyper-car-dependent development pattern that will be crippled by energy shortages, these places will have additional problems with failing water supplies and an inability to grow much food locally. They will be severely depopulated.

Southern California is in a league of its own as an unsustainable urban hypertrophy with an overlay of intractable ethnic conflicts.

The "wet" Sunbelt—east Texas to Florida—presents a somewhat different but equally grim picture. Most of the investment made there over the past half century is precisely the kind of car-dependent dreck that will lose value the most severely. Orlando, the Atlanta metroplex, Houston, Miami—these places are toast, damp toast, if I may be allowed a moment of levity. I also view these states as containing cultural drawbacks, for instance a bias for hyper-individualism at the expense of community and the romance with firearms in the defense of that hyper-individualism—not a good recipe for civic cohesion.

I view the Northeast, the Pacific Northwest, and the upper Midwest east of the short-grass prairie as having the best chances for the maintenance of civilized life, despite the challenges of home heating. The Rocky Mountains you can pretty much forget about. On the whole, I think life in our small towns and small cities will be a better bet than the big-city scene, which is liable to be rather turbulent.

>> Can the real estate industry safeguard itself against your predicted trends?

Well, no, not really, since I do not believe it will survive in anything like its current form. In the decades ahead, we will be lucky if we can redevelop individual building lots and fix some bridges. Also, you can pretty much forget about manufactured and modular building materials. The future will be pretty much about building in regional materials found in nature and at a very modest scale or increment of development. Young people can learn some traditional skills and bone up on classical architecture, which necessarily requires a precise knowledge of tectonics in materials like stone, brick, and wood.

>> Can the individual homeowner safeguard himself/herself against the trends?

An awful lot of Americans are going to be stuck with tragic misinvestments—4,000-square-foot [370-square-meter] McHouses that they can't afford to heat, located in suburban outlands too distant from services, job centers, perhaps even public safety. The woes of the recent creative financing binge are well-known and don't require elaboration, except to say one can easily imagine orgies of default and repossession. These could have pretty gnarly political repercussions, too, since they represent a kind of organized swindle by way of negligent oversight.

>> Are there any opportunities for savvy companies and real estate investors coming out of these trends?

I don't think groups organized in this way will continue to be "players" in the ways we are familiar with now. Overall, we will be experiencing massive contraction in wealth, business activities, economic expectations, and the scale of operations in everything.

>> When do you expect your predicted trends to really affect the United States?

I think we've already entered the zone of difficulty and that these dislocations will be palpable in earnest within five years—and probably sooner where the real estate sector, per se, is concerned. I think the collapse of the housing bubble has quite a way to go still in this calendar year, 2006, and will continue downward long after that.

The permanent global energy crisis is already underway, but will get big-time traction in the next five years as well. While these events sound frightening, and may entail great vicissitude, the eventual outcome may be a far more fit society. We will have to be more self-reliant. We will have to work shoulder to shoulder with our neighbors to stay alive, and we will sing our own songs.

WILLIAM A. McDONOUGH

William A. McDonough is a well-known advocate of green buildings and sustainability. He is the founding principal of William McDonough + Partners, Architect and Community Design; cofounder and principal of McDonough Braungart Design Chemistry (MBDC), a product and process design firm; and partner and senior adviser at VantagePoint Venture Partners, a venture capital firm. He is the author of *Cradle to Cradle: Remaking the Way We Make Things* (2002).

"If anyone has done any math, they will understand how valuable the green agenda is economically, and that if they don't adopt it, they are probably not an intelligent fiduciary as a developer or owner."

A complex and controversial man who is justly celebrated for his ability to popularize environmental and sustainability issues, McDonough began actively designing green buildings in the mid-1980s and has worked on sustainable development around the world. Thus, he has a unique understanding of the state of green buildings today, the sea change in the development of green building materials, and even the importance of bedouin tents.

>> **Do you think that green buildings have reached the tipping point—where they are becoming the preferred norm, rather than the exception?**

We are certainly feeling that we have reached a tipping point in our office. We used to get two or three requests a week to do green work, and now we get the same number every *day*. We also see that our own leadership has spawned a number of firms that are also working in the green space. So, we are no longer feeling so alone in the forest. We have lots of competitors that are fiercely engaged in going after work, using green criteria as part of their proposition.

If anyone has done any math, they will understand how valuable the green agenda is economically, and that if they don't adopt it, they are probably not an intelligent fiduciary as a developer or owner.

Certainly, for an owner who is constructing a project for their own use, the productivity gains for their employees, which is their highest cost, more than offset the cost of the entire building, not just the green features—and sometimes in only one or two years. The numbers are compelling. A 1 percent increase in productivity can pay for green features. A 10 percent increase in productivity can pay for the building. Yes, the *building*.

We see 4 percent to 16 percent increases in productivity in our buildings, and it's usually higher in clerical activities like call centers and marketing operations, because they get daylight and fresh air. The highest value is typically in a manufacturing context.

>> Tell me more about the fiduciary issue for owners and developers.

It's very important. Because of our firm's history of interest in indoor air quality since the early 1980s, we have seen the lawsuits over indoor air quality complaints, which were settled out of court because they didn't want to create a scare or a precedent.

Anybody with half a wit will not want to expose themselves to contingent liabilities. Anybody in an executive position will want to be both cognizant of and render visible their contingent liabilities. If I am a CFO, and I have a potential lawsuit that would cost the company $100 million or affect our insurance coverage, I must let the shareholders know. I just cannot leave it floating out there.

So, sick buildings will be more and more of an issue of contingent liability for the owners and definitely in the marketplace. The banks won't touch them. Who will want them? They're expensive—like having a Superfund site built on your property.

Smart people will want to show that they are not negligent. As more and more owners and tenants become aware of these issues, there will be a tipping point where people are rendered liable because they *should* have known. At some point, it will be common at ULI [the Urban Land Institute] for the more advanced members to treat this issue as ordinary course of business. The best protection from liability is to do the best you can.

>> Why is this shift to green buildings occurring after such a long incubation period? After all, pioneering architects, like you, were designing sustainable buildings in the 1970s and 1980s.

Thomas Jefferson said that revolutions happen when you get a critical mass of 5 percent of thought leadership. So, that what's happened: at least 5 percent of the building industry has recognized that green building is fundamental to the enjoyment of life, liberty, and pursuit of happiness—not to mention profit—in the building field.

It has taken this long to reach the critical mass. But we're here at that point: green buildings and best practices exist now. Take a look at the 10.4-acre [4.2-hectare] green roof for Ford [in Dearborn, Michigan]. The green roofs we did for Ford, Mayor Richard Daley in Chicago [the City Hall], and the Gap [in San Bruno, California] were the first. Once they were done and proven, anybody could be second, or third, or fourth. The first example gave other people the license to practice. A young architect at a firm can say, let's do a green roof; rather than being seen as loopy, the young architect is now seen as smart.

>> What sectors or building types are leading the green transformation, and why?

Typically, it's buildings with names on them, because those people, those companies, have a comprehensive view of their self-interest. So, it's typically the non-spec owners and developers constructing for their own account—the corporations that celebrate people as their primary resource, like the Gap in San Bruno.

Now, take all the solar collectors going onto the roofs on Google's headquarters [in Mountain View, California]. That's what a responsible corporation should do. They're not stupid. Their job is getting the top PhDs at Stanford and similar universities. The cost of solar collectors is chump change compared to recruiting value because Google has one of the highest rates of return per person—nearly $1 million—if they recruit the right people.

We must also respect that people and companies have different bottom lines. You must respect that people come to green buildings in different ways—saving money in energy, reducing liability, boosting productivity, or feeling good about green rather than pink marble in the lobby.

>> What are the challenges to green buildings truly going mainstream?

The primary impediment is the perception that green buildings cost more, without any kind of comprehensive understanding of the real value that will be generated. It doesn't take long for an intelligent person, a person with high school math, to run the numbers on green agendas. [They have] immense payback.

All sustainability, like politics, is local. An example: one of the most valuable things is a green roof. We got a project approved in California because it had a green roof. Earlier, the city had decided that the stormwater system couldn't handle any more stormwater runoff. They were going to reject any more development because the infrastructure had maxed out. When they saw our building, with a nine-inch- [23-centimeter-] thick green roof, they said build it since the water runoff would be less than existing runoff from the site, which had an artificial surface.

We put native grasses on our roof, so from a bird's perspective it was better—and, of course, it was better for the city.

>> **The U.S. Green Building Council's LEED [Leadership in Energy and Environmental Design] standards have become the benchmark for green buildings. Can you suggest any improvements in the LEED rating system?**

The LEED standards are a great start because they give a benchmark against which people can measure a building's performance. But any checklist is always ready for improvement. For example, the LEED checklist gives points for recycled content in carpet and other products. But it doesn't look at the qualitative question: are there harmful materials like PVC [polyvinyl chloride] in the carpet? You could be recycling a carcinogen.

So, in many cases, we need new design of things. That's why we are looking at integrating "Cradle to Cradle" practices into LEED, where we can get innovation points for new, more sustainable products. Warren Buffet's company, Berkshire Hathaway, has the capital to invest in intelligent market steps, and in the case of carpet, it owns Shaw Industries, the largest carpet manufacturer in the word. They can invest in retooling. They are getting out of PVC in carpets. They could have said, "We cannot afford it," or "PVC is good for you," but they didn't. They just made the change.

Countries around the world are starting to ban PVC. So, for Shaw, why make a product that they cannot sell in global markets? So they made a fundamental business decision that respects the reality of the current global business environment.

>> **What about China? By 2009, the country is projected to produce more greenhouse gases than the United States, and it has suffered major environmental disasters. Can it be a leader in green technology?**

China is a supernova, which is exploding and imploding simultaneously. The environment is collapsing while the economy is exploding. The rivers run black. You can eat the air. You can feel it on your tongue.

So, China holds the key to this green issue—that is, when China decides to make solar collectors in huge numbers. That will make solar energy cheaper than burning coal. That's got to be one of the fundamental steps in resolving their air problem, which is very visible in particulates.

When China comes on line with solar collectors cheaper than coal, it will be one of the greatest gifts to the U.S. For every one job in manufacturing collectors, you will create four jobs in installation and maintenance in whatever country they are installed.

China wants to create jobs for itself, create new markets, and reduce its own pollution —to solve all kinds of problems at once. How close are they to doing that? Six years and $3 billion away.

My job is imagining the perfectly exquisite in order to create the practically impossible. The perfectly exquisite outcome would be for China to put $3 billion into solar technologies immediately, looking for the way to make equipment that can mass produce solar collectors on a scale at which generating kilowatt-hours from the sun produces energy cheaper than the burning of coal. That is the assignment of our species at this moment in history. And China is the only place where this can happen.

In the end, China will make the equipment that makes the solar collectors, then ship it to the U.S. for assembly and final production. We have to tool up a piece of equipment that costs $100 million to manufacture here, but can be built in China for $10 million. So, you manufacture the solar equipment in China, and bring it here to carry out the actual production, which will create manufacturing jobs here, enable us to reduce oil dependency, and then generate more jobs to install and service the collectors.

The thing in the next ten years after that will be logistics. Why not [produce a solar collector] locally instead of shipping it across the ocean? So, I think the Chinese will build factories all over the United States in the next 50 years, just like the Japanese have done with cars. If you'd said 50 years ago that the Japanese would build factories in the U.S., people would have laughed at you. Now, of course, various states and their governors chase the Japanese carmakers when they are planning new facilities and give them tax breaks.

>> Do you have any favorite green buildings or developments? Are there best-practices projects that have inspired you?

I'm always delighted by architect Norman Foster's work. Very high end. [It's] not a conventional practice, but I am inspired by the fact that he worked with Buckminster Fuller and really understood what Fuller was trying to do. I am inspired by Richard Rogers. They both have sustainability in their hearts.

I am particularly fond of bedouin tents, which are made from goat hair. They have magical properties. First, the tent is black, which is surprising in the desert in 120-degree heat [49 degrees Celsius]. But it provides deep shade, so it protects you from UV rays. Your sensible temperature drops from 120 to 95 degrees [35 degrees Celsius]. Because the tent is black, it causes convective currents on its outside, which cause the air to rise. Even though you are in a place with no breeze, you get a breeze moving through the tent because of the coarse weave.

The open weave is so loose that you get tiny points of light. You get a beautifully illuminated interior—a great place to read. The color and light are beautiful.

The bedouin tent has other sustainable features. Goats are ruminants that eat what humans can't, and give us meat, butter, and wool. Finally, the tent is biodegradable.

>> What are your predictions about sustainability? In ten to 20 years, how will sustainability affect the real estate industry?

Given the fact that young people see sustainability as common sense and don't understand why we would do it any other way, in 20 years these practices will be considered normal behavior.

I have CEO clients who are thinking this way. Because they are 45 years old, not 55 years old, their world and perceptions are different. That's a ten-year gap, but it might as well be the Grand Canyon.

Einstein said that no problem can be solved by the same consciousness that created it. So, clearly these people have a different consciousness than the people who created the problem that they are trying to solve.

>> What do you hope your legacy to be?

I think [it will be] my buildings and the cities we are designing, certainly. That's kind of obvious because I am an architect. But it's really the many minds I've changed. That will be my legacy.

BJÖRN STIGSON

Björn Stigson had over 20 years of international business experience when, in 1995, he was appointed president of the World Business Council for Sustainable Development (WBCSD), an international organization with 200 member companies from more than 30 countries that are committed to sustainable development through economic growth, ecological balance, and social progress. He also serves on boards and committees advising everyone from the Chinese government to the Dow Jones Sustainability Index.

"Concern with ecosystems, including fresh water, is going to produce more regulations and incentives concerning where one can build, what one can build, and how one can build."

As president of the WBCSD, Stigson works with 200 companies around the world that are actively pursuing best practices in sustainability. His activities give him an invaluable perspective not only on the international state of green buildings, but also on the most effective green incentives and regulations, how sustainability policies can make business more competitive, and the future of the real estate industry in this era of growing public demand for change at all levels of the built environment.

>> **Sustainability is becoming an increasingly important principle and action around the world. Witness the growing concern about global climate change and the increasing popularity of green buildings. Who or what will be the most effective "green change agent" that drives sustainable principles more fully into the mainstream?**

Reality is the most potent change agent. A reporter for the *Economist* recently asked me why all our members wanted to be on the side of the angels. I said that they wanted to be on the side of reality.

Managing sustainability issues is becoming crucial in managing a business. Where is a factory's water coming from; its energy supply? How can we manage carbon in a carbon-constrained world? Is a business plan that requires shipping goods vast distances viable in a world of expensive energy?

With a number of countries' populations stagnating and aging, companies must do more business in the developing world where we can see population growth. This need brings in both the social and the environmental side of sustainable development. It is the companies that think they can focus on old business models that will need the intervention of angels.

>> What is the largest, most significant role that corporations can play in sustainability?

Corporations provide much of the innovation and efficiency that society needs to progress. The WBCSD members are positioning themselves to prosper in a market where sustainability issues matter. As they do this, they provide a powerful business voice for change in the right direction and powerful examples from the ways in which they manufacture, sell, service, report, build, and maintain their plants and buildings. Our members have a total annual turnover of some $6 trillion and reach about half the world's population with a good or a service every day. So they are powerful message generators.

>> Do you want to see government regulations require companies to become more sustainable in their real estate practices, in their operations, and other aspects of their business?

So much of what needs to happen requires new or improved technologies, and most of these technologies need policies and regulations to encourage their development, dissemination, and use. In a sense, technology and regulations are two sides of the same coin. In terms of policies, I am thinking of policies such as building codes and product performance standards. This is particularly true in getting new energy technologies into the market. Paths of sustainable progress cannot be achieved without business, but they cannot be achieved by business alone.

Our Energy Efficiency in Buildings [EEB] project has established a vision of all buildings being energy neutral, carbon neutral, and cost-effective by the year 2050. A lot of the technology to get there already exists, but it will take new government framework conditions to get it widely used.

The Millennium Ecosystem Assessment, in which the WBCSD was very involved, found that almost two-thirds of "ecosystem services" were being degraded. The word *services* refers to the provision of things like fresh water, food, fiber, and a predictable climate for agriculture. So we are speaking of the basic needs of civilization. Reversing this degradation will doubtless require some new regulations on the development of real estate all over the world.

>> You said recently to a gathering of government ministers in Nairobi that "Governments must quickly establish the policies that will allow business to invest more in a clean energy future." Did you mean that current policies slow or prohibit the development and use of clean energy technologies, building materials, and practices? If so, what do you consider the most important policies that should be established?

It is very simple. Why should business invest in equipment that decreases carbon dioxide emissions if there are no policies requiring or rewarding it—either regulations or emissions-trading markets? Why should electricity utilities encourage their customers to be more energy efficient if this means they simply sell less of their product? Why should companies develop next-generation nuclear plants unless policies back their commissioning?

>> What incentives will have the most impact in driving sustainability into the mainstream? If these incentives have not been introduced yet, what should they be?

Every time a group of thoughtful people gets together to think about sustainable development, they find themselves championing a few basic incentives. I am thinking now of the Brundtland Commission, the CEOs of the original Business Council for Sustainable Development that re-ported to the Rio Earth Summit, and the U.S. President's Council on Sustainable Development. These were very different groups, but they all wrestled with the same basic notions.

One incentive would be implementing full-cost pricing: that is, for example, if you buy a car battery, the price should include the cost to society of eventual disposal of that battery. Another incentive would be moving away from command-and-control regulation toward more use of market solutions and economic instruments to keep people and companies constantly improving. This includes also taxing more heavily the things we do not like, such as pollution and waste of resources, and taxing less heavily the things we like, such as jobs.

Movement in these directions would provide great incentives for innovation and de-ployment of more efficient technologies.

>> You've mentioned that the vision of the WBCSD's Energy Efficiency in Buildings project is to make all buildings around the world—new and existing—energy neutral, carbon neutral, and cost-effective in less than 50 years. Many people in the real estate industry would insist that that is an unrealistic goal. What makes you think we can change the real estate industry's practices, government regulations, and people's attitudes to accomplish your goal?

There is no law of nature that prevents us from achieving this vision; it is a question of will and determination. The target of a moon landing was "unrealistic." So was the concept of splitting the atom. And much of the technology for the sort of buildings you describe already exists. I think society has reached a tipping point in terms of doing something about climate change that is as emotional as it is scientific. And this emotion is going to drive what politicians see as realistic. Those in the real estate industry who are ready for rapid change are going to be the winners in the next few decades. Those whose view of reality is stuck in the 20th century will be the losers.

>> How will the growing interest in sustainability affect the real estate industry? Do you see different impacts in various parts of the world?

Concern with ecosystems, including fresh water, is going to produce more regulations and incentives concerning where one can build, what one can build, and how one can build. Concern with climate change will affect how buildings are heated and cooled.

>> Do you think that the real estate industry will soon be forced to construct buildings only with sustainable and alternative building materials?

The word *forced* and the linking of *sustainable* and *alternative* show the sort of 20th-century thinking I was talking about. I hope governments will develop the sorts of incentives to which I referred that will make it in the interest of the real estate industry to use energy-efficient materials. Customers will demand it. And *sustainable* will not be *alternative*, but will be mainstream. This is already happening

>> The WBCSD is pursuing ambitious programs for research and public education about sustainable best practices, such as the Energy Efficiency in Buildings work. Why is WBCSD taking this role?

The *real* WBCSD is not the small secretariat in Geneva but our 200 members that lead and drive our program. No project gets started unless the members call for it and unless at least two members agree to chair the effort, thus putting their own and their company's reputation behind the effort. Companies tend to join at the CEO/chairman level, and most of these people are passionate about sustainable development and getting the word out.

George David of [Hartford, Connecticut–based] United Technologies Corporation and Bertrand Collomb of [Paris-based] Lafarge pushed for the creation of and have led the Energy Efficiency in Buildings project, while the secretariat plays a coordinating role.

But there is also a business case for such efforts. These leaders have positioned their companies so that they can be more competitive in a world where sustainability issues play a crucial role. They are more eco-efficient, they do more with less, and they are more in tune with the needs of society.

>> **Has the WBCSD thought about programs that educate workers about sustainability at its member corporations so that they can carry that information into their private lives?**

We have given a great deal of thought and effort to this, and it is a major concern of our members. If the CEO of a company is an advocate of sustainable development and people in middle management are cutting environmental or social corners, then a company can get in deep trouble very quickly.

We helped develop a computer program called Chronos, which anyone at any level in any company can use to learn about sustainable development from a business viewpoint. Some of our members have customized the program so that it better fits their operations. Shell made it appropriate for an oil company.

Every year, the WBCSD organizes a Young Managers Team from member companies. We bring together about 30 rising talents under 32 years old. These people decide what they want to do, and they contribute to the overall work of the membership. They also take sustainability messages back into their companies and spread them through the younger staff.

We also have at each of our twice-yearly meetings a Learning by Sharing session in which members educate others on sustainability topics of mutual interest. We have found that so many of our companies are implementing sustainable development in various ways, and we are increasing our efforts to spread these examples and cases throughout the membership, getting them into company newsletters and onto Web sites.

>> **The WBCSD has a worldwide reach. Are you aware of any company that has instituted a broad-based green culture, as well as green real estate practices? Are there any examples of best practices that you would like to mention?**

You put me in a tough spot. As president of the organization, I hesitate to single out a few companies without mentioning some of our other members. I think it is safe to say that this concept of sustainability—meeting the needs of the present without compromising the abilities of future generations to meet their needs—is so vast and complex that no single company has operationalized it, if you will pardon the expression.

There are, however, many examples of best practices, and it is these that we try to spread through our Learning by Sharing work and our case study library. But these best practices tend to depend on corporate concerns and situations. Eskom, the South African electricity utility, for example, was required by the government to get electricity to poor people, so it has pioneered metered systems that allow poor people to pay as they go.

The Swiss-based cement company Holcim is concerned with the ways in which its products are used after it sells them. So, it has established a foundation to improve the use of cement in construction. The Mexico-based cement company Cemex works with NGOs [non-governmental organizations] to sell bags of cement to poor families, and it also offers advice on how to use the cement to build or improve homes.

Many of our members are pioneering efforts on biodiversity swaps, so that when the siting of a plant or building decreases biodiversity in one area, the company can conserve or even increase biodiversity in another area.

>> The U.S. media usually focus on the United States, Europe, and Asia in their sustainability coverage. Can you identify any successful—and inspirational—sustainability lessons in Latin America, the Middle East, or Africa that have not gotten U.S. coverage?

In addition to the South African and Mexican companies I have already mentioned, the Latin American holding company GrupoNueva has developed a drip irrigation system for poor farmers in Guatemala and has pledged that, by 2008, 10 percent of its business will be with poor people in poor neighborhoods.

The Britain-based mining company Rio Tinto is training people so it can hire locally in countries like Australia—where indigenous unemployment is high—and it is making local firms part of its supply chains all over the world. The international phone company Vodafone is introducing mobile banking solutions in Kenya, Tanzania, and elsewhere. I could go on.

But these are just the big companies. We have a network of more than 55 national BCSDs, our national partner organizations, stretching from China to New Zealand and from Chile to Mozambique. Each of these is pursuing and promoting sustainability at a national level.

>> Can you offer predictions of where sustainability will be in ten to 20 years and how it will affect the real estate industry?

It is so hard to predict what *will* happen. Multilateralism seems to be at a low ebb. The governments of several powerful and important nations seem unable to deliver sustainability solutions. The main sustainable development drivers are globalization, energy, and climate; the future directions of giants such as China and India; and the development of the global markets. One can throw in a host of other issues such as the decline of ecosystem services, especially water.

Managing all of these will require powerful new multilateral efforts and serious public/private partnerships combining government, business, and civil society. No single part of society can create a sustainable world on its own. We need partnerships between the best of government, the best of business, and the most pragmatic civil society organizations, which will require enlightened leadership from all parts of society.

JAIME LERNER

Jaime Lerner is an architect and urban planner. He served three terms as mayor of Curitiba, the capital city of the state of Paraná in southern Brazil, which has become a model of sustainability, social betterment, and economic growth. He then served two terms as governor of Paraná. He founded his own firm, Jaime Lerner Associated Architects, and the nonprofit Instituto Jaime Lerner, which focuses on urban management strategies.

"People seek complex solutions when simple ones often work better. . . . A city is not as complex as people tell us. There are a lot of 'complexity sellers' around the world. We should beat them with slippers."

As a consultant to the United Nations and to cities and countries around the world on sustainable urban and regional development, few people better understand what makes for a successful and humane city than Lerner. In this conversation, he discusses issues ranging from mass surface transit to sustainability challenges and opportunities in Latin America and China. Often challenging conventional wisdom, he emphasizes that bigger is not always better, and that more money can be less effective than limited money if it is spent unwisely.

>> What are the most serious sustainability problems in the world?

Many people are starting to be concerned about the seemingly impossible sustainability issues worldwide. Sometimes, we start to feel like terminal patients, like there is nothing we can do about the problems.

My feeling is, the most serious sustainability problem facing the world is failing to understand the role that cities can play. What are the main problems of carbon emissions? Most of the problems are related to our misconception of the city, particularly to mobility and to the misuse of the automobile. It's simply not enough to have green buildings, and it's not enough to have new sustainable materials. Instead, it's in the conception of the city, and of urban transport, where we can begin solving the problem.

Besides the normal problems of cities—like housing, education, health care, the care of children, safety—there are three main environmental issues that are fundamental, not only for one particular city, but for all of mankind. The three main environmental issues are mobility, sustainability, and social diversity.

Let's speak about mobility. I am concerned about how, in every city, we are postponing the problem. We know that cars are responsible for such a large percentage of carbon emissions. We know that we have to provide good alternatives through public transport, but new and effective manners of public transport are hardly even discussed, let alone implemented.

Every city in the world can improve the quality of its mobility in three years—that's the normal term of a mayor. I'm sure of this, from my experience of working on cities for 40 years. I have to tell you, it's not a naive position; it is possible. All I am doing in many cities of the world as a consultant is giving the testimony that this is possible to do.

Many places are trying to solve the problem of mobility through costly systems, which take a lot of time to do and need subsidy. In New York, they have been talking about building the Second Avenue subway line for 50 years. Now that the talk has started up again, it will take 20 years—that means 70 years from the original idea to completion. [Construction on the line began a quarter century ago, but the tunnels were sealed when work halted.]

The Second Avenue line is supposed to cost US$3.8 billion. But it would not even transport more people than the light rail line in Curitiba, Brazil, right in front of my house, which we built in less than two years!

I am sure that the future of urban transportation is in surface mass transit—in a surface system that has the same performance as a subway. You can give a surface system the same performance as an underground system, but you can construct it much faster to serve more passengers with higher quality. I can tell you, because I did it. Now, over 80 cities are implementing systems like the ones that I implemented in Curitiba.

The key concept of urban mobility is that different types of transportation should never compete in the same space. And that is a good concept of mobility—trying to make what you have better.

>> What about sustainability as the second great problem of cities?

If you and I want to help create a more sustainable world, what is possible for every person to do? There are five commandments of sustainability.

One, use your car less. I'm not saying, don't use it. Just use it less in your routine itinerary. When you can, take public transit. Of course, you must have a good alternative transit system in the first place to do that. Every city in the world must offer that alternative. If not, we are really in trouble.

Two, either live closer to your work or bring your work closer to home. It will be impossible to continue our current mode of living—of living in one place and working on the other side of the city or having leisure on another side of the city. Cities must have an integration of functions. We cannot waste energy, including our own energy or time, always going back and forth.

Fortunately, today, the generators of jobs—the industries and services—are diminishing in scale. The major industries—food, services, and so forth—can be closer to your home. And they are no longer noisy or dirty. That's a good asset for our cities now and in the future.

Third commandment: separate your garbage. Simple.

Fourth, we have to understand that sustainability is the integration of saving and wasting, where you save at the top and waste less on the bottom. So, the more you save, the less you waste. If your waste is zero, your sustainability goes to the infinitum.

Fifth and finally, an important issue, have multiple uses for all urban facilities. We cannot afford to have downtown districts empty for 16 hours a day or a big arena used just ten times a year. An arena could be a farmers' market in the morning, or serve university uses, or be used at night for big events. It's incredible that they are used just ten times a year. Multiple uses make the city more compact.

>> And finally, what about the third major environmental problem that you identified—diversity?

A city is more human when it mixes urban functions—living, working, and leisure—when it mixes ages and income. The more you mix uses, ages, functions, and incomes, the more diverse it is, the more human.

We must have diversity, not only in ages and incomes, but also in religions and backgrounds. If you have a contact with your neighbor, you are not an enemy; you coexist. It is a healthy coexistence.

I like better the expression of the former president of Portugal, Mario Suarez: we have to globalize solidarity. The city is the best refuge of solidarity. That means if a country, every government, doesn't have a general view about their cities and a general view about people, my feeling is—history shows us every time—when we try to solve the economy, we try to work on the economy separated from the human settlements, we have disaster. When we are speaking about Latin America, it's a severe problem of detachment.

>> That said, what course should political and community leaders take to boost sustainability? Or for you are these issues directly tied to all politics, not just environmental issues?

How can we be closer to people? We must propose a high quality of life—meaning a goal above a mere economic one. Many times I was watching or listening to debates between candidates for president in many countries, and the big discussions were about numbers. For example, "I propose more millions of jobs than you."

My own feeling is, never did I see a discussion of the whole scenario for a whole country or a state. I was in Lima, Peru, once, and I saw written on the wall, "Enough Public Works, We Want Promises." It was a joke, of course.

In most countries, there's a lack of creativity and innovation. But you know what the main problem is? People seek complex solutions when *simple ones* often work better. What are the secrets of my city? I would say commitment to simplicity—that is, not being afraid to be simple, because a city is not as complex as people tell us. There are a lot of "complexity sellers" around the world. We should beat them with slippers.

The second approach is not wanting to have all the answers. Why are people so ambitious to have all the answers? If you want to have all the answers, you will never start. So, if you want to have innovation—it's 50 percent of the process, the start— why? Give the people a chance to correct you. That's the main issue: listening and not losing your creativity.

>> Where does Latin American excel in comparison to other nations or regions in solving sustainability and growth problems? What lessons or best practices does Latin America offer other nations?

I can give you a quick answer: the lack of resources helps Latin America to be more effective, more creative. You are more creative when you have less. That is, if you want to be more creative, take out a zero from your budget. If you want to be really creative, cut two zeros.

We cannot cut programs that are tackling serious problems, however. I could never cut our education and health care programs when I was mayor. I tried to make a creative solution on sustainability with the money that was left.

>> Where does Latin America fall behind other nations in solving sustainability and growth problems?

For our needs, we have to find quicker answers. We are very fast-growing countries; we don't have enough time. We have to understand that it must be fast, it has to start. Other nations, without this growth problem, can have more time.

>> What about of lack of environmental laws in some Latin American countries?

It's not about passing regulations or even taxing people. Rather, it's convincing people. They have to understand the result of their attitude. If you can explain, if people are convinced, they will help you. It's not trying to force by law or by taxing. If you force too much, they will always try to find a way to evade the law.

>> **You have worked as an urban planner in China. What do you think of its industrialization and rapid urbanization? Is it good, is it bad, or a mixture of good and bad?**

I know China, but not well enough. China is a very complex situation. If you look at Shanghai, it is more like a *Flash Gordon* landscape. In other issues, they are mostly like the *Blade Runner* landscape. You can go from *Flash Gordon* to *Blade Runner* very easily.

If China wants to commit to a more sustainable policy, they will commit. They have this will. It's an incredible country. That's my hope, that they want to commit more to a more sustainable world. They can do it faster, but there are still big, big problems there. I have a lot of hope that they can. If they have a big commitment, they have this kind of will to make it.

>> **Do people worldwide need to change their attitudes or their values about what's desirable and what's not if we are going to successfully tackle the truly daunting sustainability challenges?**

Every country, including China, is trying to build the tallest building in the world. The *Guinness Book of Records* names a tallest building in the world. We should change that rating to the most sustainable city in the world!

I am obsessed about one idea: teaching children about their cities, trying to make them understand their own cities. At Curitiba, we started with the separation of garbage. We taught children in our schools for six months. They went home and they taught their parents. That was an incredible experience.

And we need a Museum of Sustainability in many cities—in fact not a museum, but a place where we have sustainable games, where we teach the five commandments about the cities, how many carbon emissions from your house or to your parents' job. You will have a more sustainable world with that kind of education.

>> **Can the many nations that suffer from widespread poverty, warfare, and serious disease improve their environmental and growth problems? Is sustainability a "luxury" that some nations cannot afford?**

That's a good question. Sustainability is not a luxury, it's a need. In fact, the more poverty we have, the more we need sustainability. Sustainability has to do with solidarity, having solidarity not only with your own generation, but also with the next generations.

>> **Your leadership as mayor of Curitiba and your work in many fields have received praise in the media and won many international awards. What do you hope your legacy will be?**

I don't want to talk about my legacy or my favorite thing I've done. Let me say, sometimes, you become frustrated because you cannot achieve your dream. But don't be frustrated if you cannot. Be sure. If you commit yourself with your dream, you can be sure sometime this dream will touch you, go around you. It will say, "I am your dream." It is your second chance. Don't throw it away.

When sometimes you have a dream for your city, but you don't understand your dream of your ideas, don't be frustrated. Just commit more and more, work more and more. Deeper and deeper this dream will turn around you, and it will touch you a few years later, and it will tell you, "Remember I am your dream." That's your second chance.

HANK DITTMAR

American-born Hank Dittmar is chief executive of the Prince's Foundation for the Built Environment, the London-based charity established by the Prince of Wales to teach and demonstrate the principles of traditional architecture and urban design. He is chair of the Congress for the New Urbanism, a founder of Reconnecting America, and author of *The New Transit Town: Best Practices in Transit-Oriented Development* (2003).

"We ought to be very suspicious of people who try to treat sustainability as a green brand to be exported just as we have exported the Western model of sprawl across the globe."

At a time when the media showcase green buildings—as long as they're new, pricey, and loaded with the newest technologies—Dittmar bursts the green bubble to discuss the reality of true sustainability, the failure of "gadgets" to create truly green buildings, the challenges of commoditization, the dangers of green branding, the importance of looking beyond individual buildings to their neighborhoods and communities, and the importance of tradition.

>> **What do you think of the sudden emergence of green buildings as a new force in the real estate world and a frequent subject in the media? Are green buildings a fad, or are they here to stay?**

Yes and yes. While there is a substantial amount of faddism to the green buildings movement, the need for greener buildings and greener neighborhoods is compelling and vital to the planet, and the movement will not go away.

Too much of green building is about technological fixes. At least here in the U.K., many green buildings are normal buildings with green gizmos tacked on. Little attention seems to be paid to the question of whether steel-and-glass curtain-wall buildings can ever truly be sustainable no matter how many CHP [combined heat and power] plants or wind turbines are stuck on them.

While it is certainly a step in the right direction, for example, for Wal-Mart to green one of its stores by incorporating environmental features, if it is located by itself in a sea of parking on an arterial roadway not served by transit, and its customers all must drive from a 30- or 40-mile radius [48 to 64 kilometers] to shop there, is it truly green?

It is the need to go deeper that has led the Congress for the New Urbanism, the U.S. Green Building Council, and the Natural Resources Defense Council to work together to create the LEED [Leadership in Energy and Environmental Design] standard for Neighborhood Development [LEED-ND].

>> **Do you see any roadblocks standing in the way of green buildings fully going mainstream? Or are their economic and environmental benefits nearly an unstoppable force at this point?**

The U.K. government has made a commitment to zero-carbon buildings by 2016 and has begun the process of revising building regulations to move toward that goal. As building codes are a state responsibility in the United States, it would be nice to see Governor [Arnold] Schwarzenegger [of California] and northeastern governors like Ed Rendell [of Pennsylvania] take up the challenge of zero-carbon buildings as well. Even if they don't, I think that the standards set here in the U.K. by the Building Research Establishment [BRE] and in the U.S. by the U.S. Green Building Council are shifting the market. Greener urbanism will hopefully be driven by the LEED-ND standard and by government action to reflect the greenhouse gas impacts of driving.

>> **Has the green building movement focused too much on individual buildings and overlooked the broader problems of automobile-dominated suburban development? Are sustainability advocates missing the bigger picture of sprawl?**

I have been working on climate issues actively since 1995 when President Clinton appointed me to the failed White House task force on the issue. The experts all said land use and transport strategies were too hard, and they argued for a mix of taxes, fuel economy standards, and technological fixes.

We are slowly making progress on this, but if you scratch a green builder, you will find lots of enthusiasm for gadgets and very little for urbanism. Partly it is that "boys like toys"; partly it is the residue of the modernism project and its belief in mechanistic solutions; and partly people think that urbanism involves asking people to sacrifice by giving up their cars, shopping only in skanky food co-ops, and living without yards and with stairs too close to neighbors. We are not getting the story out about the many successful, vital, walkable, mixed-use communities being built by new urbanists and ULI [Urban Land Institute] members around the country. That is why we have to teach people about choice, quality of life, affordability, and wealth creation.

In the long run, greener urbanism will succeed because it will improve the quality of people's lives and save them money, and not primarily because it will save the environment or provide us with the tools for the long emergency.

It's not that I don't believe Jim Kunstler on peak oil or Al Gore on climate change, but . . . attraction works best. "Try it, you'll like it" is better than "do this even though it hurts, because it's good for the planet."

>> **You work for Prince Charles, who deeply believes in traditional architecture. How does that belief support the broader mandate of sustainability?**

As defined by the [United Nations'] Brundtland Commission [whose report, *Our Common Future,* was published by the Oxford University Press in 1987], sustainability means "meeting the needs of the present without compromising the ability of future generations to meet their own needs." It is through the marriage of tradition and ecology that we link past, present, and future generations and demonstrate that, far from being a fad, green urbanism is truly about taking the long view. We believe in tradition as a living thing, beginning with what has worked well in the past and evolving it to confront and respond to the problems of the present day.

In the foundation's urban projects, we acknowledge contemporary issues, accommodating the automobile while celebrating the pedestrian and recognizing that separated zoning may have made sense when factories were tanning animal hides, but that mixed-use makes sense in today's creative, knowledge-based economies.

As the Prince of Wales said in a recent speech to the British Home Builders Federation: "The drive for eco-excellence is, or should be, a key feature for new homebuilding. One might assume this will mean more modern design. But the *Evening Standard* recently pointed out that most people prefer traditional designs for their homes, so an overtly high-tech style will only have limited marketability or curb appeal. And I think it makes greater commercial sense to design an eco-excellent house of vernacular appearance that tells some local story."

>> **Do we need a different real estate model to achieve more sustainable buildings and communities? Doesn't our formula-driven real estate industry stand in the way of green principles? What about building codes, financing, appraisals, leasing practices?**

Our current financial models are based upon the idea of the time value of money, an approach that deeply discounts future benefits and costs. This issue is magnified by the fact that real estate has been commoditized, particularly on the commercial side, so that people are buying shares of portfolios rather than of estates [development projects]. At the end of 2006, the Prince of Wales launched the Accounting for Sustainability project with a large group of corporate partners. The project seeks to find ways to integrate sustainability into both on- and off-balance-sheet corporate and government reporting.

Sir Nicholas Stern's *Review on the Economics of Climate Change* for the British government, also released in December 2006, found that the benefits of an early response for the world's economy were too great to ignore. Minor changes in discount rates triggered massive changes in the level of return from early investment. The problem is one of collective responsibility and individual response, and this means that government must set some clear and consistent standards and expectations.

Practices in the development industry will change as more information becomes available and as other industries begin to shift. Once the insurance industry responds and once the cost of transportation rises, then many aspects of our development paradigm will shift. Value-capture strategies, long-term approaches to development, and town management are all growing aspects of industry practice.

We are looking closely at the way the most successful, beautiful, and dense parts of the U.K. were developed originally, and we are finding that most were developed on long-term leases by titled families that owned the land, which developed urban design and architectural codes for the speculative builders. This model seemed to have worked very well for 200 years in promoting long-term value, encouraging maintenance, and supporting mixed use.

>> Are there any cities or nations that are leaders in sustainability? Are they valid role models for other communities?

We can learn from one another right across the board, but one of the first things we ought to learn is that the tools and techniques for creating sustainable communities may be cross-cultural, and the principles of walkable, mixed-use communities and legible beautiful places may be universal. Truly sustainable places are derived from a connection with local identity, building culture, climate, ecology, materials, and culture. We ought to be very suspicious of people who try to treat sustainability as a green brand to be exported just as we have exported the Western model of sprawl across the globe.

>> Do you have any favorite green buildings or sustainable communities, besides Poundbury?

Taos Pueblo comes to mind. It's been sustained, largely by the sun, for 900 years.

Our own work at Upton outside of Northampton [60 miles (95 kilometers) north of London], where the foundation did the charrette and initial master plan, is incorporating compact, mixed-income, and mixed-use traditional urbanism, sustainable urban drainage, and a high degree of green building.

Watch this space, though, because the work that Leon Krier, Robert Adam Associates, and the Duchy of Cornwall are doing at Newquay in Cornwall and the project that we are doing with Paul Murrain and the developer Red Tree at Sherford outside of Plymouth promise to take sustainability to the next level. Prince Charles is challenging all of us to do better.

The NRDC [Natural Resources Defense Council] building in Santa Monica [California] by Moule Polyzoides is not only beautiful but a benchmark in green building, as are their TOD [transit-oriented development] projects in Pasadena and South Pasadena. Calthorpe Fregonese's plans for Austin, Salt Lake City, and southern California, and their emerging work in Louisiana, demonstrate that to be truly sustainable we have to confront economies, transport systems, and land use at the metropolitan scale.

>> What has been Poundbury's contribution to architecture, to planning, and to sustainability?

Poundbury has, quite simply, broken the mold of conventional development in the United Kingdom. In place of a single-use housing estate, Poundbury is an active, vital community with 1,200 residents at present and 750 jobs, growing to 5,000 residents at buildout. Thirty percent of its houses are affordable—both rented and shared equity—and the affordable units are "pepper-potted" throughout the community so that they are indistinguishable from the exterior. Factories—a chocolate factory, cereal factory, and electronics supplier—are imbedded within the blocks and designed so that they blend into the community. There is no street-sign clutter in Poundbury as the road design serves the purpose of taming the auto within the neighborhoods. And the architecture reflects the tradition and the materials of Dorset, the county in which it is located.

Poundbury has also performed in the market with houses typically selling at a 5 to 10 percent premium over similar homes in conventional suburban developments. When Prince Charles proposed to do Poundbury, he met with the U.K.'s leading house-building companies and they told him, "Nice idea, but it will never work." Today, the Prince's Foundation is partnering with the British Home Builders Federation on educational and benchmarking programs to improve the quality of community building and sustainability of the volume builders. In announcing the partnership, the Sunday *Times* headline read "Prince Charles Was Right All Along!"

>> The Prince's Trust Web site says, "We're a U.K. charity that helps young people overcome barriers and get their lives working." How successful is the Prince's Trust in this goal? How does sustainability—in its broadest sense—fit into this mandate?

The Prince's Foundation for the Built Environment is one of 17 charities for which the Prince of Wales is president. He founded 15 of them personally. Taken together, they represent an interconnected approach to sustainability across all of its dimensions: youth and elder opportunity, education and skills, corporate social responsibility, the built and natural environment, arts and crafts, and health. The charities work both in the U.K. and internationally. The Prince's Trust is one of our sister charities, and it is the largest of the Prince's Charities.

The trust celebrated its 30th birthday last year, and during its time it has helped young people start thousands of successful businesses and has built a mentoring network across the United Kingdom.

>> Where do you see sustainability—in the broadest sense of the word—in ten or 20 years? Are today's young people the ones who will transform sustainability from an ideal into an accepted everyday practice?

Sometimes, I feel like I will spend my life undoing the mistakes of my generation and the generation or two before me. We have had an enormous amount of work to do just fixing all of the things that were trashed in the middle of the last century.

The kids coming up today will be unencumbered by the residue of the modern project, and they will be working in a world of fairly clear limits. But they will not find those limits confining. They will work within them to create places that are truly worth living in because they reflect the materiality and the presence of local cultures, environments, and economies while tapping into a truly global storehouse of knowledge and tools.

>> How will it affect our built environment—in the U.K., the United States, around the world?

We'd better start getting it right in the United States, Great Britain, and Europe as we can't really expect other countries to do better unless we set an example. By nature, I am rationally skeptical and constitutionally optimistic, and so I know that creating livable, walkable, resource-efficient places will be a long, hard slog. But I wake up every day excited by the progress we are making both in the U.K. and the U.S. and abroad.

A more sustainable built environment to me means that we ought to be able to tell where we are—city, suburb, countryside, or India, Mexico, or Indiana—at a glance, because it is clear that the buildings and the form of neighborhoods has evolved in response to climate, ecology, and culture. To do this, we will have to solve what Andrés Duany [cofounder of Duany Plater Zyberk & Company and the Congress for the New Urbanism] calls the problem of large numbers, "creating flexible tools for development that can respond to differences on the ground." Such tools as design codes, pattern books, and community engagement are all key here. It is an exciting and worthwhile challenge, and an area where I hope ULI can continue to lead.

ELIZABETH C. ECONOMY

Elizabeth C. Economy, director of Asia studies at the Council on Foreign Relations in New York City, is a renowned expert on Chinese domestic and foreign policies, U.S.-Chinese relations, and global environmental issues. She consults for several U.S. government agencies, has lectured and taught at several universities, and has appeared on the *Charlie Rose* show on PBS. Her latest book is *The River Runs Black: The Environmental Challenges to China's Future* (2005).

"The real challenge for China, and frankly for the world, is . . . to reform its political economy in a way that makes it easy for local officials and businesses to do the right thing."

China has the world's largest population, its fastest-growing economy, and one of its most degraded environments. The country both offers tremendous opportunities and faces tremendous challenges in the area of sustainability. Will the Chinese, for example, emulate the post–World War II U.S. model of near-universal car ownership and suburban sprawl, and suffer all the resulting environmental consequences? Or will the Chinese benefit the world by mass producing green products and technologies? Economy provides valuable insights.

>> **China is the biggest environmental player—and puzzle—on the planet. Are you optimistic or pessimistic about its progress on various environmental issues?**

It is tough to be overly optimistic about China's current environmental situation and the potential for improvement in the near term. The country tops the world charts on several measures of environmental pollution and degradation and is exerting a profoundly negative impact on the global environment in the process. With the continued emphasis on growth—somewhere around 10 percent annually—and an understandable desire to raise the living standard of the 800 million or so people that have yet to become part of the Chinese middle class, it is difficult to see how China is going to turn things around.

On the positive side, there has certainly been an uptick in the rhetoric emanating from China's senior leaders concerning the importance of addressing the country's environmental problems. Particularly with the 2008 Olympics around the corner, Beijing is intensely concerned about the environment. China promised a green Olympics when it won the Olympics bid in 2001. It is embarrassing for them now to be in a position of uncertainty over whether they will be able to offer the athletes and spectators clean air and water, much less a cutting-edge demonstration of a green Olympics.

>> Where are the Chinese excelling on the environmental front? Where are they a role model for other nations?

The Chinese excel at experimentation. They love to try out new ways of doing things. They might introduce solar heaters in rural southwestern China, grow sweet sorghum for biogas in northeastern China, or try out a novel water purification system. Small-scale experiments are a staple of China's environmental protection effort.

Unfortunately, things become rather more difficult when these experiments are expanded to the rest of the country. Then, a variety of other challenges—corruption, pricing issues for natural resources, the political pressure to grow the local economy—come into play and typically undermine wide-scale adoption efforts. In addition, China tends to approach environmental protection with a campaign mentality that means that important details of implementation are swept aside in favor of meeting unrealistic targets.

>> How degraded is the Chinese environment? Doesn't the title of your book, *The River Runs Black*, convey the enormity of their problems?

The truth is that the title of my book only begins to convey the magnitude of China's environmental problems. If you were to travel throughout China, you would see the full range of environmental threats. The air quality is probably the first thing you would notice. China has five of the ten most polluted cities in the world. People in Beijing, for example, often develop a hacking cough throughout much of the winter and spring as a result of the air pollution.

Land degradation is also an extremely important problem in China. People often think that China is simply going through the process of development that the U.S. and Europe went through 50 years ago, but the reality is that China's environmental degradation did not begin 25 or 30 years ago. Rather, it has been centuries in the making, and an easy place to see that is in terms of the land. By the mid-1800s, entire swaths of northern China were deforested, contributing to a process of desertification that continues today.

Right now, China, which is roughly the same size as the United States, is one-quarter desert, and the desert is advancing at a rate of 1,900 square miles [4,900 square kilometers) per year. In fact, the Gobi now sits only 125 miles [200 kilometers] from Beijing's doorstep. This desertification process is producing tens if not hundreds of thousands of environmental migrants annually. Entire villages in northern China are being subsumed in sand.

Even with these grim statistics, though, if you were to ask someone in China what the most serious environmental problem is, he or she would most likely say access to clean water. About 70 percent of the water that flows through China's cities is unfit for human consumption, and 30 percent of the water that flows through China's seven major river systems is not able to be used even for agriculture and industry. Just about half the population drinks contaminated water, and 190 million Chinese drink water that is so contaminated that it is making them sick.

>> **Does China's authoritarian, highly decentralized political system contribute to these environmental problems? Can it be part of the solution? Or does the system both help and hinder progress on the environmental front?**

Frankly, the Chinese government has proven virtually incapable of getting much of anything done on the environment. It passes law after law, regulation after regulation, and new initiative after new initiative, and the environmental situation continues to deteriorate.

Beijing has very little control over what local officials do. The problem is that there is very little in the system that makes it easy for local officials and businesses to do the right thing. Natural resources are priced below replacement cost, meaning that there is little incentive to conserve. Fines for polluting enterprises are so low that businesses would rather pollute and pay the fines than adopt the appropriate pollution control or treatment technologies mandated by law.

There is no political incentive in the system to protect the environment. Local officials are evaluated on their capacity to grow the economy, not protect the environment, and since they are not accountable to the people in any direct fashion, it is tough to create change.

>> **Is the Chinese building boom as big as it seems to casual observers? Shanghai must have more construction cranes than any other city on Earth right now.**

It is probably fair to say that China is in the midst of one of the greatest social experiments of our time—urbanizing 300 million people, or roughly the entire population of the United States, between 2000 and 2020.

This means an enormous amount of building—not only of apartments and offices, but also of infrastructure. Urban residents use 250 percent more energy than their rural counterparts. To meet this demand, China is bringing one new coal-fired power plant on line every week. Roads are being built everywhere. By 2020, the country will have paved over 40,000 new miles [64,400 kilometers] of highway. Urbanization will also place huge pressure on the water supply in many regions. Right now, China is building three grand-scale canals to transport water—as much as flows through the Colorado River—from the Yangtze to cities in northern China.

>> How fully have the Chinese adopted energy efficiency and other green features for their new buildings? Are the regulations really being followed and enforced?

The Chinese government, in particular the Ministry of Construction, has called repeatedly for Chinese developers to adopt green building standards. The country is adding about 2 billion square meters [21.5 billion square feet] of floor space every year and spends as much as 45 percent of its total energy on the construction and heating and cooling of these buildings. As it stands, Chinese buildings use about two-and-a-half times more energy than buildings in comparable climates. If the country is going to make any headway in reducing its reliance on fossil fuels, more energy-efficient buildings will have to be a significant part of its future.

Everyone points to the Ministry of Science and Technology building in Beijing, which uses 70 percent less energy and 60 percent less water, as the prime example of what can be done. Thus far, however, only about 4 percent of China's largest buildings have adopted energy efficiency measures, and there are only about ten or so projects country-wide that have either received or are registered for the internationally recognized Leadership in Energy and Environmental Design [LEED] certification. Again, recognizing the higher upfront cost for such buildings, there is virtually no incentive or real disincentive for building developers to do the right thing.

>> Why are the Chinese repeating some of America's worst 1950s and 1960s urban renewal mistakes in their big-city building booms? The Chinese, for example, are leveling human-scale historic neighborhoods and ramming expressways through their cities.

This is a tough question to answer. I think it goes back to our earlier discussion of the imperative of growth in the Chinese system and a lack of political control from the center. Some cities are trying to do it better, often with assistance from the international community, but it really depends on having a proactive mayor and money. Zhongshan in southern China, for example, is a lovely little city that has worked hard both in urban planning and historic preservation with the assistance of Singapore to develop a modern green city that has preserved some of the traditional architecture. Qingdao in northern China is another good example of trying to get it right.

It is tough to make the case, too, that quaint stone houses without adequate electricity or running water should not be replaced by homes with all the modern conveniences. There is no doubt, however, that it is tragic to consider that centuries-old homes—really the history of the country—are being razed in favor of truly appalling gleaming new white boxes that will look horrible in just a few years' time due to their shoddy construction and pollution.

At the same time, constructing eco-cities and villages is all the rage right now in China. Experimenting with new building materials, developing a state-of-the-art public transportation system, and using renewable energy for a significant portion of the cities' energy needs will all ostensibly be part of these eco-cities. Again, whether these experiments work and whether they can be replicated, only time will tell.

>> **On the broader environmental front, the Chinese seem to be embracing many of the worst U.S. practices. One thousand new cars are added to the roads of Beijing every day. Fast food restaurants like McDonald's and KFC are opening dozens of drive-through restaurants in China each year.**

Whatever challenges there may be in our relationship with China when it comes to trade or foreign policy, we are clearly of one mind when it comes to commercialism. Bright lights, big cities, and private cars all appeal to the Chinese consumer. Golf, which draws on already scarce water resources, is a hugely popular pastime. No matter the calls for a less material world by Chinese environmental leaders, the Chinese people seem to have spoken.

>> **How are the Chinese trying to reduce their growing dependence on fossil fuels?**

The Chinese are mandating that 10 percent of all energy come from renewable sources by 2010. Wind and solar power are going gangbusters right now, and China is on a perpetual hunt for nuclear power deals. At the same time, the government wants to reduce energy intensity [energy consumption per unit of gross domestic product] by 20 percent between 2006 and 2010.

Unfortunately, they already missed the first year's targets. The plans are good, but the truth is that Beijing has already acknowledged that it plans to double its coal and oil consumption by 2020. So, a reduction in fossil fuel dependence really isn't in the cards.

>> **What about global climate change? What are the Chinese really doing here?**

On the plus side, Chinese companies are eager to take advantage of participating in the Clean Development Mechanism under the Kyoto framework and the opportunity to access new technologies or investment to limit their greenhouse gas emissions. China has more such projects in the pipeline than any other country. Any progress China makes in expanding the use of renewables and enhancing energy efficiency will contribute to diminishing its expected greenhouse gas emissions.

On the downside, China, like the United States, is unwilling to sign on to any agreement with targets and timetables for reducing its emissions. In such a framework, I expect that the International Energy Agency's estimates that China will surpass the United States as the largest emitter of carbon dioxide in the world by 2009 will be right on target.

The real challenge for China, and frankly for the world, is something I mentioned earlier: it is for China to reform its political economy in a way that makes it easy for local officials and businesses to do the right thing. Both the political and economic incentives need to be in place, and they are not. Until then, we are going to continue to see ambitious policies with utterly failed implementation.

It is also the case, however, that for the United States to have any real leverage, or even any real credibility with the Chinese, we need to be doing a much better job on these issues as well. But that is probably a topic for another conversation.

S. RICHARD FEDRIZZI

In 1993, S. Richard Fedrizzi became the founding chairman of the U.S. Green Building Council (USGBC), and in 2004 was appointed president and chief executive officer. He also was one of the founders of the World Green Building Council (WGBC) in 2002. He is on the boards of the WGBC and the United Nations Environment Programme's (UNEP) Sustainable Buildings and Construction Initiative.

"I just came back from Australia, where climate change has meant years of severe drought. The country right now is in a state of panic that there is not going to be enough water for them to feed themselves, to drink, or to bathe themselves."

In June 2007, green building was already booming in the United States and around the world. In this conversation, Fedrizzi discusses the remarkable growth of the USGBC and green construction, global climate change, sprawl development, and regulatory and green building trends. He also addresses such key issues as whether commercial tenants will pay more rent for green workplaces; how the USGBC will accelerate certification under the Leadership in Energy and Environmental Design (LEED) program for companies that construct many near-identical buildings, like bank branches; and the trends he foresees in the coming decade.

>> **Today's media are filled with green building coverage. More and more cities and states are mandating LEED ratings for new buildings. Are green buildings becoming the preferred norm, not the exception?**

I believe that the idea of green building has turned a corner. Why? I'm looking at different indicators than just the number of green buildings and the number of LEED certifications. I see changes in industries like insurance.

The USGBC chased the insurance industry for almost ten years trying to get it to take us seriously, but one summer's losses from Hurricane Katrina tipped the industry, and now at least ten insurance companies are focused on green buildings. Some, like Fireman's Fund, are offering significant programs for renovating after a catastrophe. If a renovation is more than 10,000 square feet [930 square meters], it must be rebuilt to a LEED standard. AIG Insurance, a massive insurance company, is now looking at green building incentives for residential and being able to offer discounted rates for green projects.

Insurance companies are getting it. That, to me, is a massive step forward. And it's just one example of many indicators.

>> Do you see the shift toward green buildings reflected in rentals and sale prices? Will companies and professional firms pay a somewhat higher rent for green workplaces? Will investors pay a premium price for those properties?

We have immense amounts of information proving that it does not cost more to go green, at least at the first two levels of LEED. Certified and Silver can be built for not a penny more than conventional construction. And yet, those properties command a premium in the marketplace.

Property owners have the ability to lease out those spaces in record time at higher lease rates than they've enjoyed before. They can market them and have the ability to retain tenants or their employees longer in those spaces and create a very significant business model.

We are trying to educate folks that if these buildings don't cost more to construct, then the end user like a corporate workplace or homebuyer should not necessarily have to pay more because a space is green. But those are market dynamics that need to play themselves out.

>> In just seven years, the USGBC has grown from 600 member organizations to 8,000 member organizations today, and from 12 LEED buildings to nearly 5,500 projects registered for a LEED rating. How is the USGBC managing its rapid growth?

We're doing a number of things to manage the growth that we're experiencing right now. Technology is a central part of our strategy, whether it's LEED online, or our ability to run all of our internal program applications through SAP [Systems, Applications, and Products in Data Processing, an enterprise resource planning software product created by SAP AG of Walldorf, Germany].

We're also working with organizations to help us figure out outsourcing LEED certification. If we are able to bring in private sector organizations like engineering and architecture firms, but also USGBC chapters and cities and states that have expressed interest in becoming able to perform LEED certification, we can exponentially grow our ability to serve our market.

>> The USGBC has been working to create LEED standards and mass certification for production homebuilders and developers. How far have you gotten?

With LEED for Homes, we have to find a model that can literally certify millions of homes. Having 13 distinct organizations that are taking the certification city by city is working quite well, but it's just the tip of the iceberg. We need hundreds or even thousands of individual certification bodies in every locale to get the kind of critical mass that we're looking for.

>> How is LEED going to be updated to be more responsive to a project's geographic location and climate?

LEED must address a number of unique aspects of projects, including bioregional aspects of where these buildings are being built. With new tools we are developing, all of the design parameters will no longer be bound by a seven-year-old rating system that made you treat your building in Arizona as if it were being built in the Pacific Northwest. All of the things we've learned over recent years are going to be put into this process to make LEED a much more elegant and more responsive system. We look at LEED as a continuous improvement product that will always evolve.

In the newest version of LEED, we've established a new framework to look at a concept we're calling "virtual bookshelf." As you sit down to design your project, no matter where it is geographically, you put the parameters into a wizard type of application on your computer and it would identify your site and the kind of structure. It would address questions like: How big is it? Where is it facing in regards to wind and sun patterns? What are the use patterns? What's the expected longevity of the building? What are the parameters of this building that make it unique?

The wizard would then pull off of a virtual bookshelf 11 or 12 out of 200 or 300 volumes that would be the basis of how you construct and design and build your building. Your rating will be like a snowflake, absolutely unique to your building.

>> How is USGBC addressing global climate change?

Our organization—from its board of directors down through its staff—is focusing all its energies today on climate change. More and more people realize that the problem we are seeing right now is a real problem and that we must provide immediate and measurable solutions.

Climate change is having real effects on people today. I just came back from Australia where climate change has meant years of severe drought. The country right now is in a state of panic that there is not going to be enough water for them to feed themselves, to drink, or to bathe themselves.

We have made a declaration of eight distinct elements of the program that we are working on right now to combat climate change. Any building, for example, that gets a LEED rating will have a 50 percent reduction of CO_2 [emissions] compared to traditional buildings.

To ensure a sustainable future for our children, the USGBC is underscoring this challenge with a commitment to the following: by 2010, there will be 100,000 LEED-certified commercial buildings and 1 million certified homes; by 2020, just ten years later, there will be 1 million LEED-certified commercial buildings and 10 million certified homes.

>> The 110th Congress has proposed bills that focus on reducing vehicular, industrial, and utility-company greenhouse gas emissions. Most of these measures

overlook buildings, which generate over one-third of the U.S. greenhouse gas emissions. How do we get commercial and residential buildings onto the national climate change agenda?

Just after entering office, [U.S. House] Speaker Nancy Pelosi made a very strong statement that green building needed to have higher visibility within the federal government and Congress. She wants to carefully examine the opportunity to green the Capitol building as a first step to show what green buildings can mean to the rest of Americans.

We have the ability now to make some significant changes. Right now in almost every one of our 50 states, there is significant traction in green building through LEED adoptions and entrepreneurial solutions. If members of Congress look at their home districts or states, they will see some phenomenal examples that they can bring to the national agenda.

>> Dozens of cities and several states have mandated that new public buildings—and in many cases the major renovation of public buildings—earn a specific LEED rating. Now, Pasadena, Boston, and Washington, D.C., have mandated that private buildings over a certain size soon meet green standards. Is that a new trend—regulatory insistence that private buildings meet green or LEED standards?

I think the mandates are a new trend. But I think it's also important that we don't forget the existing trend that is working in a number of cities—encouraging the private sector to build green and allowing the owners of the buildings or the projects to experience the real positive benefits, through incentives, without mandates or high costs to the cities.

The best examples that I can give are accelerated permitting and density bonuses. There are 22 cities right now that offer accelerated permitting and greater density [for green projects].

One example that I love is the Lowe's home improvement store in Austin, Texas. Lowe's built a LEED Gold store that uses 40 to 70 percent less energy and 50 percent less water [than a conventional big-box store]. Lowe's was very excited, because the store was permitted in three months, and it usually takes about 15 months to permit a store in Austin. They calculated a profit of $85,000 per day from that store. So, that store saved $3 million just by building LEED Gold. The interesting part was the store cost $2.85 million to build, so Lowe's essentially got a store at no cost. The store has tremendous performance metrics associated with it and tells a story that will help transform the market. Similar examples of incentives driving green building are happening all across the country.

There are other options than regulation to increase green building. When you force things on people, they will try to get around them, but when you give them opportunities and incentives, they will find every way they can to pursue them. It's human nature.

>> Several excellent and proven green building standards are currently operating in the world, like the U.K.'s BREEAM [Building Research Establishment Environmental Assessment Method] and Australia's Green Star programs. Yet, LEED seems to be the standard that more and more countries like Canada, India, and Mexico are choosing to adapt for their own use. Why is LEED proving so popular internationally?

When we adopted LEED for the U.S., we actually looked at other programs like the BREEAM program from the U.K. and the Austin [Texas] Energy Green Building program. We tried to figure out a program that would make the most sense for the American market—that would get people's attention and not be so onerous that it discourages people. And as a result, I think we've achieved significant impact with LEED, not just in the number of buildings that are certified, but also with the 38,000 LEED accredited professionals. This shows that the standard is intuitive and gives people the ability to understand the integration of products, services, and systems to reduce costs and generate social benefits.

In the U.K., the BREEAM program has been very successful, and the Green Star program in Australia is a hybrid rating system of BREEAM and LEED. Everyone is trying to make the best version of a program for their locale. It's interesting to me that our program would be so easily understood and accepted in India. The Indian government, when I spoke to them a few weeks ago, said they love the LEED rating system. Certainly you would expect that in Canada, but to me India was a surprise. Some think LEED is more easily understood, and its simplicity makes it more easily applied in different markets.

>> Is the USGBC going to forge more alliances with other organizations to achieve similar green goals?

Absolutely. We are facing problems that as a species we have never faced before. There is no single organization today that has the ability to undo the horrific climate, toxicity, and human health–related issues that we are facing. We have made it part of the DNA of our organization, ratified by our board, that we are going to collaborate at every level as often as possible.

We have strategic alliances right now with ASHRAE [American Society of Heating, Refrigerating, and Air Conditioning Engineers], AIA [American Institute of Architects], BOMA [Building Owners and Managers Association], IFMA [International Facility Management Association], ASID [American Society of Interior Designers], ASLA [American Society of Landscape Architects], and many of the NGOs [nongovernmental organizations] that are involved in sustainability at different levels. We are trying to achieve what I call the "grizzly bear effect"—where, if we link arms and yell loudly, we appear larger and more powerful. We need to make ourselves heard.

Through collaboration, we can make meaningful progress. If we do not collaborate and instead have turf wars, then we will find ourselves in a very sad position in the next ten to 25 years.

>> **I've always thought green buildings are only half the solution to reducing energy consumption and achieving environmental benefits, such as slowing global climate change. What is the USGBC doing to transform our antigreen sprawl development patterns?**

The LEED rating system and now LEED for Neighborhood Development [LEED-ND] are instrumental in helping people understand the negative impacts of sprawl, that a green building [constructed] on a greenfield is not necessarily something to be proud of.

Real green building happens when existing developed land is once again treated with respect, where people have the ability to re-create connections and neighborhoods, utilize mass transit, share energy services—even look out for each other's security. Redesigning our neighborhoods is one of the most important things that green building will lead to.

I think it needs to be understood that if there is no preexisting footprint, in my strong opinion we should not be using that land for anything other than possibly growing food, if necessary. I am horrified by the current public debate over whether we use land to grow our food or for our energy supply. If that becomes the debate of the future, without realizing that we have other alternative and renewable energy sources that don't utilize our agriculture stock, then we've lost the battle.

>> **What new green building trends do you see that would surprise people following the evolution in green development?**

When I think about trends, I think the most important new trend is a return to common sense. People are finally utilizing information on energy, water, waste, toxicity, and site usage that was *not* developed by USGBC 14 years ago, but was developed by solid practitioners maybe 100 or 150 years ago.

I believe that we are now reclaiming our souls. We are going back to the roots and understanding how structures nourish us as human beings, whether it's a person at home, a worker on the job, a child in school, or someone who's healing in a hospital. We are finally taking seriously how human beings are affected by the buildings where they live, work, and play. We are respecting the right of children to have clean air and clean water and daylight.

As we take that knowledge and apply it in everything we do, the trend is that we've again reclaimed our souls. We are designing the right buildings at the right time in the right place and understanding that the human being is what it's all about.

PAUL HAWKEN

Paul Hawken is executive director of the Sausalito, California-based Natural Capitalism Institute research group. He is also a well-known environmentalist and entrepreneur who founded the Erewhon Trading Company for natural foods and the Smith & Hawken garden supply company. His newest book is *Blessed Unrest: How the Largest Movement in the World Came Into Being, and Why No One Saw it Coming* (2007).

"The media are presenting green as the new black, which is fine, but what we are talking about is a cultural change that comes about as a result of deep reflection about values, community, and identity."

For more than 40 years, Hawken has worked on environmental, economic, social, business, and green development issues—far longer, and with more success, than many of today's "green gurus" who are, by comparison, Johnny-come-latelys to sustainability. His depth of experience, his global understanding, and his work as a consultant for companies and governments on economic development, industrial ecology, and environmental policy provide important insights on sustainability and the built environment.

>> **Your Web site says that since age 20, while you were still in school, you have "dedicated your life to sustainability and to changing the relationship between business and the environment." What exactly do you mean by that statement? And why did you embrace this life cause at such an early age?**

Maybe it was the formative years I spent in the Sierra Nevadas. Maybe it was growing up in California and seeing development destroy places I loved—places where one night there were frogs and mockingbirds, and the next day bulldozers. But whatever it was, from early on, the disconnect between nature and business was obvious, and I have spent my life addressing it.

At age 20, I started my first company, and its purpose was to develop sustainable methods of agriculture and cultivate a market for the products. It's called the natural foods movement now, but at the time it was not so clearly defined.

At that time, the U.S. food system had reached a low point. The chairman of the Department of Nutrition at Harvard, Dr. Fred Stare, happily promoted sugar, canned foods, and chemical additives, and sat on the boards of companies that encouraged dietary habits that lead to obesity, Type 2 diabetes, and heart disease.

What I was doing—linking health and food quality to land and water quality—was simply beyond the pale in his eyes. He thought we were nuts, and not the edible kind. It was a time in America when there was a gleeful disconnect from material life and nature. Food, real estate, transportation, and commerce itself were not viewed from a systemic point of view, but as autonomous economic sectors that could transcend natural limits.

Dr. Stare called us food faddists and said that eating organically grown food was experimental and potentially dangerous. I would respond that because the 3,000 food additives and pesticides used on and in our food were pretty much all invented since World War II, he was the wild-eyed radical on the loopy fad diet. Our customers were the true conservatives and were eating the way humankind had evolved over millennia.

>> In the past year, corporate America seems to have embraced sustainability as a correct—and profitable—strategy. When did you sense this shift in attitudes? Can you share any case studies?

As far as I can tell—and my evidence is purely anecdotal—something shifted just over two years ago [2005]. I could tell because of who was calling me, and what they were saying. Companies and CEOs that you would not associate with any environmental awareness began to make inquiries that were serious, top-level explorations of the future.

This was a very different response than the defensive greenwashing that was often seen in the 1990s. The obvious case study is Wal-Mart, the largest company in the world. Even their most dogged critics believe their commitment to the environment is the real deal, and they would be right.

>> Is corporate America's embrace of sustainability genuine? Or does the depth of commitment differ from company to company?

That still depends on the company, and to a large extent the values of the CEO and his/ her relationship to the board of directors. When you are responsible for a huge pile of assets and brand equity, you get understandably cautious and conservative. Despite the fact that commerce benefits from rapid change, most companies resist it in the belief that resistance will protect them.

In the past, the environment was seen as a secondary issue that could be put off into the future. However, if you are management, your responsibility is to plan for the future, and one by one, leaders in business are coming to realize that business as usual will lead to ecological chaos and thus economic ruin, and that to be a responsible business requires a strategy that incorporates both environmental uncertainty as well as environmental restoration.

In short, understanding the environment and transforming the company's relationship to it has become a fiduciary duty. Of course, once you understand that, you get the prize in the Cracker Jack box: moving toward a sustainable world is the most exciting, innovative opportunity that has come along since the advent of the industrial age.

>> What is your opinion of the commercial real estate industry on the sustainability front? Do commercial developers and investors "get it"? Or, again, does it differ from company to company?

It differs vastly, not only from company to company, but country to country. There is Sweden—and then there is Dubai.

My current favorite is Joe Van Belleghem of Windmill West Company, who has partnered with Vancity to create Dockside Green at the upper harbor in Victoria [British Columbia], surely one of the most advanced and thoughtful green developments in the world. Joe has continuously pushed himself and his partners to be problem solvers and to use environmental constraints as a doorway to innovation.

Development always faces a cap-ex [capital expenditures] versus op-ex [operating expenditures] dilemma. The profit motive combined with market forces favors minimal capital expenditures—always a detriment to green development. True ecological development requires a leader and a team that approach the development with dogged attention. These upfront planning costs pay off because when you get it right, the higher costs can be lessened and the higher value is manifestly apparent to buyers.

>> What about the residential developers—not the custom homebuilders, but the big mass-market developers who construct the vast majority of U.S. housing? Are they introducing sustainable principles into their products?

I am not as familiar with this sector, but I think it is evident that the residential housing industry is bringing up the rear. People are struggling to buy into a very expensive real estate market, and the exigencies of the market require cost control and rapid turnaround once construction commences.

Current lending practices rarely factor in reduced energy and water use as part of overall ownership cost, and thus they discount the value of solar panels on the supply side and energy-saving technologies that work on the demand side. This is a shame, because the vast majority of the nearly 2 million new houses built every year will become white elephants—homes that will need extensive retrofitting to adapt to a carbon-constrained future. Money saved in the purchase price will come back to haunt owners later.

Just as we should be building fleets of plug-in hybrid electric vehicles that will get 400 miles per gallon [170 kilometers per liter] in order to address energy costs and national security, we should be doing the same in the housing market: building highly efficient, carbon-sipping homes. Instead, we are building the residential equivalent of Lincoln Navigators and Hummers.

>> What about our sprawl development patterns? How can we really have an economy and society that values sustainability when sprawl gobbles up greenfield land and mandates an automobile-dependent lifestyle?

We either have concentrated areas of people in cities, towns, or villages, *and* a viable countryside, or not. Sprawl doesn't fit on the landscape of a viable, sustainable future.

We are building future ghost strips, and they will be eventually abandoned for two reasons. First, they will be too expensive to get to, and second, intelligent developers are creating mixed-use residential and commercial centers that favor pedestrians rather than Detroit, and this is what people *do* and *will* want. It doesn't mean suburbia can't be retrofitted. It can.

One of the trends that has been overlooked is localization. There is a rapidly growing movement to shorten the distance between supply and demand on almost every level, from food to fuel. Bill McKibben's new book, *Deep Economy: The Wealth of Communities and the Durable Future* [2007], is an excellent look at this movement and the thinking that informs it.

We cannot afford a rapidly growing global economy, because it is extraordinarily wasteful of energy, resources, and even people. We are moving toward locally sourced food, power generation, fuels, transport systems, and even currencies. Bill McKibben is the same author who was largely overlooked by the business community in 1989 when he wrote *The End of Nature,* a prescient forecast of the effects of global climate change, and it would be just as easy to dismiss these ideas today—just as my ideas about creating local organic food webs was ridiculed by Harvard in the late 1960s. But I would suggest that author/prophets such as Bill McKibben have been stunningly accurate in their writings in the past—far better than any of our media pundits who rarely think beyond the next calendar year.

Companies hire consultants to teach employees to think outside of the box, and yet when the outside-of-the-box ideas show up, it becomes apparent that thinking usually has migrated to another box.

>> What are the major roadblocks to the mainstreaming of sustainable principles?

One of the obstacles is cost and price. The federal government provides considerable subsidies to the carbon fuel industry but whipsaws the renewable energy industry with on-again, off-again incentives.

I do not see the Iraq war as an ideological contest, but an oil war. We simply would not be there were it not for the oil fields in and around the country. The eventual cost of the war is projected now to exceed $1 trillion. For that amount of money, we could have provided the incentives to the business community to completely transform their automobile fleets to plug-in hybrid electric vehicles getting hundreds of miles per gallon and powered by 10 million new wind turbines largely placed in the Midwest, benefiting farmers and Native American populations. We could have provided the means and incentives for coal-fired utilities to employ technologies to sequester carbon from their stacks.

We could have altered the economics of homeownership to favor sustainable materials and renewable energy. Finally, we could have provided the incentives to ensure that every building constructed would be carbon neutral within 15 years. This would have provided 1 million dignified family wage jobs and boosted our economy, security, and, no doubt, our self-respect.

Thus, the major roadblocks to sustainability are ourselves. Sustainability is much talked about but little practiced. When I was photographed for the *Vanity Fair* green issue in 2006, they flew in a photographer from London to San Francisco, rented an 11-passenger van with driver that held six other people flown in from New York to assist the photographer, including a makeup artist even though no makeup was required as I leaned against a tree in the woods by my house. During the whole shoot, the driver sat in the van with motor idling.

The media are presenting green as the new black, which is fine, but what we are talking about is a cultural change that comes about as a result of deep reflection about values, community, and identity. One of the real breakthroughs is occurring in the religious community, which increasingly sees sustainability as a way to express care for the sacredness of life.

Another large obstacle is business. Our government is corrupted by money, and overwhelmingly the money comes from business or people made wealthy by business. This skews the electoral process, decision making, and the exercise of power. Just as we enshrined a necessary separation of church and state in our Constitution, we need a separation of business and state. Government also needs to stop politicizing science, which goes back to governmental corruption.

In order to solve problems, you need good data and good diagnosis. This cannot be done when science advisers who once lobbied for ExxonMobil are redlining drafts of federal studies on climate change.

I believe business is now taking a leading role in creating a sustainable future. It is also time for business to take a role in cleaning up its relationship to governance. This requires leadership.

>> What are the most effective ways to promote sustainability? Is it government mandates? Is it education? Will business be the green change agent? Or will it be the organizations covered in your newest book, *Blessed Unrest*?

Sustainability is a systems problem. Thus every node of the system needs to be addressed, from business to education, from church to state. There is no Archimedean lever to be pulled. We need everything and everyone to pull this off, not just business. Just as we often don't know what we don't know, we can't see what we can't see.

The new book addresses humanity's magnificent and collective response to the deterioration of the environment and social well-being. For years as I traveled and spoke to groups, I would meet people and social entrepreneurs who were part of the nonprofit world, better known as social benefit organizations. It occurred to me over the years that I was encountering thousands of organizations addressing the environment and social justice that I had never heard of. So, out of curiosity, I began to find out how many groups there were. Despite government registries and the like, there were no good data. I started to do my own research and was surprised—shocked actually—at how many groups there were.

When I say groups, I include citizen-based organizations, research institutes, NGOs [nongovernment organizations], faith-based organizations, foundations, educational organizations, networks and alliances, [United Nations] organizations, and village-based organizations. I discovered that the movement to address climate, poverty, deforestation, water, hunger, peace, human rights, and conservation is the largest social movement in history, as well as the fastest-growing movement in the world—a vast social landscape that is under the radar of the media because it is atomized, ubiquitous, and composed of mostly small groups.

This collective response is what I address in *Blessed Unrest*. It is essentially humanity's immune response to political corruption, economic disease, and ecological degradation, and it is unlike anything we have ever seen. We overlook it because we focus on ideologies and concentrations of power, whether it is religious extremists, terrorist organizations, or neoconservatives.

But as destructive as these groups have proven to be, they actually have a very small base. What is different about this movement that is working to heal the wounds of this world and reimagine our relationship to each other and the sacredness of nature, is that this movement is not about trying to amass power or authority. It has no central leadership, no leader, no doctrine, no ideology. It is about ideas, and the difference between ideas and ideologies is that the former liberate and open up possibilities while the latter constrain and dictate.

This movement has a long and deep history that is not taught or understood, and it has legs and momentum. There are at least 1 million organizations that comprise this unnamed movement—over 100 million people working actively every day affecting directly the lives of billions more. In essence, it is a phenomenon not yet well understood. We are not just localizing economies and food systems; the world is localizing the nexus of change.

To illustrate the depth and breadth of this movement, we created at my Natural Capital Institute WiserEarth.org, an open-source platform of the organizations, people, resources, events, and more. "Wiser" stands for World Index of Social and Environmental Responsibility. We also created WiserBusiness.org—which catalogs resources, best practices, and companies that are striving toward sustainability—after which we will create WiserGovernment.org. We are moving from a world created by privilege to a world created by community. All of these organizations are allies to those companies that authentically care about their communities and the environment and, as Joe Van Belleghem at Dockside Green and Lee Scott [chief executive officer] at Wal-Mart discovered, can be enormously helpful in propelling change and innovation.

VIVIAN LOFTNESS

Vivian Loftness is a researcher, author, educator, and architect who has worked for more than 30 years to improve the quality of the built environment. She is a professor at Carnegie Mellon University (CMU), where she has headed the School of Architecture, helped found the Intelligent Workplace building research laboratory, and helped develop the Building Investment Decision Support (BIDS) tool.

"If we are willing to invest our cars with his-and-her thermal controls, individual ventilation controls, operable windows, task air, and task lighting for two hours of use a day or less, why are we unwilling to invest in our workstations where eight to ten hours of productive work must take place?"

Existing buildings outnumber new buildings by 100 to 1, yet most of the attention from developers, corporations, and the media has been on new green buildings. Loftness discusses not only the importance of turning existing buildings green, but also the tremendous value and green opportunities to be found in historic buildings—particularly those constructed before buildingwide electricity and heating, ventilation, and air-conditioning systems were common— and the many sustainable design lessons they provide.

>> In much of your work, you stress the importance of reusing existing buildings. What buildings best lend themselves to green renovations and optimal long-term green performance?

Historic buildings and buildings that predate air conditioning were designed for today's green features, from shading to daylighting. All we have to do is bring these buildings back to their historic functionality.

Our historic buildings, for example, were originally designed to use extremely low— if any—amounts of electricity. Their high ceilings, large and plentiful windows, and wide hallways, for example, bring natural daylight to the core of the building, which means you don't have to use electric lights at all during the day.

The 19th- to early-20th-century buildings were also typically quite heavy, often with beautifully crafted stone and masonry facades. Heavy buildings hold on to the cool of the night and suppress the heat of the day, offering what is now known as time-lag cooling. In addition, pre-air-conditioning buildings were designed for wonderful cross-ventilation, taking advantage of natural breezes and a stack effect supported by belvederes. It is a great loss when old buildings are renovated with sealed windows, dropped ceilings, and forced air conditioning rather than using the building's historic features to keep the building cool.

Of course, new buildings can take advantage of the very same features: shading, daylighting, cooling with thermal mass, and natural ventilation. Although energy-efficient lighting fixtures are important, the most efficient light source is daylight. While it's important to have efficient electric lighting, the best option is not to turn it on.

Our Intelligent Workplace lab at CMU, for example, is a very-low-energy workplace. One day, the power went out on campus. We looked through the windows and saw students trickling out of the other buildings. That's when we realized the power was out. We'd had no clue before because we are a daylit facility and we use natural ventilation and we use laptops. So, we just didn't know.

>> What should companies look for in historic buildings if they want to turn them into green and efficient workplaces?

The first step is to evaluate the craftsmanship and quality of the shell, structure, interior, and the space available for introducing new services, plus, of course, location, location, location. Some of the basics include:

- good floor-to-ceiling height;
- adequate and accessible vertical shaft space;
- generous lobbies and circulation areas;
- adequate satellite closet space, or generous circulation areas to borrow from;
- a generous structural grid size, with not too many necessary fixed walls;
- if air conditioning has been installed, adequate duct size and cooling capacity;
- separate ventilation systems for heating and cooling;
- access—or opportunities for access—to operable windows;
- access—or opportunities for access—to natural daylighting and outdoor views;
- irreplaceable craftsmanship;
- a good pedestrian-oriented, mixed-use neighborhood.

>> What are some of the most effective strategies following a green renovation to reap the full benefits of a green building?

The most obvious first step is commissioning the lighting and mechanical systems, including daylight and natural ventilation systems. The payback for commissioning is outstanding on energy costs alone, and it also contributes to better air quality and thermal comfort.

Commissioning is a term developed by the military to ensure that the designers of a sophisticated ship take responsibility to test it on the open seas and transfer their expertise to those who will be responsible to run the ship from then on. Thanks to LEED [Leadership in Energy and Environmental Design] standards and energy renovations in general, we have a new discipline—commissioning agents who improve the mechanical and lighting systems' performance from 10 to 50 percent.

>> Where do energy service provider companies come in?

The biggest challenge to renovating or even updating an existing building is the shortage of cash. In the last two decades, a new industry has emerged that provides both the expertise and the capital for building energy renovations in exchange for a share in the energy savings. This works because we have been so energy wasteful in our buildings and the savings are so significant.

>> You have said that people are rediscovering former building engineering solutions to help them turn buildings green. What are some of those solutions?

We have become so used to the "brute force" method of cooling, ventilating, and lighting our buildings with continuously running equipment that we have lost touch with the engineered "natural" systems from the previous generations of designers.

Pittsburgh's Allegheny County Courthouse [completed 1886] by noted architect Henry Hobson Richardson, for example, has daylit courtrooms, heavy walls for time-lag cooling, and most amazingly, underground cooling tubes. The courthouse, which predates air conditioning and even electric light, is naturally stack ventilated and cooled. Each of the four stairways framing the corners of the building's courtyard acts as a stack. As hot air naturally rises, the stairways pull cool air from the underground tubes up through the courtrooms and out through the roof. It is both an incredibly simple and an incredibly sophisticated system.

The Pension Bureau Building [completed 1887] in Washington, D.C., now the National Building Museum, is another icon of sophisticated daylighting, natural ventilation, and natural cooling systems—in an even hotter climate. While beautifully restored to the eye, the original thermal, light, and air systems in this building have not been brought back to their former glory.

>> Your building design and engineering preferences for green renovations keep cutting off at 1950. What's wrong with the commercial buildings constructed from the 1950s on?

The biggest change that occurred in the 1950s was the invention of buildingwide air conditioning. This meant that we could truly ignore nature and create artificial environments indoors, anytime and anywhere. Designers became sloppy. We designed unshaded, lightweight, and sealed buildings with deep floor plates. The buildings were placeless. They often were built at the lowest possible cost as well, so craftsmanship disappeared.

There are several things wrong with this shift in our built environment. First, these buildings are always energy wasteful. Second, they're often unhealthy. You would be scared watching a fiber optic camera move through the aging ducts in a 1970s sealed building, from the air intake on the roof sitting in a pool of standing water, through ducts with debris and growing organisms, to a diffuser that is black with dust or mold. It is not only that the air-conditioning ducts are buried and inaccessible; it is that we underfund the maintenance of those hidden infrastructures.

Third, these buildings are often least cost and inflexible without the generosity of corridors and lobbies and stairwells that make historic buildings such ceremonial and social meccas.

Finally, one of the greatest losses in our shift to sealed buildings was the lost connection to our natural environment—the dappled sunlight and shade, the floating breezes, the celebration of seasons, the sounds and smells and touch of specific places.

>> Should we just demolish all the cheap 1950–2000 buildings and start over?

While it is environmentally critical that we do not continue to abandon our older buildings, it doesn't pay to renovate every building. Companies—and cities—must identify those buildings where the renovation investment will ensure the revaluing of a naturally comfortable structure, a beautifully crafted building, or a rich mixed-use neighborhood. In some cases, gut rehabilitation can take all of the embodied materials and create a new building that is magical. Re-visioning the least-cost, uncrafted, and sealed buildings of the late 20th century can bring neighborhoods back to life.

>> Your Intelligent Workplace research lab work focuses equally on greening the individual workplaces within existing buildings and on creating new green buildings. Why?

It is time for businesses, governments, and institutions to reinvest inside buildings—rather than just in new infrastructures and least-cost shells—to ensure easy technological and organizational reconfiguration coupled with workplace quality and craftsmanship.

Every affluent Western nation *except* the U.S. guarantees each worker access to a window. Those countries have no concept of the back office, or the basement office, or the center core office, or the *Dilbert* office where workers have no access to daylight, outdoor views, or even fresh air, much less individual temperature controls.

If we are willing to invest our cars with his-and-her thermal controls, individual ventilation controls, operable windows, task air, and task lighting for two hours of use a day or less, why are we unwilling to invest in our workstations where eight to ten hours of productive work must take place? We must begin to invest *inside* buildings.

>> What must be done to help green buildings—both historic and new—adapt to and support future technological and organizational changes, as well as human health and well-being?

First, we must unseal our buildings. We need to design for daylighting, natural ventilation, shading, natural cooling, and passive solar heating—reconnecting each building occupant with the natural environment and the uniqueness of place.

Second, mechanical and lighting systems should be designed to be off as long as possible while providing comfort and healthy conditions when nature cannot. To accomplish this, we must abandon the large zone approaches to thermal conditioning and lighting, which are intended to blanket hundreds of people with adequate environmental quality. Instead, we must move toward individual workstation-based provisions for ventilation, cooling, heating, lighting, data, power, and voice to ensure that each worker has environmental and technical service regardless of workplace changes.

Companies must eliminate their fear that individual controls will result in anarchy. When Alexander Graham Bell first announced the telephone, he had a vision of a phone in every home. The shocked response was that this was an impossible vision that would require every person to be a switchboard operator! As numerous studies have shown, individual controls ensure more satisfied and productive workers, and lower energy usage.

Third, we must recognize that our infrastructures need to be as dynamic as the changing building functions, walls, and furniture. It is imperative that mechanical and electrical systems not be embedded in the building, inaccessible, undersized, and unmaintainable. Instead, we should make these systems "plug and play" with just-in-time purchasing of technology as we need it, rather than employ redundant safety factors: a track light system whose fixtures can be relocated as needed, for instance, rather than downlights embedded in specific locations. Flexible infrastructures also rely on the separation of ambient conditioning needs for temperature and light from the higher levels of task conditioning needs.

Finally, we should reinvest in quality and craftsmanship, both to reinvigorate U.S. industry and trades and to greatly enhance the quality of architecture housing our offices, schools, courthouses, and hospitals.

>> You have said that companies undertaking a green renovation or constructing a new green facility should go beyond the building. What do you mean?

The location of your building is as important to our environmental success as the design of the building itself. America is not only sprawling, it is sprawling in single-use complexes: office "parks," and school "parks," and shopping "parks," and gated housing subdivisions. The amount of driving needed to move through our daily lives is growing every year, which has led to almost ten parking spaces for every car in most states.

One goal for the green construction or renovation of buildings is to rethink land use. We must make a commitment not only to reuse our existing buildings, but also to reuse our existing lands and infrastructures, create density, and diversify with mixed uses.

Instead of consuming more virgin land for single-use activities like office parks, shopping malls, movie complexes, and warehousing connected by increasingly congested roads, it is time for us to rediscover our main streets and town planning. Not only will this spur the environmentally sound greening of existing buildings and neighborhoods, rather than abandonment, but we will also recapture the craftsmanship and grandeur of our historic buildings. Whole-life neighborhoods from Dockside Green in Victoria, British Columbia, to Noisette in Charleston are using infill development to revalue our built-environment inheritance and create new visions for our sustainable future.

>> What will happen to cars in these green urban places?

The empowerment of owning a car will not be lost, only the necessity to use it for all of your family's mobility and the necessity of getting locked in traffic congestion for hours. Imagine the empowerment of a ten-year-old joining a pickup baseball game on his or her school field without needing to be driven to the game. Imagine the working parents who no longer are forced to commute one to two hours a day. They'll have time to coach Little League or soccer, or attend their child's dance recital.

Because we have moved away from mixed-use, whole-life community design, America is in a state of transportation poverty today. For many destinations, the only access is by car, a mode of transportation that is energy intensive, pollution generating, time consuming, and accident prone. Moreover, a substantial percentage of Americans are too young, too old, or too poor to own a car.

If we can imagine a future where walking, biking, skating, boating, light rail, and high-speed rail are as richly supported as driving, we will have achieved a far more sustainable, healthy, and celebratory lifestyle.

DAVID GOTTFRIED

David Gottfried cofounded and was the first staff president of the U.S. Green Building Council (USGBC), which had more than 10,000 members and 70 regional chapters in mid-2007. He was also a founding officer of the World Green Building Council (WGBC). Now, he is senior vice president of sustainable development for Thomas Properties Group in Los Angeles.

"Why aren't we willing to pay for quality and true value in our buildings, especially since we spend most of our lives indoors and the quality of the space affects our ongoing health and happiness in so many ways?"

Few people have been as intimately involved as Gottfried in the history of the USGBC, the Leadership in Energy and Environmental Design (LEED) program, the WGBC, and the growth of green building from a fringe movement to a worldwide phenomenon. In this conversation, he provides his unique perspective on history, current challenges, investment opportunities, and the critical importance of education and rigorous accreditation.

>> **The U.S. Green Building Council now has over 10,000 members and 70 regional chapters, and its LEED program has become the accepted standard for high-performance green buildings. How was the USGBC viewed by the real estate industry and government when it was founded in 1993?**

The USGBC began with a vision of creating a coalition of the U.S. building industry to transform the market toward green. Remember, there was no definition of green then and, likewise, no U.S. green building market, so Mike Italiano and I started from scratch. Our ambitions were huge, and our funds and staff were almost nonexistent.

We began by pitching the vision to product manufacturers in order to fund the startup of the organization. We proposed that they'd pay year-one dues and a charter member initiation fee. For a billion-dollar-annual-revenue firm, the payment was $10,000 in dues and a $15,000 initiation fee. Smaller firms—including architecture, engineering, consulting, building owners, and utilities—paid much less. In order to establish membership balance from the beginning, we recruited nonprofit professional and environmental organizations for a low annual dues level and no initiation fee.

We successfully raised $125,000 within a few months of our April 1993 organizational meeting at the AIA [American Institute of Architects] national headquarters in Washington, D.C. There were representatives from about 60 firms in attendance. Some of those enthusiastic attendees are still on our board and active in the organization now, 14 years later.

Even though we didn't have a track record, glossy brochures, an annual budget, or proven nonprofit executive-level staff, many supported us from the beginning. These tended to be visionaries themselves—professionals who had studied the state of the world, who remembered the 1970s energy crises, who followed the first Earth Day in 1970, and were early recyclers. These early pioneers were mostly architects, engineers, environmentalists, professional society executives, and a few product manufacturers.

It took years for us to finally get more mainstream members to join us, including those that represented building owners, banks, insurance companies, brokers, appraisers, lawyers, and property managers. Since our founding, we've made substantial progress in these areas, but we still have sectors in which our membership representation is weak.

The federal government, at least a few of the agencies, was supportive in the beginning. The first one to the table was NIST [National Institute of Standards and Technology], a branch of the Department of Commerce. It even hosted our first few green building conferences and federal government green building summit. We also received early support from the EPA [U.S. Environmental Protection Agency] and Department of Energy. A few years after our launch, many of us worked on the greening of the White House and Old Executive Office Building under President Clinton's leadership. One of the more difficult tasks was to specify energy-efficient windows that could not only meet the stringent historic preservation guidelines, but that were also bulletproof.

That all helped to boost our credibility, even though our organizational infrastructure was weak and took years to grow, at least when you compare that growth to the current explosion.

There were many organizations that weren't supportive in those early years. Some thought that we were controlled by product manufacturers, even though each firm only received one vote—the same as every other member—despite the dues paying differential. A few of our professional society partners were also skeptical of our motives and our broad mission of bringing together the entire industry within our 13 sectors of membership. I think a few of them wanted to adopt a similar approach for their own organizations. We also had no track record, so that diluted our credibility. I believe many took a wait-and-see attitude and then joined us several years later. Many property owners and their trade groups thought that green building was just another niche that would add cost, delay projects, and increase risk. They therefore refused to take a seat at our table. I smile as I reflect that they are mostly all our close partners at this point.

>> What did your family think of your work in the fledging green building movement?

My family thought I was crazy when I announced that I was quitting real estate development and construction management to start a green nonprofit. This is especially true when I informed them that I was working for free, and also funding the startup costs of the new organization. My father, who is always looking out for my best interests, said "That's a great gimmick, but don't come home when you're starving."

My brother Rick was a big early supporter and had even met Amory Lovins [chairman of the Rocky Mountain Institute] before I had, and lived in one of the first green housing developments, Village Homes in Davis, California. Over the years, as we slowly climbed up the steep mountain, my Dad and Mom became two of my biggest supporters, especially when our home city of Los Angeles adopted a LEED Silver requirement for government buildings.

However, green was a different ethic than my parents' generation. They worked hard to help us get into the best schools, to earn professional degrees, and to have successful careers. Being the founder of an environmental nonprofit and its first president didn't seem like a stable job, let alone one that could earn enough to provide for a family, much less a home, college education for my children, or retirement.

I often remarked that I'd taken on the risk of an entrepreneur, but invited a board to tell me what to do, and then gave away all of the intellectual property and stock to the public. I came to realize that I was offering a different type of wealth than I was taught.

>> When—and how—did the green building movement gain traction or momentum? Was there a specific event or series of events? Were there some key buildings?

It was really the development of the LEED green building rating system that spurred a definitive growth in membership and in public awareness. LEED was born with key assistance from the Department of Energy, which provided grants of around $800,000 in the late 1990s. Their support—both in money and in name—helped make us real.

The greening of the White House and working with President Clinton also anchored and helped establish us. A few years later, we partnered a few conferences with the AIA, and that gave us additional exposure and credibility. Our first Federal Government Summit in around 1994 was also a big success.

>> What are the current roadblocks to the greater construction of new green buildings?

First, we do have reason to celebrate: we now have over a billion square feet [92.9 million square meters] of LEED-registered buildings [awaiting final certification] across the various rating programs in the U.S., divided among 13,000 projects.

However, we still have far to go. The LEED registration figures represent only about 6 percent of the industry.

I still see many barriers to greater adoption of green building principles and LEED, starting with a lack of education. Many building owners are still early in their education about sustainable development.

The problems blocking the spread of green buildings aren't necessarily technical, but in the development process itself. We really need to change how we budget, schedule, hire, and manage professionals, and, in particular, how we utilize our development budgets to achieve the highest life-cycle value. Often, we take the life-cycle value out of our buildings for the sake of a lower first cost, and we don't look further into the operational stage of the building. This short-term—and often linear and segmented—orientation can result in enormous resource inefficiencies and thwart occupant health and productivity, which is even more costly than the building cost.

Speculative development has its own challenges for achieving a high LEED score, and it takes an open and creative mentality to achieve success. I'm pleased to say that a few great developers are achieving LEED Gold and Platinum award levels at little or no first cost increases and premium returns on investment.

Building tenants and their brokers are also just beginning to learn about green and its benefits to their occupancy: lower expenses and improved employee productivity. The more they are educated about these significant benefits, the more they can demand a high level of sustainability from landlords.

It would also help if tenants would pay more for green space. I don't understand why they would not be willing [to do so]. We pay more for better cars, bigger and more luxurious homes, fancier suits, and faster computers. Do we request the payback period or a zero cost premium for these commodities? Why aren't we willing to pay for quality and true value in our buildings, especially since we spend most of our lives indoors and the quality of the space affects our ongoing health and happiness in so many ways?

It sure would help the green movement if banks required environmental performance standards for their loans and insurance companies required environmental performance standards for their insurance policies.

>> What are the specific roadblocks for green improvements for *existing* buildings? That's where we really need to cut energy use and reduce greenhouse gas emissions.

The average age of the existing building stock is around 30 years. Most of these buildings are Class B or even C. They require full systems upgrades to bring them up to modern and green standards of quality and performance efficiency. This package of work might include a new building skin, roof, windows, HVAC [heating, ventilating, and air-conditioning] system, lighting, plumbing, and electrical service and appliances. The cost for these items is significant. It's also possible that the older building is located in a market where the rent level won't support such a high redevelopment cost; the return on investment won't pencil out. This is a barrier to pursuing a high level of green for some of the older buildings.

Even still, all buildings can adopt many measures that are extremely cost-effective and have fast payback periods. This includes lighting retrofits, installation of efficient fans and motors, window films, carpet with recycled content, low-emitting paints, solar shading, and new energy-efficient appliances and fixtures. In many instances, the local utility company can help figure out the program and also provide rebates. If a building owner desires solar power, a third party can be brought in to pay for the system and even lower the monthly energy bill. Purchase of green power is fairly cheap and can help an owner offset the building's carbon footprint. The vogue these days is to be carbon neutral.

Many high-profile tenants demand Class A space. Can we make the average 30-year-old building into a Class A space? Traditionally, we've often just torn down the building and replaced it with a larger modern one. Our waste mentality is pervasive in how we live and consume. This mentality needs to change, and a great place to start is by saving older buildings and redeveloping them cost-effectively to give them a second and third life. These buildings contain so much embodied energy. From an environmental standpoint, cleaning them up and modernizing them into highly functional assets is such a savings. Renovation represents a fundamental shift in how we view our built environment. Many of our older buildings, especially the ones dating back decades, have beautiful architectural features that aren't common in today's buildings, such as extensive operable windows that provide daylighting and natural ventilation.

LEED-EB [Existing Building] was introduced to the market as a single building certification, as were the other LEED rating systems. The USGBC is now shifting its approach with its LEED Portfolio partners program. This pilot program allows a firm that has many buildings in its ownership portfolio to apply LEED across all of its buildings. I believe it's important that owners apply environmental management principles to all their assets and strive for continuous annual improvement.

As we've learned from environmental management systems such as ISO 14001, the key to environmental improvement is to create a system, establish a base case of performance, create goals for improvement, and then set along the path for change. Sustainability isn't a destination, it's a journey, and the LEED program needs to move in this direction, as do all building owners and property managers.

>> What are the major risks of investing in green buildings, and how do you address or overcome them?

Investors want to achieve their desired return on investment, and developers are tasked with achieving that return. So, green buildings can't lower the average market return for an asset class. In fact, the opposite needs to occur: we should achieve higher rates of return for pursuing a high level of green. Even though many of us believe that this is possible, the market hasn't yet proved through credible case studies that this can occur. The data are very scarce. We need more private developers who have completed a LEED building to share their numbers with us.

We do have good statistics justifying the cost/benefit ratio for energy efficiency and commissioning. It's not hard to justify the payback period for water- and waste-efficiency measures. In turn, we can then begin to apply these savings and financial benefits to the entire building. However, there are several building owners who are creating LEED Gold and Platinum buildings and doing this within their typical budgets. One project in Victoria [British Columbia]—Dockside—sold out approximately 75 percent of the initial condominiums on the first day, and at elevated sales prices.

The LEED documentation process and associated energy modeling and commissioning work does still add first cost. I'm not sure, however, that it's so fair to add in the energy modeling and commissioning fees as part of LEED. They should be part of all projects and the scope of work added into the base contracts for the architect, engineers, and contractor. I'm optimistic that the remaining LEED documentation costs will come down substantially as owner teams take on more of the work of the consultants, and software vendors produce tools that make it much easier to document a project. The USGBC-managed review process will also be streamlined and still be effective and credible. As with all new innovations, the future cost is not usually indicative of the past, especially during those early startup years where the innovation slope is steep.

If managed poorly and brought to the project late, embarking on a green initiative can add cost and delay the schedule. It's best to start upon the project's inception by determining the green goals, conducting an early LEED brainstorming charrette, and filling out the scorecard. Even of greater importance is to hire the team with a green performance goal and requirement in their contracts, and educate the project manager to understand the integrated design process and how the various elements of sustainable design come together.

>> **In your experience with both the public and private sectors, where do you see the greatest potential for leadership in bringing green buildings into the mainstream?**
We really need to create cost-effective programs that address our existing building stock in order to mitigate climate change. As I mentioned earlier, owners need to put their entire portfolio into the green game. Successful LEED-EB case studies and the measures the project team employed need to be shared. If we could aggregate our green product and system procurement, that would also help bring down the first cost. There's a huge opportunity for a few new firms to take on this procurement project and start with the LEED-registered buildings and tenant spaces. The same can apply to LEED-Home pilot projects.

The commercial building industry is still inefficient in how it specs and bids. There's opportunity for up to 25 percent cost savings or more. Local governments can do the same by banding together. This approach works best for commodity products like carpet, ceiling tiles, solar, bathroom fixtures.

A friend of mine at a large bank once negotiated for the purchase of many commodity-type building products direct from the manufacturer at an average cost savings of 40 percent. I know in my own consulting work that I've achieved an average procurement savings of 25 percent by dis-intermediating the supply chain.

If I were a lender, I'd require a minimum level of LEED certified as a prerequisite for obtaining construction financing for a new building. If a customer wants a loan to buy an existing building, the lender should require that they commit to LEED-EB as well to ensure high-performance operations. And the same requirements could be applied to obtaining property insurance.

These requirements aren't onerous, and they even contribute to lessening the lender and insurance companies' liability. If Bank of America, Wells Fargo, or another leading financial institution were to require this, I believe the others would follow. And, in turn, the cost of LEED would come down. I believe the USGBC could further streamline the process to complement this bold move.

Sustainability should be a prerequisite for all educational institutions. A student shouldn't be able to graduate without understanding the basics, including the state of the planet and its systems, and the methods for regeneration. These lessons apply to all fields and students at all levels.

I believe the LEED-Accredited Professional [LEED-AP] exam and designation should progress to a much more robust level. I've proposed that we invent a GBC accreditation program that goes far beyond what we now require. It would include several testing modules spanning professional breadth, depth, and LEED within each discipline area, as well as sustainability practice experience and continuing education requirements. The USGBC is beginning to look at many of these expansion ideas in its program.

The depth requirements could be partnered with each of the professional societies, who would administer that portion of the GBC requirement to their constituencies. The designation could become global through the adoption of the program by the World Green Building Council. This would unite and integrate our sustainable building education on a global basis, becoming the first integral professional accreditation.

>> Some real estate developers and investors argue that regulations are not the right step. They say that incentives or market forces should drive the acceptance of green buildings, not the "heavy hand" of government. What do you think?

Do we really have time to wait, given that buildings account for such a large percentage of greenhouse gas emissions?

Time is of the essence for the world if we are to stop global climate change. We must adopt a full array of transformation tools. The palette needs to include both regulations *and* incentives, as well as improved building codes, education and training, better information, case studies, effective procurement, more green products, better financing and insurance rates for green building, and many other programs and strategies that will accelerate achievement of higher-performance buildings and spaces.

In terms of incentives, I like tax credits, height and density bonuses, parking reductions, accelerated building permitting, and real estate tax reductions like they did in Nevada.

Widespread adoption will only take place with all these measures, whether government or market driven.

>> A number of cities—Boston, Washington, D.C., and Pasadena, California—have enacted regulations to require that new or renovated *privately* owned buildings above a certain square footage meet green criteria. Do you foresee such measures being enacted by other cities or counties, and how quickly?

Yes, I foresee this trend increasing its momentum, but it's not moving fast enough. Building codes need to change much more quickly to address the urgency of global warming, as well as our other environmental imperatives, including waste, water, and materials efficiency, and improved indoor environmental quality.

>> USGBC CEO/president Rick Fedrizzi has said that today's LEED Gold building will be tomorrow's standard green building. How can developers and architects plan new or renovated buildings today that won't be outdated in the near future?

As I mentioned earlier, sustainability is a journey and not a destination. You simply cannot seek a LEED-NC [New Construction] rating, and not develop and implement a green operations and maintenance plan. I'm a fan of continuous commissioning and monitoring and verification. You've got to ensure the building's performance and also make way for continuous improvement. That's key. Buildings need to be designed for future upgrades in systems—whether solar, fuel cells, lighting systems, HVAC, or other items that will become outdated.

The basic tenets of green building should also be integrated into the core and shell of the property. This includes a high degree of daylighting, high ceiling heights, solar shading, passive solar performance, and the opportunity for natural ventilation and individual control.

I believe we can invest significantly more time and budget into the training of our staff so that they are progressive in their designs, management, and ongoing improvement. We should also reward our staff and consultants for continued performance, including the three areas of the triple bottom line: economic, environmental, and social equity.

I think we can do a lot better in the social area, and begin to understand that humans can also be humane. I call it the "E revolution": putting the "e" back into the word *human*. Doing so will not only make you more money as the world continues its rapid shift toward embracing sustainabilit; it will also change your own life by adding meaning and ensuring a better future for those who are not yet here to defend themselves.

JULIAN DARLEY

Julian Darley is president of the Sebastopol, California–based Post Carbon Institute, which conducts research, develops technical tools, educates the public, and organizes leaders to help communities respond to the challenges of fossil-fuel depletion and climate change. He wrote *High Noon for Natural Gas: The New Energy Crisis* (2004) and cowrote *Relocalize Now! Getting Ready for Climate Change and the End of Cheap Oil* (2005).

"That's what we've done effectively: bring this planet to its knees. We've used our energy and tools and undoubted cleverness to destroy this planet."

In this conversation, Darley discusses a wide variety of issues critical to the real estate industry, from the impact of peak oil and natural gas to currency instability and revaluing rural areas. He focuses in particular on localization—returning to pre-oil development patterns that put everything human beings need within a five-minute walk of where they live. Outspoken, knowledgeable, informative, and entertaining, Darley provides abundant food for thought.

>> The Post Carbon Institute has focused its efforts on helping local governments, communities, and individuals prepare for—and adapt to—the post-carbon world. Why should we plan for a post-carbon world?

One meaning of carbon in this case is carbon dioxide, and also methane and various other greenhouse gases. Getting beyond putting out greenhouse gases would be a good idea, as an increasingly large number of people agree—although, it would've been an awfully good idea if we'd agreed on this 40 years ago or more.

It would be a really good idea if we didn't burn any hydrocarbons at all, but they are incredibly useful. We have built a giant infrastructure that needs them in order to function. To have a safe transition to something else, we will need to find some substitutes at some level for the nonrenewable hydrocarbons—that is the hydrocarbons that come from fossil fuels like oil and natural gas, and also coal, of course.

We shouldn't be burning hydrocarbons for several reasons. First, and a well-known critical issue, is the global warming caused by carbon dioxide emissions from carbon fuels. Second, we use these bountiful energy sources to go around tearing up the planet and fighting terrible wars. We've used it to rip up forests and agricultural land and put down concrete and asphalt and giant cities. Basically, we've gotten better and better at destroying the planet that we all rely on to sustain human life.

Finally, the sources of fuel that we are burning are limited, temporary, and unsustainable.

When animals find what the worlds of physics and ecology call "free" energy—it isn't *free* in terms of price, I mean it is *available* energy—they increase their population as much as they can to use all the available energy in their ecological niche. If that available energy keeps flowing along and nothing intervenes, that population can stay at that high level. What usually happens in nature, however, is that other things do intervene and very often that available energy supply was a peak. It does not last, and you get a classic population boom and then decline or collapse.

This goes on in nature all the time. It's normal practice, and it's probably been going on for 2 or 3 billion years—as long as we've had life on this planet.

Now, when you're a human and you get your hands on a large amount of available energy—coal, and then oil, and then natural gas—there are three key things that happen. First, you have those three sources provide 85 percent of your industrial energy. Second, that means you can do a monumental population boom. And third, on top of that, you start building a giant economic system, cultural system, and food system. You build absolutely everything on the availability of that energy.

Then, you rather later discover that that system doesn't have a boundless supply of energy. That's a problem. It's foolish to grab the first available energy source, which is what all animals do, including us, because most of these sources are only temporary. And that, of course, is what we are finding with peak oil, peak natural gas, and now, more than likely, peak coal as well.

An even more troubling argument, which not many people think about, is: okay, so we've got this main form of energy—oil, natural gas, coal, hydro—what do we do with it?

We go around tearing the planet up. We fight terrible wars. I mean, everything from the First World War onward has depended on oil, and some would say was *for* oil anyway. All the modern mechanized warfare depends on oil.

And we use oil to rip up forests and agricultural land and wild lands. We tear it all up and we put down concrete and asphalt and giant cities, and we mine everything, and we use all this big energy—that is, oil, coal, natural gas, uranium, and big hydro—to destroy the planet.

That's what we've done effectively: bring this planet to its knees. We've used our energy and tools and undoubted cleverness to destroy this planet. And we're doing a pretty good job of it as far as I can see. We're doing it very quickly and very impressively. If that was our aim, to really wreck this place, we are doing an A-1 job.

>> **Peak oil is a term you use a lot. As I understand it, peak oil means that oil production has a cycle. When an oil field reaches the peak of production, from then on the level of oil supply and production will decline. You claim that the world is reaching its peak of oil production, that the peak may come well before 2010, and then oil supplies will begin to dwindle, making them more scarce— even unavailable in some locations—and more costly. What problems will peak oil create around the world?**

It's clear now, I think, to almost everybody that we are in the bumpy plateau of oil extraction. The peak period of oil production is now. The question that's beginning to arise is when the bumpy *decline* will occur.

We are already feeling the pre-shocks, as you get with earthquakes. As demand tries to exceed production, we see wild variation in the price of oil. What that does eventually is constrain demand, and the economy starts to cool off, and energy prices start to come down again. The moment that happens we open the throttle again, and then we bump up against the production limit and prices shoot up and then we need to cool down again. This is one of the reasons the plateau is bumpy, and the decline will be bumpy and disruptive. We are starting to see this back-and-forth whipsaw rippling into the economy and currency, with many stark problems arising.

There is a much closer connection than people realize between currency and energy. Money is really a proxy for the flow of energy. This is one of the reasons why we've been working on energy-backed currency at the Post Carbon Institute. Currency instability, the instability of American currency, has many causes, but one of them is we are covertly energy-backed. As we start to get into more and more trouble with oil, I think we will start to see more and more trouble with the dollar as well.

Another indicator is the liquidity of speculative money that chases around looking for the next best "pump and dump." There is still a lot of liquidity ready to chase oil up and then down again, and you can't do this when there is ample supply, so this is another indicator that we are in the bumpy plateau.

>> **Your 2004 book *High Noon for Natural Gas* focuses on the peak of natural gas. What are the impacts of this trend?**

North American natural gas production peaked in 2001, and it is now in undulating decline. The decline of natural gas is particularly important for property owners and real estate professionals because of its importance for heating and air conditioning.

The peak of natural gas poses a major problem also for Europe, one area that is particularly dependent on natural gas, especially exports from Russia.

Russia has the world's largest deposit of natural gas, it is one of the world's largest oil producers, and it is doing just what everyone else would do if they had that much power. It's about all Russia has got. If the only thing you had was oil and gas, what would you do? Russia feels really threatened by America and NATO, so it applies the only pressure it has got to nearby nations like Belarus and Turkey and Georgia.

Europe has done it to itself. It is hideously dependent on natural gas. It has no one but itself to blame for getting into this jam.

If Europe is foolish, they will allow themselves to become more dependent on Russian gas and oil, making them more vulnerable politically and economically as those supplies become more scarce. People were telling Europe that natural gas would peak and decline, and they didn't listen, just as America didn't listen. It's probably human nature, and it's certainly in American culture. We don't want to hear bad news that actually affects us.

>> **While many national and local governments and individuals may not have understood the peak oil phenomenon, they have recently come to understand that we must try to reverse global climate change by significantly reducing consumption of fossil fuels. Wind farms are rising around the world; photovoltaic systems are being used, even mandated, in many countries; geothermal and biomass systems are beginning to proliferate. With all of these renewable energy sources expanding at an impressive rate, won't they counterbalance our declining oil supplies? Won't they mitigate the problems you have forecast?**

We are jolly late in trying to do that. America was one of the leaders in renewable energy in the 1970s, but things changed in the 1980s and America gave up a lot of work in renewables.

The argument that renewable energy sources alone will solve the problem is the "grand substitution" argument. It's also wishful thinking.

Renewables will help, but in the real and practical world, can we get enough renewable energy from sun and wind and soil to substitute for all the oil, gas, coal, big hydro, and uranium we use now? Almost certainly we physically can't. To put it bluntly, there are too many people on the planet demanding too much stuff in a system that is too spread out.

It's not just the amount of population; it's the level of consumption. People in England or Canada or America consume many times the amount of energy of people in developing countries. One child in America consumes as much energy as 50 children in the Far

East. There are too many of us consuming too much stuff because we've built a system which relies on consuming too much energy. The whole system is too greedy and wasteful, top to bottom.

>> **Do you think it is possible for developing nations to recognize the broad challenges, spot our mistakes, jump past them, and create a new, better model of the world?**

Yes, it is possible. One of the biggest problems so far is that everyone is copying the model of endless growth. The world is trying to copy a kind of southern California way of life with a climate that most people don't have. Even in Europe, where they have strong central cities, they have copied sprawling patterns as they expand. Dublin is a classic example—the heart of the Celtic Tiger. They went in for explosive economic growth and they got horrible traffic. Ireland is running out of energy fast. It has torn apart its social structure to rush after economic growth.

We're fighting the laws of nature and thermodynamics, and we can only get away with it for a short time.

There is a wonderful essay I would recommend by the late British biologist and geneticist J.B.S. Haldane called "On Being the Right Size." In all of nature, size and scale are critical. With all our clever technologies, we have still made everything too big. We need to get our city sizes down. We need to densify—to build four to seven stories high with the buildings connected. We could have combined heating and cooling like they do in many parts of Scandinavia, but only if we have four- to seven-story buildings all joined together.

>> **So, we come back to real estate and how we've designed our buildings and cities. What are some of the land use patterns that are necessary for communities to enable them to cope with global climate change and scarce traditional energy sources?**

One of the big questions is: are we really any good at settled life? I don't think we are well set up mentally to cope with settled life. We grew for a million or more years as hunter-gatherers. Are our brains really suited to settled life? Once creatures start settling and staying in the same place, they need to manage themselves quite differently.

Once we settled with farming and fire, we needed to change the way we did things. That's been the problem. Ever since we settled, what we do is make a big mess—sewage problems, diseases, crime, social problems, bad city design, and so on—and expect someone else to clear it up.

This is really where it starts to get into buildings and real estate and how we've laid our cities out. This is the great question of the age.

The CNU [Congress for the New Urbanism] and other groups have thought seriously about how we laid out cities. But the deeper question is: was it a good idea in the first place?

In order to be humane and decent about it, we need to find some transitionary path out of our settlement problems, which will probably take 100 years. But we need to act fast. If you start thinking down at that level, I think it changes the way you approach things.

We've built in a lot of the wrong places, the hottest and driest places with no water—like Las Vegas and Los Angeles—even San Francisco, which has no rain all summer, and much of the southwestern United States. When you stick trillion-dollar infrastructure in the wrong places you'll have trouble.

Many of these places use a lot more air conditioning. It's jolly uncomfortable at 95 or 100 degrees, especially when you need to work hard. We don't take a siesta the way people used to do in hot climates. It used to be that 12 to 4 p.m. was the common time to stop and relax and have a bit of a sleep. Humans seem well-suited to having a sleep in the afternoon. But even in Spain and Italy, the influence of the Anglo working way is driving out the siesta, and that is driving their need for more air conditioning, more energy.

We still need buildings, settlements, and cities, but we need to do it smarter—build with much more density and in smarter places that make ecological sense. And we need to carry out retrofits of the existing built environment, move away from horizontal suburban layouts, and get density back up again. Build four- to seven-story buildings connected together around squares and blocks with internal gardens.

This disastrous linear strip mall idea condemns you to use a car. If your shopping district is two miles [3.2 kilometers] long, you're bound to use a car, whereas, if your shopping district wraps around a block or square, you could walk 400 yards [365 meters] with shops all around and then arrive back home again.

Europe offers some good examples because most of its cities were built pre-petroleum. This pre-petroleum layout will give Europe an advantage over America, whose cities are largely petroleum-based cities.

America can borrow complex design ideas for how to lay out cities and rural areas from Europe to help retrofit its built environment, and at the same time export its ability to be generous and innovative and say yes to good ideas. One of the greatest things about the U.S. is that Americans are amazing at saying yes to ideas. This makes America a great place to be if you have lots of new ideas. Frankly, there is nowhere quite like California when it comes to saying yes to innovative ideas. And that's one reason why we are doing our work here.

There is no ideal way of living. Settled living doesn't fit human nature, so this is going to be a bit of a mess. We should stop searching for perfection and have a better time with it.

>> Do you think your suggestions are realistic for the United States? What you are describing, will Americans go for it or will they have no choice?

I've thought about this long and hard. I've lived in Europe and Canada and all over the U.S. I've started to think that this is the only choice, based on the evidence. Will Americans go for it? At the Post Carbon Institute, we're trying really hard to persuade people that this retrofit of the built environment is practical and realistic and could be a much better way of life than what we've got. If we do nothing, real ugliness may ensue. I don't recommend that. Chaos is not pretty.

>> You mentioned rural development patterns. Can you expand on that?

City dwellers have looked down their noses on rural dwellers for hundreds, maybe thousands, of years. Why is looking down on farmers a really bad idea? That's where our food is coming from. If we're going to have a chance at this thing called sustainability, we'll have to get all our resources in a renewable way, including our fuel, feedstocks, fiber, and our food. The bulk of it will come from rural areas.

We should really be revaluing our rural areas. These places are the most wonderful places we've got. We should treat farmers and rural people really well and value them highly.

People who know how to grow things, for fuel, for fiber, or feedstock, or fertilizer, or grow our forests back should be valued at the top of the economic and social pyramid. I recommend Richard Heinberg's paper called "50 Million Farmers" about bringing back farming and respect for farming.

We need to protect the farmland and the people who work in [the fields]. We should put no more asphalt and concrete on growing land. That means if we need to build a farmhouse where there wasn't one, we ought to de-pave and un-tarmac a more than equal amount of land—maybe ten times more. How about de-paving a few carparks?

>> It seems like a lot of this comes down to dependence on cars and the internal combustion engine. What do you think we should do?

At the core of all this, which a few architects and planners get, is the five-minute circle. The pre-petroleum cities in Europe were based on the five-minute circle: how far you can walk in five minutes—or about a quarter of a mile [0.4 kilometer]. All of human life should be based on getting its daily needs within a quarter-mile radius. This is the essence of relocalization: get your daily needs from as locally as possible, preferably within walking distance.

We must relocalize. Right now, we're getting everything—from garlic to gaskets—from China. And their prospects are looking grim. There is a risk that China will have an economic, energy, environmental, social, and political meltdown. They're trying to hold things together until the 2008 Olympics, but the situation is looking terribly unstable.

Localization is really difficult to do for humans who insist on having 6.5 billion people on the planet and millions of people in a city. Once you insist on doing that, you need mechanized transport—whether horses and trolleys, or trams, or cars, or buses, or subways.

Given that cars make bad cities, it is a bad idea to design a city around the car, which is what we've done in America. Gasoline- and diesel-powered cars are most likely to be going away. We'll do a bit of biofueled vehicles, but it behooves us to start thinking about the city after cars. European cities offer some great examples. Rome, Copenhagen, parts of San Sebastian, parts of Munich, and Cologne and Paris all have car-free downtown areas. These places all managed to do it. I would say: America, you can do it too. You can get rid of the cars downtown. It's possible.

I'm worried about American cities that don't have subways. They give you a much better chance in the coming post-carbon, post-petroleum age.

That points to the need for a comprehensive transit system that should include metal rails *par excellence*. One of the things I want to bring back into people's thinking, especially planners and architects, is to bring back metal rails. There are many many reasons for this. It's much easier to get electricity to an electric rail system than to wheels, like a trolley. Aside from barges, trains are the lowest-friction method to move things around, and that can really bring down energy costs. Also, it constrains development patterns. Once you have rails in and you use that as your pattern, then that tells you where to put your buildings. That stops us from sprawling.

I will assert that you can reduce greenhouse gas [emissions] and still maintain mobility by using more transit rather than the car.

Ideally, like Paris and other places, the transit should be underground, which promotes walking in the city, keeps vehicles off the roadways, and makes it much easier to become car free. But you also need above-ground rail. We need to bring back electrified railways across the nation, including streetcars and interurban rail and electric trolley buses as well, like San Francisco. Then, fill in with walking and bicycles, and some electric delivery vehicles and some small electric cars. That is a much more powerful way of doing a city.

>> What is the Post Carbon Institute doing to fix these problems?

We are working with people from many walks of life—institutions, government, business, and citizens—to build a multilayer, integrated, strategic response that makes sense. A response that is scientifically practical but has enough political and human appeal that people will start to adopt this long but fast and urgent transition to a post-carbon world. We have a number of major programs underway.

We work at the public policy level through initiatives like the Oil Depletion Protocol, first developed by Colin Campbell in 1996 and written about by Richard Heinberg. The protocol is very ambitious and calls for a 3 percent annual reduction of petroleum consumption. This would lead to a halving of petroleum consumption in the next 25 years. The Post Carbon Institute is working on getting this policy deployed at the city level and United Nations level.

Our Global Public Media Internet channel [www.globalpublicmedia.com] is a public service system for a post-carbon world. We try to inform the public and policy makers by interviewing people who've thought about and analyzed very carefully the grave problems we face and some of the possible solutions. Our Post Carbon Cities program is working on a book, *Post Carbon Cities: Planning for Energy and Climate Uncertainty*, that addresses many of these issues. [The book, written by Daniel Lerch, was published in 2007.]

We also have the Energy Farms Network, in which we are looking at the kind of farms and gardens that we will need in this coming century to get our vital materials—food, fiber, fuel, feedstock—as locally as possible. That means thinking about agriculture in a different way—a way that aims to use no petroleum and as little water as possible, and has private citizens using their gardens differently.

Our Relocalization Network has 160 groups in 14 countries around the world, citizens coming together in recognition of the peak oil problem—specifically, people working in cities and rural areas to help people help themselves, to help them understand the full nature of the problem, and to start responding.

And, of course, the Post Carbon Institute, a think tank and umbrella organization, is key to the work of integration. We humans have broken the world into millions of parts—a clever technique that can do useful things. But now is the age of reintegration. The Post Carbon Institute is the force behind getting this integration work deployed at the city level and the United Nations level.

CHÉ WALL

Ché Wall was the founding chair of the World Green Building Council (WGBC) and was chairman for five years. Under his leadership, the WGBC helped establish green building councils in several countries, including the United Arab Emirates and Mexico. Wall is managing director of Sydney, Australia–based Lincolne Scott, a building services and environmental engineering consulting firm.

"Only a year ago, the question tenants most frequently asked was, 'How much do I save if I reduce my green commitments?' Now, the only question tenants ask is, 'How much more will it cost to increase my green credentials?' This is a huge shift in the perceived value of green investment."

In the year and a half since Wall last sat down to discuss sustainable development (July 2006), the green building movement has changed dramatically. Green buildings have entered the mainstream in many cities because of rising energy costs, increasing concerns about global climate change, and the structures' proven financial benefits. Wall discusses the latest green building trends, the importance of greening the existing building stock, and green building leaders and laggards around the world.

>> How has the green building landscape changed since our last conversation?

The green building movement has matured a lot since then. There are a number of significant developments.

First, the World Green Building Council model of an industry-led organization with broad stakeholder engagement is proving increasingly infectious. In addition to our five founding members, we now have 11 robust councils, including the councils in the United Kingdom, the United Arab Emirates, Brazil, and New Zealand. Significantly, about 30 additional councils are forming in countries including Germany, China, and South Africa, which proves that the council model works whatever a country's political, socioeconomic, or bioclimatic structure. The council model is clearly adaptable to suit individual countries' needs.

Second, this rapid expansion of Green Building Councils demonstrates that the responsibility to create a sustainable built environment and ensure a sustainable future has been recognized globally; it is not just an issue for developed countries. I think this expansion is also revising that old green mantra "think globally, act locally." The World Green Building Council model says "think locally"—each market is different and requires local leadership and solutions—and "act globally"—leverage your peers and don't reinvent the wheel.

Third, as industry demonstrates its concern for the environment and joins with government and academia in the green choir, people are starting to listen. When a major bank adopts the highest green building standards into its workplace strategies—like the ANZ Bank [Melbourne, Australia–based Australia and New Zealand Banking Group Ltd.] did for its 900,000-square-foot [84,000-square-meter] office building in Melbourne's Docklands district—it creates cascading changes far beyond those workplaces.

The bank's competitors suddenly take sustainability seriously. The bank's developers and landlords have to deliver those green building standards in their facilities to retain the bank as a client and to strengthen the perception that they are at the forefront of green, which will snare the most attractive blue-chip lease commitments. The contractors and suppliers to those developers and landlords have to provide the highest level of green if they are going to retain their clients. Local, state, and even national government—which has been leading the way to green by example—must benchmark their own commitments against the bank's green standards. When these serious change agents become engaged in green buildings, the race to green very quickly moves to a whole new level.

The speed with which green changes are adopted is also faster for industry. Government policy is mostly reactive. When it comes to addressing global climate change, for example, policy positions are formed in response to perceived public opinion. The politicians who create those policies only have to face the market once every four years in an election. Public companies, however, face the market daily, and they are valued by their future earnings. Climate change has become a significant intangible on which the market appraises a company. Thus, companies must quickly adopt climate change policies if they are to remain competitive.

Fourth, the number of organizations implementing sustainable building-oriented projects is proliferating rapidly. The World Business Council for Sustainable Development [WBCSD] has launched its Energy Efficiency in Buildings project, the United Nations Environment Programme has started the Sustainable Buildings Construction Initiative [UNEP SBCI], and the Clinton Foundation's Clinton Climate Initiative [CCI] has launched its Energy Efficiency Building Retrofit Program.

What is most important is that these bodies complement each others' efforts. The WGBC focuses on market behavior, the WBCSD focuses on products, UNEP leans toward policy, and the CCI has a political capital and mayors' network. The WGBC convened a meeting between these parties in late 2006 to start the dialogue, and initial progress has been excellent.

I am concerned, however, that the UNEP SBCI could still aspire to the development of a global building rating scheme. A global scheme is attractive on the surface, but it raises serious problems. Each region has its own unique climate, development, and environmental concerns. For a global building rating scheme to meet every market need is an impossible task. It would struggle to deliver workable solutions and benefits to each market and run the risk of creating local market confusion and poorly calibrated solutions for the problems of each region, which would produce a negative outcome. The Green Building Council model, on the other hand, is successful specifically because it works with local markets, climates, environments, and development issues.

Fifth, a huge change is the shift in how corporations now think about the environment, which I attribute to a combination of Al Gore's film *An Inconvenient Truth*, the U.K. Government's *Stern Report* [Sir Nicholas Stern's 700-page *Review on the Economics of Climate Change*, prepared at the request of the U.K. Chancellor of the Exchequer and issued on October 30, 2006], and the February 2007 IPCC [Intergovernmental Panel on Climate Change] report. Each of these engaged with a broader audience than was previously reached and did so with a clarity of message and an urgency that is hard to ignore. Climate change risk is now being discussed at the board table.

Finally, in the real estate sector, reports from McKinsey & Company [a New York City–based global management consulting firm] and the IPCC report in May identified a cost abatement curve for greenhouse gas emission reductions. Both reports stated that the building sector was the most financially attractive strategy that provided the greatest scope for significant emissions reductions.

>> Does this mean the thinking about green buildings has matured also?

Absolutely. Only a year ago, the most frequently asked question tenants asked was, "How much do I save if I reduce my green commitments?" Now the only question tenants ask is, "How much more will it cost to increase my green credentials?" This is a huge shift in the perceived value of green investment.

In addition, we now have many green buildings. If I look at my home market of Australia, the figures are fairly staggering. Green Star [the Australian green building assessment and rating scheme] has about 30 percent penetration in new office tenants' briefs and I would estimate a 70 percent penetration by area. This sounds like a huge number, but it highlights our next problem: how to stimulate the green refurbishment of existing buildings.

>> Why are existing buildings so important?

In any year, Australia will typically add 2 percent floor space to the downtown office markets. Existing buildings comprise 98 percent of those markets. We have shown that green is not difficult when managed in a capital spend budget, and indeed tenants are starting to pay extra for their green aspirations. The challenge with green refurbishment—or rehabilitation as I prefer to think of it—is that there needs to be a catalyst for the upgrade.

A traditional asset management strategy will replace building systems when they fail with a drip-feed capital spend over a number of years. The problem is that you inevitably end up with a shinier and slightly more efficient version of the system that was designed when the building was originally constructed. That is unlikely to provide the big energy savings and greenhouse gas emission reductions the industry needs and that clients are starting to demand.

The only way the property sector will make deep cuts to the emissions footprints of our cities is to replace the technology in existing buildings with the systems being installed in new green buildings that reduce emissions by up to 50 percent. At 30 the Bond [the Lend Lease headquarters in Sydney], for example, the chilled-beam air-conditioning system and efficient lighting system helped reduce that building's carbon emissions by 48 percent compared with the average Sydney office building. It is interesting that such technology is also the most suitable for retrofits, because it has relatively small spatial requirements, enabling it to fit in the tightest ceiling voids and vertical risers.

The *Stern Report* stated that buildings are responsible for 50 percent of all greenhouse gas emissions at the power station. While the commercial office market is not solely responsible, it is likely to represent at least 10 percent of power station emissions, making it a more polluting sector than transport. If we can slash the commercial sector's emissions by 50 percent, we will reduce our total emissions by 5 percent. Retail and industrial can make similar reductions, which will make deep cuts in our greenhouse gas emissions purely on the demand side.

>> That sounds good, but where is the catalyst to make the required changes?

I think owners of the better-quality existing buildings will investigate environmental rehabilitation urgently to ensure they are not faced with a rapidly shrinking market as tenant briefs make high-level green nonnegotiable. This will likely be done at the next leasing term.

There is a great example of a major tenant, IAG [Insurance Australia Group], which went out to the Sydney market for about 35,000 square meters [377,000 square feet] of a Five Star Green Star office accommodation. The owners of their current building, however, bid for IAG's tenancy with an investment of some $20 million [Australian, US$13.3 million] in upgrades to achieve a Five Star Green Star rating. The result is IAG committed to another ten-year lease in the same building and the building owners pulled off a master stroke—a fully leased building for another ten years for only $20 million. The re-lease is believed to be an Australian first. More important, it is likely that a new building to meet the brief would have cost at least $100 million [Australian, US$88 million].

Despite this success story, we still need incentives to accelerate green rehabilitations and get the corresponding reductions in greenhouse gas emissions. The method championed by our Property Council is to accelerate the depreciation of assets that were purchased to reduce the environmental impact of a building's operation.

The other method that would work is a building carbon emissions trading scheme. We are already seeing major resource companies factoring a shadow carbon cost into investment decisions in anticipation of the inevitable. When a scheme is finally introduced, it will radically affect the return on investment for major capital spending.

The state of New South Wales introduced the world's first carbon trading scheme some years ago, known as NGAC [New South Wales Greenhouse Abatement Certificate]. This created a new market for entrepreneurs. One company offered free installation of compact fluorescent lamps in homes in return for the homeowners assigning the company the carbon credits for the life of the lamps. The company replaced 3 million bulbs in one year, which is demand reduction on a massive scale, and it had plans to offer solar hot water upgrades, too. It created employment for 240 people and provided greenhouse gas abatement with no cash cost to the customer.

This shows how investment decisions become a completely different paradigm when a value is placed on carbon.

Unfortunately, our previous federal government, which had not taken action on climate change, tried to recover its damaged reputation this year and announced a national carbon trading scheme for 2012. No details or targets were given except that New South Wales's state-based scheme would be abolished. The result? Uncertainty about the future value of state-based credits led to the collapse of the carbon market and the company had to lay off its staff overnight.

This salutary lesson says more about the lack of government leadership in Australia than the weakness of carbon trading schemes. What is most important is that if there is a market, it should allow for demand-side credits to provide the market stimulus required to slash our buildings' carbon footprints.

>> **What do you think the effect will be on Australia of having Kevin Rudd as a "green" prime minister? Will it affect the collapse of carbon trading in New South Wales?**

There is a real sentiment of change in the air as to how Australia might participate in the global environmental debate. The actions so far have been significant. The first act of the new government, immediately after being sworn in, was the ratification of Kyoto. Then Rudd and no less than four cabinet ministers went to the United Nations Climate Change Conference in Bali in December.

>> Which countries are today's green building leaders, outside of the early adopters like those in northern Europe?

This is a tough question. I see many countries demonstrating leadership in complementary areas. We have the U.S. to thank for the Green Building Council model and for helping to mature that model into a major political and industry force. The U.K. is leading in sustainability legislation through policies like mandated zero-carbon homes. And without any parochial bias, I believe Australia is now leading in the corporate sector's engagement in green and the transformation we have seen in its procurement of green workplaces.

>> Which regions are lagging in green building development, and why?

As a generalization, I would have to say that countries with emerging economies and countries with undeveloped economies have the toughest challenge. With the emerging economies, their move toward green has to be done in the context of an urgent need for infrastructure and an improved quality of life. We should also remember that the countries that are leading are coming from a starting position of high environmental impact. Therefore, the opportunities to create significant change and benefits are huge. Finding the best paths is their only challenge.

But when your spending power is low and your baseline environmental impact is significantly lower than your peers, it is not a reasonable expectation that you lead the green charge.

>> What can the countries that are green building leaders do to help the lagging nations, particularly those struggling with potable water scarcity, rising energy costs and/or unreliable energy supplies, minimal infrastructure, and poverty—i.e., the countries that need green buildings the most?

The short answer is: get your own house in order and stop suggesting that any green action that can be taken locally is insignificant when the growth of China and India is considered.

The longer answer is: focus your efforts on the domestic market you understand, help local green building efforts in other countries, and share freely any intellectual property you created in the process of fixing your domestic market. The last thing that the lagging regions need is to be dependent on expensive imported products or expertise. Once the local capacity is in place, then provide financial assistance.

>> Which of the countries that are just beginning to embrace green buildings excite you the most, and why?

I think New Zealand is exciting at the moment, and I am optimistic about the potential of Asia, in particular Thailand.

New Zealand is a relatively small economy that has a strong connection to the environment. Within one month or so of the launch of its Green Building Council, the federal government mandated a local version of Green Star for all of its future accommodation needs. This is something we have seen succeed at municipal and state government levels in other countries, but only after the industry has embraced the tools. For the New Zealand government to lead like this was astonishing and very commendable. I think the New Zealand market is small and nimble enough to demonstrate a lot of innovation, and I expect we will continue to be impressed by their achievements.

My interest in Thailand lies with the fact that they are showing a lot of interest in sustainability, and they are coming from a very different starting point. We celebrate graywater recycling systems in the West. Many office towers in Bangkok already have on-site blackwater recycling—not because they went green before anywhere else, but because they do not have the sewage infrastructure we rely on. Market transformation from such a different perspective is very exciting.

>> So, are you optimistic about the worldwide state of green?

We know that for every year we fail to invest in serious reductions of carbon emissions the task just gets harder and more expensive. I am confident that common sense will prevail.

Everyone knows where we have to go, but we are still searching for the most direct route. The most important need right now is an exemplar—a market that moves quickly to rehabilitate its existing stock and create some world-class new green buildings. If a hard-nosed commercial market does this without depending on legislation to act, then the rest of the world's markets will take notice.

I am hoping that Australia sees the global opportunities from such a leadership position and continues to innovate in the field, but I would be just as happy if another country put the pieces together.

ROBERT S. DAVIS

Robert S. Davis is the visionary founder and developer of Seaside, Florida, considered the birthplace of the new urbanist movement. Today, he is a principal in the Arcadia Land Company, which specializes in town building and land stewardship. He also is on the boards of the Congress for the New Urbanism (CNU), the Seaside Institute, and 1000 Friends of Florida.

"We'll need to develop a system of producing new towns and cities that are almost as pleasant to live in as our old cities. It will take time for them to rival older cities, because time is such an important process in marinating and simmering urbanism."

From Pienza, Italy, during the Renaissance and London in the 18th and early 19th centuries to Kansas City, Missouri's Country Club District of the 1920s and the HOPE VI projects of the 1990s, Davis discusses the key building blocks for successful community development, the hits and misses of the new urbanist movement, the challenges of the status quo, and how to change America's unsustainable development patterns.

>> **New urbanism and smart growth incorporated many sustainable development principles 15 to 20 years ago. Yet, they did not capture the widespread attention like green buildings and sustainability today. Why?**

Complexity. Sustainable urbanism is complex, just like sustainable ecosystems. Green buildings, in contrast, are actually relatively simple to evaluate and their greenness is relatively simple to create a report card on. Another reason is the history and politics of the Congress of the New Urbanism.

Back in the 1990s, the CNU board had a continuing and heated set of debates about whether we should be issuing report cards or making judgments about the quasi-new urbanist developments out there as opposed to the ones we considered legitimate or fairly faithful to the principles the charter embodied. The people who were ambivalent about whether we could do that effectively won out. The issue was essentially tabled.

Now, there's a pilot project, between the CNU and the U.S. Green Building Council [USGBC] to come up with a LEED [Leadership in Energy and Environmental Design] Neighborhood Development model for scoring neighborhood developments. It turns out there's an excessive demand on the part of developers for this legitimization. The criteria for evaluating neighborhoods are still a work in progress, but there is clearly a demand for neighborhood report cards, based on the overwhelming number of applications received.

I think it's a great idea, and I think we [CNU] ought to be doing this. The USGBC has managed to publicize the notion of sustainability of buildings clearly and more effectively than CNU has done with its emphasis on neighborhood design or ULI [Urban Land Institute] has done with its more recent emphasis on smart growth.

If you look at the numbers, if we're really serious about achieving anything like energy independence or reducing carbon dioxide emissions, we have to address our development and transportation patterns. So, the best thing we can do to try to reduce emissions and gasoline consumption is to change our land use patterns so that passenger cars become a much lower percentage of trips made by people, and transportation in general can be a lower percentage of emissions.

>> What are the greatest challenges to new urbanist development?

It's actually a set of interlocking challenges that essentially represent a system that has grown up over the past 50 years to plan, underwrite, finance, and develop conventional suburban sprawl.

This system has many components, particularly planning and zoning codes throughout the country cranked out by a couple of operations.

First, the transportation engineers that put out a book that makes it safe for transportation engineers around the country to do their planning and make judgments. Second, a set of fire marshals who have become very comfortable with the efficiencies of very large fire trucks, and with them come large turning radii and difficulty in dealing with narrow streets.

Third, the transportation system is changing very slowly from the [federal] to the local level. It is geared to improve mobility by increasing the number of car lanes. Mobility is often not even a key concept. The system is really about vehicular traffic.

Then, of course, there's the financial system, which has gotten much more complicated with the commoditization of real estate. That system is imploding now, and it's difficult to see in the dust and rubble what will come out of it.

The failure of the financial model, however, may raise a few opportunities for change. There are several reasons why the model imploded. One is that the financial instruments were very complex, but only in the way that a shell game is complex. They were trying to hide the reality of what was going on. The actual underwriting of the mortgages themselves required an incredibly simplistic approach to what was financeable, and it actually entrenched the single-use kind of monoculture approach to the development of land, because it was much easier to underwrite a single-family house, or strip center, or warehouse. It was a model that everyone could understand.

The problem with that model is that it produces development that is not very sustainable as real estate investments over the long term. Sustainable real estate investments are in places like Georgetown in Washington, D.C.; or the Upper East Side in Manhattan or most of New York City, including the outer boroughs; and certainly in places like the Country Club District, which J.C. Nichols, a founder of ULI, developed over a 40-year period.

J.C. Nichols is one of our heroes who should be honored and studied as we think about redeveloping America's cities. He did a very slow, long-term investment, not worrying about the internal rate of return, but simply knowing that if he put a lot of energy and money into the initial phases of development that it would pay off over the long term. And it did. Even during the Great Depression, the Country Club District held its values better than other developments.

We need a more sustainable financial model, as well as a more sustainable model in ecosystem terms. Complexity is key to that model; time is also key to that model. It actually is much safer to develop relatively slowly without taking enormous risks at any given time than to throw up a single 40-story high-rise or develop 1,000 lots at a time and put up several hundred spec houses at a time.

Of course, now the national homebuilders are learning the problems of scale and leverage when things go bad. My sense is there is an opportunity to revisit scale, time, and complexity.

>> Which communities in the United States and around the world do you admire for their quality of life and sustainability, besides the Country Club District in Kansas City?

Almost all of the 1920s developments of ambition in every community are inspirations for me and ought to be for us now. They dealt with automobiles, which will probably be a reality of life for a while longer, but they did so in a way that was urbane and elegant. Shaker Heights outside Cleveland, Forest Hill Gardens in Queens—those neighborhoods are still some of the most desirable places to live in each of their metro areas.

Or Coral Gables, as it might have been. George Merrick, its founder, had a great vision for his city, but he was unfortunate in his timing. The 1926 hurricane wiped him out. There's rather less of Merrick's imprint on Coral Gables than if he'd had three more years and been wiped out instead in the 1929 stock market crash.

Other models are neighborhoods in Georgian London, like Mayfair and Belgravia, that were thrown up rather quickly but are complete urban neighborhoods with shopping districts, schools, churches, homes. They were constructed on leased land that the landlord expected to get back in 99 years, and then 198 years. Belgravia was mostly developed by Thomas Cubitt, one of the great early-19th-century land developers and speculators on land that is still owned by the Grosvenor Estate. It's an incredibly impressive accomplishment. These are some of the most desirable and incredibly beautiful urban residential areas in the world.

The most inspiring to me is the combination of Pienza and Rome. Pienza is the first ideal city in the Renaissance. It was a medieval hill town that was remodeled—urban renewed, if you will—by a brilliant humanist scholar who happened to have just become Pope Pius II. His close friend when he was a younger member of the Vatican hierarchy, Leon Battista Alberti, created architectural rules based on the work of Vitruvius [Marcus Vitruvius Pollio, a first-century B.C. architect and engineer], the only architectural theory that survived and came down to us, which he improved on. Pope Pius II and Alberti and [Florentine architect Bernardo] Rossellino had worked on a very ambitious plan for Rome when in the court of Pope Nicholas V. It was way too ambitious to be realized with the limited resources of the papacy at the time. They recognized that carrying on a vision that needed to be done by one pope was simply impractical.

But the ideas of improving Rome survived, and I think Pius was smart enough to realize that he could execute those ideas at the scale of a tiny village and turn it into a small town of great civic dignity. He created a model, a city of ideas, in Pienza.

The plans were then executed more or less well in a series of towns that were essentially greenfield sites, generally fortress towns. The best examples for me are the much less perfect, much more ad-hoc interventions in Pienza and Rome. The ideas got executed in Rome by a series of popes who were knowledgeable enough to carry on and modify the work, making Rome a grander place and easier for pilgrims to understand as they went from one site to another.

Later, these ideas—radial planning, legibility, grandeur, magnificence—were adopted in places like Paris, where they were carried out on a much grander scale and, I think, in a much less interesting way.

>> **Some people have said that Seaside is a pioneering sustainable community. Do you agree?**

Yes, Seaside was a protogreen community. We did a lot of things that were pretty radical at the time that we talked about in our initial brochures. But it was too early for sustainability to be at the core of our marketing campaign.

In addition to making a pedestrian-friendly place where people parked once and left their cars parked for a week, the first houses were designed as passive solar houses with south-facing porches, deep roof overhangs, cross-ventilation—the real issue is cooling—tin roofs that reflected the heat, cupolas and other strategies to let hot air out at the top of the house, outdoor showers, and clotheslines.

We required traditional natural building materials for houses, even though the norm at the time was vinyl siding and aluminum and vinyl windows, because we were convinced that the real stuff would last longer and look better if reasonably well-maintained. The houses were built up off the ground by code so the air could circulate under them and so all the drainage could be natural. We did no drainage structures at Seaside except in the downtown, and that was for our amphitheater.

We outlawed grass except for the amphitheater, croquet lawn, and Lyceum. All existing vegetation was required to be left in place except for the building footprint. Where vegetation was disturbed, it was replaced with native vegetation. We built walkovers to protect the dunes. We built way back from the dunes, which have unfortunately receded with greater storm activity, probably because of climate change. But the beach and dunes do rebuild themselves after a storm if they get the chance.

>> Aren't local land use policies a tremendous impediment to more sustainable, more attractive new development and redevelopment of existing or empty infill sites?

The reality is that, even if we can get beyond the current paralysis in land use politics caused by the unholy antigrowth alliance of NIMBYs [not in my backyard], environmentalists, and antigrowth proponents, there is probably not enough land in close-in areas in our cities to redevelop. There *are* opportunities where enough land exists in the core cities and the land is valuable enough to do the long-term expensive development.

Even so, we will need to develop greenfield sites. Joe Duckworth [president of Arcadia Land Company] is developing a greenfield site that will be its own city: 1 million square feet [93,000 square meters] of office, a large amount of housing, 1 million square feet of retail, schools, etc. It's obviously easier to do something like that in some ways, but it's much harder than a small infill site, because the financing has to be mainly equity and it's a very long project. Jason, Joe Duckworth's son, is in his mid-30s and he may live to see it completed, but Joe and I won't.

I think projects like that have enormous potential. If the country settles the immigration morass and we once again welcome the rest of world and continue to grow, we'll need to develop a system of producing new towns and cities that are almost as pleasant to live in as our old cities. It will take time for them to rival older cities because time is such an important process in marinating and simmering urbanism.

>> Many new urbanist communities offer homes at substantially more than their market's average price. Can't a developer make a profit on homes in new urbanist communities that sell for prices the middle class can afford?

Sure. For the most part what you're seeing is that homebuyers are willing to pay a premium, and why wouldn't a developer take advantage of that? There is some additional cost in developing two sets of streets—an alley/mews system and the street at the front of the house—and currently there's a little bit of a cost premium involved in going through entitlement battles. Most locations are not geared to incentivizing new urbanism and instead put many obstacles along the path to entitlements.

But there are numerous new urbanist neighborhoods that deliver market-rate and subsidized housing that's no more expensive than standard development. One of the things that most disappoints me about new urbanist public relations is that the movement is known a lot more for Seaside and projects for the gentry than it is for the scores of HOPE VI projects we completed before the Bush Administration decided that the guidelines were not written by them and therefore HOPE VI should be killed.

HOPE VI was a remarkable success. It transformed completely dysfunctional low-income housing projects into mixed-use, mixed-income urban neighborhoods that, after several years, seem to be quite sustainable.

>> What are some of the land use and transportation patterns you think are necessary for communities to adopt to better enable them to combat sprawl and cope with the effects of global climate change and declining traditional energy sources?

I think probably one of the most important strategies would be for local governments to get back into the proactive planning business. Right now in most jurisdictions we have reactive planning. It's a stupid process.

What we need to do is the sort of thing that BART [Bay Area Rapid Transit] has started doing in the San Francisco Bay area. BART is transforming a suburban transit system into a system that links a series of high-density nodes to each other and that has some parking for the suburbanites that want to drive to a station and take public transit into the center city or to another node. A lot of work done on a theoretical basis by Peter Calthorpe in the early 1990s is finally being realized in places like Fruitvale just east of Oakland where they're actually building housing, jobs, schools, and other stuff all around the transit stops and within walking distance.

As a strategy, what we need to be doing is taking the public transit we already have and creating very urban, fairly high-density development around those transit nodes. We need to be looking at new and affordable ways of creating more efficient transit, like the mass surface transit advocated by Jaime Lerner, the former mayor of Curitiba, Brazil, that is dirt cheap to develop. From a planning point of view, Lerner created a linear corridor of very-high-density development wherever he put a rapid transit system in Curitiba.

We in America need to stop being so parochial and thinking that because we're the richest and most powerful nation on the planet that we're barred from using successful models created in places in Europe and in developing countries like Brazil.

>> What other suggestions can you offer to create more environmentally sustainable communities?

First of all, we need $10-a-gallon gasoline, because it will begin to change people's behavior. Take the money from gasoline taxes and reinvest it in transit, in renewable energy, pilot projects, and, most important, in helping the less fortunate in our society to adapt to these changes because they're the ones who drive the farthest and spend the most on automobiles because they can only afford to live in exurban locations.

In the long run, we have to get beyond our paralysis of land use to do infill affordable housing for these people. In the short run, as long as these people are stuck with three or four cars per household so that everyone in the family can get to school and to work, we need to give them a tax credit or a rebate for the extra gas taxes they're going to pay while we work on the long-term solutions.

The first strategy is beginning to price gasoline, and carbon dioxide in general, at a more accurate level that reflects their environmental costs.

The second strategy would be to begin to work on a set of proactive plans by a combination of local, regional, and state-level governments, with some help from the feds, that would begin to allow urban infill sites and particularly transit-friendly sites to be developed at higher densities and with a mix of uses that would allow people, particularly the young and the elderly, to use their feet as a means of transportation.

Third, we need to deal with some of the material and life-cycle issues. Slow down the construction of throwaway buildings. In suburban construction, we're throwing up five- to ten-year buildings to house companies like Wal-Mart. Wal-Mart's strategy is to abandon that building before it disintegrates and after it has sucked all of the money out of the community and move on to a Wal-Mart Supercenter. What's left is a suburban slum occupied by lower-value tenants until it completely falls apart. It's an incredibly wasteful system.

>> What do you consider the most important initiatives for creating real and lasting change in our country's development patterns?

In my imagination, Gore gets elected president with a clear mandate to act on his new-found enthusiasm for talking to us about the urgency of dealing with climate change. That's very unlikely to happen.

I think that what will happen is a slowly growing awareness that climate change is a real issue, that energy dependence is a critical geopolitical issue, and that we need to come up with strategies beyond higher-mileage automobiles to deal with these issues.

The other thing I see happening is trendsetters are moving back to the city. The TV programs, the sitcoms that were set in suburbs 30 and 40 years ago, are almost all now set in urban settings. Baby boomers are moving back to the cities. My guess is that a lot of the kids who will be forming families over the next couple of decades are going to realize that the city is not only cooler, it's a better place to raise kids. As soon as they become active in school-board politics, we'll have the best schools in the world in our urban areas because we'll have enough parents putting energy into forcing that change.

What is most encouraging is that it's become fashionable to live in the city, just as it's always been in Europe. I think that more and more people will be moving to the city, and that will put increasing pressure on real estate prices. But that will also create lots of opportunities for redeveloping industrial sites. As the value of real estate goes up, the environmental problems of cleaning up and recycling those sites begin to be economically feasible.

We're going to see a lot more recycling of urban land, often in the most desirable places, often right on the water. The Port Authority in San Francisco owns thousands of acres on the waterfront. Eventually, they and the longshoremen will come to realize that San Francisco won't replace Oakland as the primary port in the Bay Area and they might as well develop the waterfront land to make the city better. There's a lot of opportunity out there.

MARIA ATKINSON

Maria Atkinson was the cofounder and first CEO of the Green Building Council of Australia. For the past two years, she has worked as the global head of sustainability at Lend Lease, a Sydney-based international real estate group. She also is the director of several not-for-profit organizations, including the Banksia Environmental Foundation and the Barton Group. She speaks often on sustainable development issues to universities, seminars, and conferences around the world.

"I am all for fast action on those 30-year-old, energy-guzzling, sick examples of a design and construction period we will never repeat again."

Responsible for driving Lend Lease's sustainability in 40 countries in Europe and the Asia Pacific, as well as the United States, Atkinson's green IQ encompasses everything from the accelerating advance of green buildings around the world to the challenges they face, green regulatory requirements, and global climate change. While Atkinson sees real estate opportunities ahead, she argues that it is time to move beyond pockets of green excellence to more fundamental changes in building design and operations.

>> What's different this year on the green building and real estate front compared with last year? In your job? Overall?

What a difference a year makes!

Twelve months ago, most of my time was spent advocating the need for change and meeting business managers to pitch and explain the case for sustainability. The case for action by the real estate industry on climate change had yet to be made and, as a result, any action that was taken was uncoordinated and piecemeal. As an Australian-listed company, we also had to contend with a national government that refused to ratify the Kyoto Protocol.

Thankfully, since then the IPCC [Intergovernmental Panel on Climate Change, which shared the 2007 Nobel Prize with Al Gore] has convincingly shown that buildings provide more cost-effective greenhouse gas mitigation opportunities than any other sector, backing up McKinsey's [a management consulting firm] and Vattenfall's [a European electricity utility company] cost curve on carbon abatement [the Global Climate Impact Map] released in the first month of 2007. Then, we had the launch of the Clinton Climate Initiative's Energy Efficiency Building Retrofit Program, with the backing of five of the world's largest banks. Our call for including energy efficiency in buildings in any emissions-trading scheme is finally getting some traction. And closer to home, the first act of the newly elected [Kevin] Rudd government in Australia [elected in November 2007] was the ratification of Kyoto.

So, at the start of 2008, the Green Building Council of Australia no longer needs to argue the case for green. The theme for its annual conference in February is "What's Possible Now?"

And my job at Lend Lease has become more about supporting the company's transformation into a sustainable organization, rather than explaining why we need to become sustainable.

>> Which are the leading nations in green buildings and broader sustainability initiatives? And which are the lagging nations?

With perhaps the exception of the Scandinavian countries, which have long been recognized as early adopters in all aspects of sustainability, the leading nations in green buildings and broader sustainability initiatives would all seem to have either or both of the following: regulations and an effective Green Building Council.

Dubai is a perfect example. Sheikh Mohammed [bin Rashid Al Maktoum] decreed that all new buildings in Dubai must be designed in accordance with green building principles, a Green Building Council was established, and they were on their way! Swift change is what's needed, and Sheikh Mohammed should be congratulated for demanding green outcomes in months, not years.

India has a Green Building Council and examples of green buildings, most notably Karan Grover's CII [Confederation of Indian Industry] Sohrabji Godrej Green Business Centre at Hyderabad—the first LEED [Leadership in Energy and Environmental Design] Platinum building, awarded way back in 2002 when the rest of us were still wrestling with green. Not content to rest on his laurels, Karan did it again in December last year— his ABN Amro Bank branch at Ahmedabad, which has one of the world's greenest interiors, was awarded LEED Platinum.

Clearly, India has the capacity, as do other emerging economies. But every nation, even early adapters, face challenges. India, for example, is far behind on implementing good practice codes and standards for its buildings, which get their electricity from coal-fired power plants. With no green building regulations whatsoever, my guess is that the broader real estate industry is always going to be behind the eight ball.

>> What are the leading building types on the green front, and why?

Applause for commercial and public buildings. It follows that commercial and public buildings are leading on green. Where governments and regulators show leadership and a commitment to green, the results speak for themselves.

It's why, in the Australian market, there are more green buildings in the city of Melbourne in the state of Victoria than in Sydney in the state of New South Wales. Several years ago, the Victoria state government showed leadership by mandating minimum Green Star requirements for all new government offices built or leased, and by a raft of other green building commitments.

The city of Melbourne has also shown real leadership on green buildings. They have not only mandated green building requirements for the commercial sector, but they've also put their money where their mouth is with their new office building [Council House 2]—a world-leading iconic green building and the first project to achieve the Green Building Council of Australia's maximum Six Star Green Star–certified rating for its design. This [city] leadership also proactively shared all lessons and solutions for all. It all sends a clear message to the industry, which has responded in kind.

International examples of iconic green buildings either under development or completed seem to fall into offices, new and refurbished accommodations, or community buildings—community halls, civic buildings—and there is an increase in the number of education campus buildings.

With the successful model of mixed use, which is a combination of retail, office, and residential—occasionally also with a community facility—my guess is that we will see more diverse precinct green buildings. This means we have to go beyond buildings and move into neighborhood ratings—and not just the large master-planned community rating we are all looking to create.

>> What are lagging building types on the green front, and why?

There are few green malls, few green hospitals, but most of all there are few green hotels!

The very nature of the real estate industry explains why hotels are the lagging building product—that is, the split-incentive nature of the industry, where it is more common than not that the entity responsible for developing the building is not the owner of the building, let alone the manager, and certainly not the occupant.

These split incentives are most obvious in hospitality accommodation. But it doesn't excuse them, and it's time for them to step up to the plate—or for their guests to speak up and demand green. I gave a speech at Greenbuild in Chicago last November. Chicago is an amazing city and home to numerous LEED buildings, as well as the city's innovative green roof and green homes initiatives. But frankly, the Windy City's hotels did not do it proud. Greenbuild 2008 will be held in Boston. In my Chicago speech, I had a message for the hotels in Boston: they need to step up to the challenge of ensuring they are green because the delegates at Greenbuild 2008 will be demanding green hotels as part of their personal commitment to green buildings.

Even with split incentives, if hotel patrons across the globe demanded green by voting with their feet, the sector would soon sit up and listen.

>> What are the real impediments to green real estate?

Clearly, the split-incentives nature of the industry is an impediment to green. I also see a risk-averse sector that applies the same technology as the last building and the one before that because it is not supported to innovate. There are few R&D incentives or alternative financing for choosing alternative systems and technologies.

Another impediment I see is that politicians and policy makers invariably refer to real estate as homes—nothing more, nothing less. In Australia, for example, that means that, while there are rebates for homeowners for installing rainwater tanks and solar hot water systems, commercial properties are not eligible for any such incentives.

In the U.K., all new homes must be carbon zero by 2016, and incentives are being directed at domestic solutions—but again *not* at the commercial buildings. In particular, there is nothing to overcome the costs of refurbishing existing buildings that have the potential to be green.

Those [existing buildings] that can't get there should be granted immediate approval for demolition. And before your readers react to this aggressive pro-development statement, they should know that we have the tools that can tell us whether an existing building can be green or not. I'm all for fast action on those 30-year-old, energy-guzzling, sick examples of a design and construction period we will never repeat again!

Another impediment has to be the way the industry has traditionally operated the world over. Yes, industry support for green building has grown exponentially in the past ten years. We have the technology. As Joe Romm [author of *Hell and High Water* about global climate change] said, we can go far on existing technology right now. We don't need to wait for breakthrough technology. And there are pockets of excellence.

But we will never achieve the growth in green buildings *that is required* over the next ten years as long as we seem incapable of consistently replicating best practices within individual companies, as well as between companies and across countries. It's not good enough that waterless urinals are increasingly common in the U.S. but not in Australia, just as dual-flush, 0.8/1.6-gallon toilets are the norm in Australia but single-flush, 3.2-gallon toilets are common in Chicago—at least in the hotels we all stayed in during Greenbuild.

Nor is it good enough that a real estate company can ensure rainwater collection and solar panels in one project, but the same company uses single-flush toilets and incandescent light globes in another.

The only opportunity for the change we need in the next ten years is if we work together by connecting with others across the real estate sector, within our own organizations, and between countries.

All of which leads to my final point: while we've enjoyed exponential growth, I can't help feeling that so far we've really just been playing on the fringes. We haven't fundamentally changed the way we design and operate the built form. We keep coming up with innovation that tweaks but doesn't reengineer the entire process. And while we've managed to fudge it so far, it's time for real change—for as long as we continue to resist this, I fear we will never achieve what is required of us.

We can make buildings 100 percent more efficient: 30 percent from passive design, and 60 percent from alternative heating and cooling solutions and smart lighting and metering. We can get beyond 60 percent efficiency if we can provide the power for the building through a distributed solution using the sun, the wind and, where possible, geothermal to maximize renewable energy. With this proven formula and our ten-year window to make a difference to greenhouse gas emissions, we can create jobs, develop new skills, innovate new solutions, and create healthier interior environments for everyone.

>> Where are the greatest money-making opportunities for real estate investors? Do you see the carbon trading market having an impact on buildings?

Everybody makes claims, but the majority of investment is going to technology; not enough is going to existing buildings.

Carbon trading would definitely have an impact on buildings, and a carbon trading scheme that includes the built environment would drive deep emissions cuts that would benefit everyone. It's just a question of when the politicians and policy makers are going to get that message. McKinsey, Vattenfall, the IPCC, even accounting practices have all made it pretty clear that improving energy efficiency in buildings is the cheapest and fastest carbon-abatement solution.

Carbon trading would drive emissions reductions through improvements to the energy efficiency of buildings. In fact, it's the single most effective tool to use because it addresses emission reductions that occur at the design and construction stages of both new construction and the refurbishment of existing buildings, and it drives through the split incentives that exist in the property industry.

By being able to trade and effectively make a financial return on their investments in emissions-reduction initiatives, developers and asset owners would be able to deliver deep greenhouse gas emission cuts of 60 percent *or more*. Significantly, these cuts can be achieved using today's technology.

Going further, high-value carbon credits of $34 [Australian, US$24] per ton of carbon dioxide equivalent could realistically achieve a *carbon zero* position in buildings at *nil* cost. It can work through a mechanism providing permits for design savings and offsets for operational emissions savings, with reporting and verification through Green Building Council rating tools. These tools offer a transparent and accurate measure of greenhouse gas reduction and a well-established and recognized baseline that would provide a robust and transparent method for reporting and verification for the built environment within an emissions-trading scheme.

It's a compelling case. I'm heartened that it's a case the Chicago Climate Exchange seems to have heard. The exchange is interested in including energy-efficient buildings in its scheme. But why aren't our politicians and policy makers talking about a trading scheme that recognizes energy efficiency in buildings? The question was asked repeatedly in Bali [during the United Nations Climate Change Conference in December 2007], but it seems everyone is focused on the energy industry. Every day in Bali questions would come from the floor—"What about building efficiency?"—and all the panelists said "of course," but no one from the sector was invited to show how.

It's time for the industry to demand a global emissions-trading scheme that recognizes energy-efficient buildings as the cheapest and most immediate solution to cutting greenhouse gas emissions. Just because government leaders and bureaucrats immediately think of a house—because that is often their only experience with the sector—that is no excuse to not seek out and engage with real estate and property leaders and collectively develop a strategy for recognizing energy-efficient design and refurbishment solutions as carbon credits.

>> Are we too focused on buildings and not looking at sprawl development patterns, which mandate automobile use and high oil consumption that generate significant levels of greenhouse gases?

A focus on individual buildings is appropriate, but the next step is broad block or precinct planning. We need to think beyond green buildings to green communities, green cities. In saying this, I do not mean we should abandon the green building initiatives and individual assessments. I am saying that urban densification is an emerging positive trend.

However, the pace of urban consolidation is too slow and it is not yet getting the airplay it deserves. Creative planning solutions that allow for adding height, as well as cultural and community services, to existing buildings are not yet commonplace. If mayors had to rate the sustainability performance of the cities they govern, we would see more clearly that the things I have listed here greatly contribute to a healthier, happier, and better lifestyle community.

>> What about our larger infrastructure—energy, water, waste? How can it be greened?

This is the future and, for developers, a really exciting opportunity. We will see the development industry respond to a constrained planet. Our depletion of valuable resources and creation of toxic wastes will result in society moving from its current obsession with the one piece of the real cost pie—the capital cost—to a whole pie of life or operational cost awareness.

Ultimately, developers who can find the operational value will succeed, and those who can't will not exist.

I see a bright future where distributed energy, water, and waste solutions provide a community with efficient, independent, secure, and clean solutions. I see developers in partnership with communities providing the new utility solutions, including on-site water harvesting, treatment, and reuse, and alternative energy generation from alternative fuel sources, which will start with natural gas and move to biofuels and then to a new method of efficient hydrogen extraction that I can't predict. The energy generation will be by renewable energy from the sun and wind. I see waste supporting the energy-generation solutions, and then I see a significant downsizing of waste. I see a zero-carbon, zero-waste community. What I can't see is whether we do this quickly enough to reverse the stress on the planet.

>> Is the greening of the existing infrastructure a realistic goal for developed nations?

While there is population growth and migration to existing cities, we don't have a choice. The emerging economies, however, have a much greater opportunity to provide these solutions now to all communities—rural and city. This will create employment and entrepreneurial opportunities for their people. This will also give them an advantage over existing communities that have no certainty or security over their water or energy supplies.

>> Many people worry that developing nations will repeat the environmental mistakes of developed nations—that they will construct out-of-date buildings and infrastructure today, then have to retrofit everything in ten years. Is that a real concern?

You only have to take a look at the inspired work of Karan Grover to realize that this is just nonsense. When Grover's CII-Sohrabji Godrej Green Business Centre at Hyderabad was awarded LEED Platinum, he noted that India has "hundreds of years of legacy in such construction, which we have all but forgotten" and that the building represented a revival of traditional methods presented in the modern idiom.

No, I think the only real risk is when we in the developed countries think we know better and try to impose *our* methods, technologies, and rating tools on *them*. As Karan has said, they don't use artificial heating and cooling in India—never have and hopefully never will. So, a rating tool from a developed country that references artificial heating and cooling would be nonsense in the Indian market.

That said, I think developing countries would benefit from a carbon trading market in developed countries. With so many global real estate and construction companies operating in India and China, any initiatives that would drive investment in emissions-reduction initiatives would inevitably also benefit construction activity in those markets.

I also believe the governance that was agreed to in Bali—all countries will report their carbon emissions—will facilitate best-practice building codes and pollution standards in emerging economies.

I still see architects, engineers, and building service manufacturers successfully selling the old solutions everywhere—shiny new buildings that blow hot or cold air around from the ceiling when we know this is the most inefficient and uncomfortable heating and cooling methods—and they astound me.

>> How do you design a building today, so that it is not obsolete—in green terms—in ten or 20 years?

Design for adaptability and change. Design for eventual disassembly—that is, a building constructed in 2008 can be deconstructed and then reconstructed in a different form, like our kids do with Legos. Australian architect Jeremy Edmiston of the New York–based firm SYSTEMarchitects has been exploring this concept with his modular Burst house. Deconstruct, reconstruct—that's the next intelligence. In addition, waste must be included in greenhouse gas emissions accounting.

As we move from the cap-ex into the op-ex world, we will see designs that maximize the passive heating, cooling, and comfort features, as well as attributes of the local geography. Building services will be reengineered to accommodate the distributed or on-site energy, water, and waste initiatives, which will lead to the next radical change.

More fundamentally, we need to reengineer the traditional supply chain. We need to do something about the four key elements of building—steel, concrete, aluminum, and glass. As things stand, you can't build without them, and yet each one of them is so carbon intensive to make. Clearly, we are going to have to find another way. We need to address the choice of materials from sustainable timber to nontoxic plastics and products.

RON SIMS

Since 1996, Ron Sims has served as executive of King County, Washington, a nearly 2 million-person jurisdiction that includes Seattle, Bellevue, and Redmond. Sims is also board cochair of the Committee to End Homelessness, a founder of the Puget Sound Health Alliance, chair of the Puget Sound Partnership Ecosystem Board, and an advisory board member for the Brookings Center for Urban and Metropolitan Policy.

"The field is so competitive. You either prepare yourself and compete—or you lose. There is no middle ground!"

Under Sims's leadership, and well ahead of other communities, King County has implemented major initiatives on sustainable development, open-space preservation, mass transit, and climate change. Most King County cities are thriving, and the county's bonds continue to earn the highest available ratings from the three national credit rating agencies. Sims's and King County's successes not only provide vital lessons, but also debunk several urban development myths.

>> **Why, over the last two decades, has King County been a national leader in green buildings, sustainable urban development, and combating global climate change? Is it something in the water or the air?**

The residents of King County value their environment. This is a beautiful area, and people want to protect it. We also have a number of icons here. One of them is Dennis Hayes, who is a head of the Bullitt Foundation and who was also the founder of Earth Day.

In 1988, I introduced legislation—I'm a Democrat—with a Republican county councilman, Bruce Lang, to establish an office to evaluate the impacts in this region of global warming. We were ridiculed. In fact, proposing that office brought me the worst editorial I've ever received. I never pulled the office off [as a success], but we did talk about implementation strategies without ever mentioning climate change for a long time.

Time has proven our vision correct. The *Seattle Times*, a major newspaper, came back with an article recently saying, "No one's laughing at Ron Sims now" on the issue of climate change. So, I've been very fortunate to have a responsive public and some really good friends and a significant environmental leader who's a resident here.

>> Who have been some of the leading overall King County supporters of sustainability in recent years?

There have been a number. Seattle Works, a very active nonprofit; a group called Future Wise; the Sierra Club; the Master Builders of King and Snohomish County, that's the building industry; the King County Housing Authority; the Seattle Housing Authority; the city of Seattle. I think all collectively have been leaders on this issue of sustainability.

>> And who were initially some of the skeptics?

Most of the governments were pretty skeptical. The builders actually were not. It surprised me. I once invited the environmental community and the builders into my office and said, "We can fight or we can find a collaborative way to improve the quality of life in this region." The builders wanted to build in dense areas and the environmentalists wanted to protect the rural areas and the forests and the agricultural areas. We agreed that would be our strategy, and that's been our strategy since 1996 and it's served us well.

Today, 96 percent of all King County growth is directed toward cities, and only 4 percent of it is occurring in our rural areas. We've been able to secure 135,000 new acres [55,000 hectares] of forest land that will be preserved in perpetuity. There is no pressure by the builders to build in those areas. In fact, in a collective approach, the environmentalists and the builders protect the rural areas and forested areas, and they have been putting huge pressure on the cities to support high-density development.

>> What are some of the key King County strategies addressing sustainable urban development and global climate change?

We are a growth-management county. Our strategy is to incentivize growth in the cities, whether it's through transportation, or allowing higher-density development. In our forested areas, our key strategy is preservation because we don't want another county executive 20 years from now allowing development of our more pristine areas. So, we have covenants on all those properties that make it nearly impossible for those lands ever to be developed. We hold the development rights in those areas in perpetuity, either through nonprofit organizations or directly through King County.

We focus our infrastructure development in our urban areas, and that's key. And we also have arts money. We have learned that there are certain things that work in urban areas. People want parks, they want arts, they want public transportation systems, adequate arterial systems. You put the amenities—particularly the arts amenities, and the sports stadium amenities—you put all of that in your urban areas, and you attract people to them. That's where the restaurant scene is the strongest, the shopping centers are at their strongest. We have built all of those into our urban areas, and it's paid off handsomely.

You don't put those amenities in your rural areas. So, you preserve rural ways of life; you protect your forests in perpetuity.

To sustain the county's agricultural areas, we had a meeting with all the major grocery stores, and we said we wanted them to start buying agricultural produce that is grown in our agricultural areas and make it available in their stores. Local produce is the hottest item in the stores. It is called buying from your neighbor. The stores told us what they needed—timely delivery, marketing—and we created an infrastructure, the Puget Sound Fresh Program, and now we have made our agricultural areas viable.

We used to have 13 farmers' markets, which have now blossomed to 73 farmers' markets. So, people who are growing in the rural areas can come and sell their fresh produce, or their flowers, or cheeses, or whatever else they've been working on, to consumers directly. Those markets are packed; you can't get in them.

In our forested areas, while we have prohibited commercial, residential, and industrial development, we do want working forests. So, we have very, very aggressive science-based harvesting systems in most forests so the owners make money.

We also have what we call transfer development rights. We buy the development rights of our forested areas. It's a banking system, so it's not a transaction that we have to put any money on; we become the banker of the development rights. We lock forestry companies into a contract, and they're stuck in that contract, again in perpetuity. They can still harvest, but they have to meet a very rigorous standard.

Those development rights, in turn, are sent into cities, and the cities allow additional growth on various housing projects. So, again, the development is curtailed in our forested areas and transferred to our urban areas. And that has proven to be very lucrative for us. As a matter of fact, a large forest company on its own just made a decision to sell 40,000 acres [16,000 hectares] of development rights to King County. We didn't even ask them.

>> **The King County Global Warming Action Plan [2007] predicts a shortage of potable water in King County because of less snow in the mountains, as well as more numerous and higher-intensity storms and flooding. What actions is King County taking to address those threats and protect businesses and residents?**
We are doing advance planning. We asked the University of Washington School of Climate Impact to tell us what our weather system would be in 2050. What would King County look like in an age of global warming? What would our forests look like, our spe-

cies look like, our water look like? And they concluded [in the action plan] that the snow packs here would go up another thousand feet [300 meters]. We're a snow pack–fed water system with 1.8 million residents.

The change in the snow pack will do two things. One, the rains that occurred in the winter will not freeze. So, that water will go back into the Puget Sound, and that required us to build a levee system.

Two, with the snow pack going higher, we decided that we're going to have to reclaim water here. So, our newest water treatment plant will reclaim 26 million gallons [98 million liters] per day of wastewater, and we'll apply that to agricultural and industrial areas. We also bought forests because forests are great sponges. And we're looking at some smaller reservoir systems.

So, all of that is being put in place now, before the impacts of global warming are fully realized here. We are planning on having a water supply and being able to meet the water needs of not only the 1.8 million people that are here now, but also the additional 1.7 million people that are expected to move into this region over the next 50 to 80 years.

>> **Inadequate and aging infrastructure—from roads to bridges and sewage treatment plants—is one of the critical issues facing the country today. Does King County have any plans to implement green infrastructure strategies?**

Yes, we do. We have pushed green for all public buildings. The builders have come to us on low-impact design because we incentivized that by getting those applications out the door first. They've been very aggressive because they found their market. Thirty-two percent of all housing that's newly constructed here is what we call green housing. Now they're working on policies to do LEED- [Leadership in Energy and Environmental Design-] certified housing.

We had two major developments here that are net-zero-carbon developments: one by the YWCA for low-income individuals, and the adjacent development on the Issaquah Highlands. We worked with them on putting in the bus system that they needed, which is key for green development because you want people out of their cars. We have preserved a lot of the green area they wanted as buffer space. I dealt with their water issue. So, we do the complementary infrastructure and then they do the building infrastructure, and that's proven to be very effective for us.

Low-impact development is key. Walkable communities, access to bicycle trails, smaller streets, and a lot of vegetation: we love that kind of development, and that's what we're seeing right now.

>> Public transit—particularly light-rail systems—is a critical means of reducing vehicular trips and greenhouse gas emissions. What is the status of King County's public transit system, and what are your plans for the future?

We have the fastest-growing transit system in North America. We'll eventually have a light-rail system that will go from our airport through Seattle into the east side. In the meantime, we're going to have variable tolling. We're divided by a lake, so we have an east and west King County. You go to east King County over two bridges—the I-90 bridge and the 520 bridge. One's an interstate and one's a state highway. We're going to have variable tolling on those bridges.

Variable tolling will have two impacts. One, it reduces the amount of automobile traffic, so it reduces our impact by automobiles on the climate. Two, it funds constructing a new 520 bridge, which will be like the I-90 bridge. Both will have bicycle lanes, and both will be able to handle high-capacity transit systems. The money from variable tolling will also pay for a fairly new bus transit system.

No matter what options you choose, you have to expand bus transportation. So, the state has already allocated dollars for us to do that. We are now looking at being able to move 1 million people more per year through Seattle by bus. We are one of the six cities that were selected for the urban partnership grant by the U.S. Department of Transportation. With that money we're going to buy 45 new buses, build three new park-and-ride lots, and have variable tolling. In terms of transit service, we're looking at a gross here of 2 million people just on two different transportation projects.

We're also forging a telecommuting agreement. Seventy-eight percent of the people in this region are on a broadband system of some kind, whether it's telephone or cable. A number of companies have agreed to increase telecommuting options for their employees. Safeco, the insurance company, did it on their own; they're a very large employer here. Microsoft realizes that telecommuting is what they're going to have to do, so they're going to work with a consortium of other high-tech companies and lay out a very aggressive telecommuting approach for the whole region.

As one of the larger employers here in our county, we, too, are going to do the same thing, because we believe it's important to reduce the number of people commuting by identifying those jobs that people can telecommute [to].

We already have a number of those functions ongoing. If you call the county looking for a bus schedule, you're likely to be dealing with a person in a bathrobe. If you call in to complain about how late a bus is, that person's working at home as well. We're now looking at every job we have to determine whether or not that job can be a telecommuting job. We have a union that recently agreed to aggressively advocate telecommuting among its members.

We're also working on creating remote job sites—that is, reporting to work at a King County office that is a half hour from your door. But it may not be a single office; it may be people who are all telecommuting from that office or working from that remote site away from a central court office. We can do that very efficiently. Our goal is to have as many of our employees working a half hour from their doorstep as possible.

One thing that we realized is that for the public and for our own employees, if you have to commute, you have higher health risks than if you work closer to your job. We have a *healthscape*, which is a mechanism that we use to determine the health and environmental consequences of where you live. Our goal is to give people their lives back. Rather than have them live to work, we want them to work to live.

>> Are you implementing measures to encourage close-in infill development to create high-density urbanity, and are you taking specific steps to encourage development near transit stops and transit hubs?

Oh, without a question. We did two things. One is that much of the development that's taking place comes from the development-right transfers I discussed earlier, which target infill development and increase density within existing neighborhoods. We've been very aggressive on that, along with the builders and the environmentalists.

Our bus locations are key because we realize that density requires people being serviced by public transportation. We decreased the head times. We created 15-minute head times on 35 major bus corridors that go through dense areas so that people don't have to wait very long to get their buses. We then established five rapid-transit bus routes where people only have to wait ten minutes—again along transit corridors. We run them all day, not just during peak hours. We're finding that people now report to work throughout the day, so the key is reliable, predictable, and robust transit service. Our buses right now are running full, and the number of overcrowded buses has gone up because people like the level of service. So, we have another 600 buses on order.

We also have one of the largest transit-redevelopment projects in the country. We actually built 320 units of housing over one of our park-and-ride lots. It's called the Overlake project and it's run by the King County Housing Authority. We have another one in downtown Renton. Renton wanted a new look for itself; it's a suburban area. We had a park-and-ride downtown and we allowed that to be incredibly developed, and then we bought the garage space underneath for our customers, the people who were going to take our buses. Downtown Renton was literally transformed. Then, they decided to build an arts center, markets, and restaurants.

We believe that, to succeed, it's not just building in a hub area, but developing along the entire transit corridor. Our strategy was to increase services along the entire corridor to make it attractive for increased densities because that's what the builders said they needed, and that's what the public wants, and that's been proven to be true. We also looked at our hub areas, where the light rail intersects with our bus system, and we are developing them as well. Both are going along amazingly well.

Now when we build our park-and-ride lots, we build them within dense areas either for housing or in the city or in new downtowns, or in the city of Redmond. In Redmond, we literally built the project that they wanted in their large retail area, which has offices, hotels, and motels. It's next to Microsoft. It's upscale and our system runs internal to that. I believe very strongly that if you're going to have dense areas, you have to meet the demands of their residents by providing a fairly robust level of public transportation.

>> **A lot of experts insist that Americans don't want to live in walkable, higher-density neighborhoods; they want suburban homes. That's been the ideal. Do you see a market for people buying and renting in urban neighborhoods with a higher-density lifestyle?**

Absolutely. A large house on a large lot isn't possible in King County anymore. The housing that's being developed is dense housing and it's moving very, very, very well. Even though the economy has slowed down, housing prices here have held very well. Actually, housing has gone up in cost; that's our biggest problem. People want this kind of housing.

Everybody had the traditional housing types until about 1996. Since 1996 to now, there's been a sea change in housing development, and it's remarkable. Our builders love it because they're making a lot of money. People just don't like that traditional, suburban, I-can't-see-my-neighbor kind of housing. People want trails; that's the first thing they look for. Our goal in King County is to have within a mile and a half [2.4 kilometers] of any area a major regional bicycle trail. We're putting together a rather elaborate bicycle and walking trail system and knitting all the trails together so they cross all areas of income, race, immigrant communities, affluent communities, and tie into a network that allows you to bicycle, whether it is to a lake, or a forest, or our agricultural lands, or major regional parks.

Remember, you can leave Seattle or Bellevue or the urban areas and be in agricultural areas or forested areas within a half hour! We have a defined line. We don't have urban/suburban. It is all urban and then it is rural, agricultural, or forest. And we put hiking and bike trails in those areas so people can get out of the urban areas and next to lakes. That formula has worked very, very well for this region.

But no one believed that people would move into condos and townhouses and smaller homes. People said "nobody wants to do that." And that is the hottest product right now. Downtown Seattle has turned into a condominium paradise. The people who are moving into those units are people who have moved out of those traditional suburban homes.

They are drawn to the richness of amenities: the arts—whether it's theater, or a symphony, or visual performances—or restaurants, or a sense of safety, and being able to meet people, incredible library systems, and retail systems. All that is being put into our area. The two fastest-growing areas of King County—downtown Seattle and Bellevue—defy all stereotypes! Because they are dense, they are condo-ed.

But you've got to have amenities. I went to a city recently that had just put up condos in the middle of its downtown, but there's nothing downtown! Those condos are going to fail because you've got to wrap housing around people's living amenities and public transportation systems. You've got to do that.

In King County, walkable, low-impact-design, wonderfully textured, and green communities *are* the market. The developers tell us that they are the most popular housing type in the region other than the condominiums and central cities.

>> Metropolitan Seattle is growing at an impressive rate. How does the county's comprehensive land use plan support that growth, maintain its sustainability standards, and enhance the quality of life?

Everybody thinks of urbanization using the wrong prism. They think of 1950s and 1960s urban renewal. Our plans are to have low-impact design, walkable communities, amenity-rich environments—which is why the arts are so key, because in one form or another, everybody wants those. We're putting high levels of bus service into those urban areas. That's also key.

It used to be that you could build anything. Now, we've found out that people don't like to have "anything" built. They want interesting colors, but they want them to be pleasant. They want design treatment, they want street treatments, they want a lot of vegetation, so you build that in. We're talking about a redefinition of what urbanization means. In this environment, poor people and persons of color and immigrants have to have the same kind of what we call essential quality fields and amenity investments. If we do that, we believe that we can change the look of poverty and the number of people who are poor.

There's no such thing as letting something happen because it can. We know that certain formulas work well in every community. Communities of color or communities of affluence—people want the same kind of quality of life. And that's what we are very aggressively monitoring and implementing.

We are the agency that ultimately is responsible for growth management in this region. We're the regional government. We can also influence the local decisions: we control the investment for the wastewater-treatment provider, we are the social services provider, we are the bus system, we are the public health system. So, we use our leverage to stimulate and encourage what we call the look and feel of neighborhoods. We create infrastructure; we create policies—like transfer-development rights—in the cities in order to continue to stimulate their economic growth.

When we first started down this path, people said, "Urbanization is ugly; nobody wants it." No one says that anymore! When you tell people we can get you fresh food from farms nearby? Huge! People want that. We say we can protect your water quality, and we can preserve and protect your ability to go see salmon spawn, and we can have wonderful forests. Even though we're going through a change, we can tell you that we'll have a water supply that's predictable not only now, but in 2050 so your children will have access to water, and to forests, and to amenities, and to a robust public transportation system.

That's what we are orchestrating, and people become part of that culture. It's just accepted now, whether you're liberal or conservative, Republican or Democrat. No one says "turn back the clock." It's part of our culture. It's inculcated. It's great!

>> So you don't have a lot of NIMBY [not in my back yard] problems?

Well, you always have NIMBY problems. People don't want wastewater systems, so we put one as far away from people's homes as we could. We still had community opposition, but most people have come to accept it.

Every jurisdiction has NIMBYs, but the key is that there are more people who want change, and the NIMBYs get drowned out. If I say we're going to put in a park or a trail, we don't get people pushing back on parks and trails. We have a generation coming up that says, "We don't have to live in a big house." People want good schools, so we work with the school districts. The idea is a concerted effort for what I call a new urbanism or new urbanity. We're achieving it here.

>> Do you believe that all of these measures that we've been discussing— particularly sustainability and quality of life—are laying the foundation for a prosperous regional future? Do you see that as part of your objective?

I think that *is* our objective. We want to be attractive. Talented people want a good quality of life. And everything I've described is a part of that. They want schools that work. They want housing that's nice. They want good public transportation systems. They want amenities.

I have said that the 21st century is going to be brutal. The new urbanism that you're seeing keeps you on the radar screen because that's where talent is going to move, and businesses will either expand or follow talent, which is why we've had an incredible growth in our biotech sector, our nanotechnology sectors, our engineering sectors. People are moving here. They want to move here because they like the University of Washington and the other major universities. They like the arts, they like the amenities, they like the parks, they like the trails, they like good transit service, and we will win in the 21st century.

Communities that don't transform themselves to look like us will lose badly.

People in Shanghai don't care about whether or not Seattle's on their radar screen, but their companies will move there. We're in an incredibly competitive global environment. If you're going to compete in that worldwide environment, what you've done in the past doesn't work! You've got to transform yourself and have a new game plan, and we have developed that game plan.

We want the high-income jobs here. We want the high quality of life here, and we want to continue to attract the best companies here. We want them to leave Shanghai and come to Seattle. We want them leaving India and coming here. We want them leaving Tel Aviv and coming here. We want them leaving South Africa and coming here.

We are protecting our environment, we're working sustainable systems, we're building green. We care about our carbon-emissions strategies, we're smart in what we do and how we invest our money here, and we continue to attract new companies and new residents.

>> What advice would you give to an elected official in another county that may not be as fortunate economically or environmentally as King County?

Don't sprawl. That's lesson number one.

Two, urbanize smartly.

Three, put amenities in there. Parks are key, trails are key, public transportation is key.

Overarching all of that is create cities that people can see are acting as good environmental stewards. That's really the underlying philosophy. We have got to build green and retrofit green in the 21st century in order to be attractive to businesses and residents.

A city or country really has to be green and sustainable because that's where talent will move. The same thing that happened with what we call the steel cities is going to happen in the future to those cities that insist on maintaining the status quo. There is no mercy shown in the 21st century. None! The field is so competitive. You either prepare yourself and compete, or you lose. There is no middle ground!

THOMAS L. FRIEDMAN

Thomas L. Friedman's newest book, *Hot, Flat, and Crowded: Why We Need a Green Revolution—and How It Can Renew America*, explains how a green revolution can reinvent America in this age of climate change, global economic competition, and soaring worldwide population.

"In today's green revolution, we're happy and everyone's a winner! Exxon's green, GE's green—I saw it all in their ads! Well, that's not a revolution. . . . We're having a green party. . . . You'll know it's a revolution when companies either have to change and innovate, or die— not when they can just get a new green brand."

From his New York Times *column to his presentations at the London School of Economics and interviews on* The Daily Show *with Jon Stewart, Friedman is renowned for his insights into the political, environmental, economic, and development challenges of our day, and their solutions. Here, Friedman offers recommendations on everything from outgreening Al Qaeda to helping America "get its groove back" and bringing conservatives and environmentalists together to create a more sustainable and prosperous future.*

>> **In our last interview in mid-2006, you said your goal was to redefine green as geostrategic, geoeconomic, capitalist, and the most patriotic thing you can do. Have you succeeded in that goal?**

I hope so. Only readers can judge that.

>> **Is your new book, which came out this month, an important next step?**

Well, you know the new book has a new title. I first called it *Green Is the New Red, White, and Blue*. Now, it's called *Hot, Flat, and Crowded*. What I tried to do in this book is connect five different trends that I think are going to be the defining trends of the 21st century. I put them into a single framework of a problem, and then I put them into a single framework of a solution.

My argument is that we're in the middle of a perfect storm of hot, flat, and crowded. It is a perfect storm of global warming and global flattening—that is, for me, shorthand for the rise of the whole developing world, India and China, and all the production and consumption they're now doing—as well as global crowding thanks to global population growth. In my lifetime, from 1953 to 2053 if I live to be 100, we'll go from a world of around 2.6 billion people to a world of over 9 billion people.

The convergence of hot, flat, and crowded—those three megatrends—is driving five interwoven problems: one, energy and resource supply and demand, as evidenced by very expensive oil and gasoline; two, climate change; three, petro-dictatorship, the rise of Russia, Iran, Venezuela—all these powers, purely because of the price of oil; four, biodiversity loss—we're in the middle of a massive extinction rate of species; and five, lastly, a phenomenon I call energy poverty, which is about the 1.6 billion people who have no connection to the power grid. More than a quarter of the planet still has no on/off switch in their life today.

My argument in this new book is that the convergence of hot, flat, and crowded has driven all five of these problems past the tipping point. We're at a whole new level. We see the energy supply-and-demand problem, evidenced by soaring oil and gasoline prices. We see climate change enter a whole new level. We see biodiversity loss at a whole new level. We see petro-dictatorship at a whole new level. We see the implications of energy poverty at a whole new level. How we manage these five problems is going to determine the stability or instability of the first part of the 21st century.

In a chapter that I do call "Green Is the New Red, White, and Blue," I make the argument that in a world that's hot, flat, and crowded, developing green power—green technology—is going to be *the* source of competitive advantage in the world today. It is going to be the next great global industry. It simply *has* to be in a world that's this hot, flat, and crowded. I know that for sure. What I don't know is whether America is going to lead that new industry or not.

Let's say you're a total climate change skeptic. What is indisputable is that the world is getting flat and crowded. When flat meets crowded, get out of the way! So, even if you take climate change off the table, in a world that's just flat and crowded, clean power, resource productivity, water productivity, and similar technologies are going to be the next great global industry.

>> So, water is the new oil?

Yeah! Preparing for that world is like preparing for the Olympic triathlon. If you make it to the Olympics, you may win the race. But even if you don't win the race, you're going to be healthier, fitter, stronger, more entrepreneurial, more competitive.

And that's my point. If the climate skeptics are wrong, and we prepare for climate change anyway, we'll be in a much better position to adapt and mitigate it. If the climate skeptics are *right*, and we prepare for climate change, we'll still be healthier, more competitive, more respected, more secure, and more entrepreneurial. So either way, this is a win-win.

Now, I'm not against Kyoto and these international treaties. If you can get 190 countries to all agree on verifiable climate reductions, God bless you and good luck. But that's not my strategy. My strategy is to make America *the* example of a country that grows rich, respected, secure, entrepreneurial, and competitive by leading the green revolution. More people will emulate us once we set that example than will ever follow the compulsion of a Kyoto treaty.

>> More carrot than stick?

Exactly. And my argument speaks to both conservatives and liberals. This book avowedly speaks out of both sides of its mouth.

It says to conservatives: I have a strategy for making America stronger, healthier, more secure, more entrepreneurial, and more competitive in a world that's hot, flat, and crowded. And by the way, that stuff Al Gore talks about? My strategy will take care of that as a byproduct.

To environmentalists, I say: I have a strategy for mitigating climate change, preserving biodiversity, making cleaner air and cleaner water. Oh, and by the way, as a byproduct, it's going to make us stronger, more respected, more competitive, and more entrepreneurial.

So, this is a strategy that *avowedly* speaks out of both sides of its mouth, because unless you have liberals and conservatives coming together on these problems, you're never going to generate the leverage you need in order to get to where we need to go.

>> What solutions does your book offer both conservatives and environmentalists?

The first chapter in the second half of my book is called "205 Easy Ways to Save the Earth." It's about the phony revolution we're having now. People always come to me and say, "We're having a green revolution!" I say, "Really? A green revolution? Have you ever been to a revolution where no one got hurt?"

In today's green revolution, we're happy and everyone's a winner, yeah! Exxon's green, Peabody [Coal] is green, GE's green—I saw it all in their ads! Well, that's not a revolution, because when everyone's green, that's a party. We're having a green party, and I have to tell you, it's a lot of fun. But it has no connection whatsoever with the revolution. You'll know it's a revolution when someone gets hurt. Oh, I don't mean physically hurt. You'll know it's a revolution when companies either have to change and innovate, or die—not when they can just get a new green brand. In 2007, the word *green* was the most trademarked word by the U.S. Patent and Trademark Office. What does that tell you?

The real revolution is what I call the *energy internet*, because that's what we're going to need. We're going to need a smart grid into a smart home into a smart car. The energy internet revolution is when IT meets ET. It's going to be like two huge rivers coming together.

>> How do we make a genuine energy internet revolution, and not just have another round of feel-good trademarks, press releases, and glossy magazine ads?

We look at the price signals we need to get the investments in that revolution. We make the regulatory changes we need to get the investments in that revolution. We need a strategy for clean power generation, and we need a strategy for biodiversity preservation.

And we have to outgreen Al Qaeda. The "green hawks" in Iraq asked for solar power. Why? Because they had to supply bases on the border with Syria with gasoline that was costing them as much as $100 a gallon to truck from Kuwait all the way to the Syrian border and back at an enormous risk. If the green hawks had solar power, they could take all those trucks off the road and outgreen Al Qaeda.

Outgreening your competition, finding a sustainable source for low-cost, clean power, is going to be the single most competitive advantage in a world that is hot, flat, and crowded.

I had a conversation with Jeff Immelt, the head of GE, in which Jeff at one point said— it's so obvious—"Look, Tom, we need a president who's going to set the right carbon price, set the right regulations. Everyone will scream and moan for a month, and then the whole ecosystem will adjust. And we'll just take off and everyone will make money. And America will take the lead."

>> You offer some important solutions. But what about the elephant in the living room: what about China?

Remember the movie *Speed*, where this terrorist puts a bomb on a bus? If the bus goes under 50 miles an hour, it blows up. China is that bus. If it grows economically under 10 percent, it blows up. China's challenge is to change the engine in its bus from a dirty diesel to a clean hybrid while the bus is going 50 miles an hour. It's the greatest show on earth.

>> These are the biggest challenges we've faced since World War II. Does America have the leadership to succeed? Do we as a country have the backbone and the unity to make the necessary sacrifices and changes as we did in World War II?

I believe that we've lost our groove as a country. We're not a serious place anymore, post-9/11. I believe that America gets its groove back by taking on this challenge. The world has a problem: it's getting hot, flat, and crowded. America has a problem: it's lost its way since 9/11. We solve America's problem by taking a lead in solving the world's problem—in being a role model, getting focused, rebuilding industry, education, and our country around this idea.

I end my new book by saying, "We need to redefine green and rediscover America, and in so doing rediscover ourselves and what it means to be Americans. We are all pilgrims again. We are all sailing on the *Mayflower* anew. We have not been to this shore before. If we fail to recognize that, we will indeed become just one more endangered species. But if we rise to this challenge and truly become the 're'-Generation—redefining green and rediscovering and regenerating America—we and the world will not only survive, but thrive in an age that is hot, flat, and crowded."

>> **America has many declining cities, older suburbs, overlooked towns, and forgotten regions in places like the industrial Midwest and Appalachia—places where most people work hard and play by the rules. But the rules have changed and they've been left behind. What can green do for these places and their people?**

Well, First Solar, America's premier solar company, was founded in Toledo, Ohio, and has its only North American manufacturing plant in the area. There's no reason that any of these communities can't be a source of green innovation. If I were the mayor or the governor of one of these distressed areas, I'd be setting up a green innovation zone with long-term tax breaks and other incentives to get companies either started there or located there.

At the same time, there's obviously going to be a huge domestic industry in retrofitting with green-collar jobs, because as energy bills double or maybe triple, people are going to be looking to reinsulate their homes, install solar panels on their roofs, to find any way to outgreen the competition and find low-cost green power or clean power. That's going to be a huge domestic industry here that you can't outsource. Someone in China can't retrofit your house.

There's a huge opportunity for new industries here, whether it's around solar/thermal if you're out west, or it's wind if you're in the Plains states, or it's photovoltaic if you're in any innovation zone. You know, some of our best solar companies are in places like Vermont and Ohio, where the innovators came together. That's the only way they're going to rescue these places.

>> **These new industries will also provide all kinds of jobs, from typical construction and renovation jobs to research and development.**

You go from green collar to lab suits with this industry. In a world that's hot, flat, and crowded, there's going to be lots of jobs at every end of that value chain.

But if we don't *make* it an opportunity for people at every end of the political spectrum to benefit from it—both in the employment sense and in the retrofitting sense, like making their mortgages more manageable by bringing down their energy costs—it's not going to scale. This has got to be for everybody. Otherwise, it will never generate the leverage you need to make the changes you need.

>> **Eight of the ten fastest-growing metropolitan areas in the country are running out of water—places like Phoenix, Las Vegas, and Atlanta. Other areas like the Pacific Northwest and the Midwest are experiencing much more numerous and violent storms. Meanwhile, we're investing hundreds of billions of dollars in infrastructure and private real estate development in these regions. Are we throwing good money after bad in what, over the long term, could be the wrong locations?**

That's a very important question. You can't just mitigate climate change in Las Vegas or Phoenix or Atlanta. Either you do it collectively, as a global community, or it doesn't happen, because if we do it in this country seriously, and China doesn't do it and India doesn't do it, it doesn't happen. The atmosphere doesn't distinguish between Bangalore and Boston, Phoenix and Shanghai. That's why we have to have a global strategy for addressing climate change. And we're very close.

But here and now, we have to take these off-the-chart weather changes very, very seriously—whether higher temperatures and less water, or extreme weather events like hurricanes and flooding. They will affect real estate values. They'll affect everything.

>> **Should the government be using tax dollars to put infrastructure where it doesn't belong?**

That's a debate we should be having. Should we be investing in better dikes? Should we be investing in adaptation? How *much* should we be investing in adaptation? Mitigation may be too late as a strategy.

>> **With gas prices on an up-and-down roller coaster and global oil reserves declining in some key countries, which means much higher prices when good economic conditions return, is suburbia even a viable model anymore?**

"We built a very inefficient model with the greatest efficiency mankind has ever seen." That's a quote from Andy Karsner [former assistant secretary for energy efficiency and renewable energy] of the Department of Energy.

Things are going to have to change. We're going to have to have more mass transit. In Washington, D.C., the number of people riding the subway every day has gone from 700,000 to 800,000. That's a huge leap. That's part of a big shift, provided the price of gasoline doesn't go down. People's demand is very, very sensitive to price. People go out and buy a Prius when gasoline is $5 a gallon, but they don't when it's $3 a gallon. That much is clear.

So, you've got to have a price signal and it's got to be fixed, because if it goes away, so will the demand. We're not going to get a dollar tax now, but that's what we need. We should have gas at about somewhere between $6, $7, $8 a gallon. Then you will get huge structural change. But at least put a floor in and tax rebates for people with lower incomes. Take it off people's payroll taxes so we incentivize people to work and disincentivize them to use gas-guzzling vehicles.

>> What are we going to do with all this inefficient suburbia that we built so efficiently?

The way to deal with suburbia is to change work so you work more at home. We're not going to dig up Levittown, or Bethesda, or Fairfax. But what we can do is redesign work so that people don't commute as much as they did—or, if they do commute, they do it in much more efficient ways. But something's going to have to change around here.

>> Do you see a renaissance for our poor, decrepit railroads and our mass transit, or do we have to start from scratch?

Clearly, we need to have a renaissance in mass transit. I don't know what will be the precise mode, but when 100,000 more people a day use the Washington, D.C., subway, you know something's happening. And there's going to be huge opportunities there, just as there will be around wind and solar and solar/thermal and other technologies.

>> You said earlier that we're not having a green revolution, we're having a party. What happens if we do start a green revolution? Who will be the winners and losers?

I think the winners will be the oil companies that move from crude oil, redefine themselves as energy companies, make multiple energy bets, and provide clean energy. I think that utility companies that make the move from selling kilowatts to helping people save a watt will be winners. I think those companies that change with the times will thrive.

I think those companies that don't change will wither, will be marginalized, will die. And the times, they are a changin'. I think we're in the middle of a huge shift, *provided* the price of gasoline doesn't roll back. Because if the price rolls back, the green revolution will, too.

FRANCES BEINECKE

Frances Beinecke is president of the Natural Resources Defense Council (NRDC), "the most effective lobbying and litigating group on environmental issues," according to the *Wall Street Journal*. Before becoming president in 2006, she was the NRDC's executive director and worked on its water and coastal program. Beinecke serves on the boards of the World Resources Institute and Conservation International's Center for Environmental Leadership in Business.

"We need new policies in the building arena so that we build green, reduce the demands on our power sector—which is the largest source of carbon dioxide emissions—and create incentives to green up our existing buildings."

The Natural Resources Defense Council has long stood at the vanguard of environmental issues. Under Beinecke's leadership, the NRDC has expanded its role far beyond oceans, forests, and clean air to also address some of today's most critical issues—the built environment, renewable energy, global climate change, national sustainability, and the greening of China. Beinecke brings this vital perspective to questions directly affecting the real estate industry and national and multinational corporations.

>> **The United States is in the midst of a serious energy crisis. Recently, gasoline and electricity prices reached record highs. For years, the NRDC has advocated a switch from heavily polluting oil and coal to renewable energy. Are you saying "I told you so"?**

Well, we're saying that there's a huge opportunity if only we wake up to it. Right now, the nation is once again—and this is about the third time in 20 years—focused on the fact that we need to be energy independent and that we can't drill our way out of this mess.

We really have an opportunity to grow into a 21st-century energy strategy. Our aim at the NRDC is to bring that fact to the attention of decision makers and to get that conversation going so that we can help solve the energy crisis and global climate change at the same time.

The good news is that there are a lot of venture capitalists, private-equity firms, and inventive technology people who want to grab hold of this opportunity and capture the market. We have people walking in NRDC's door literally every day with new ideas about how to solve our energy problem and how to take the lead internationally—a new solar company, a new wind company, a new technology that someone thinks can make a particular product much more efficient than it is now.

Now, the thing that has to happen is government policies need to be put in place to really unleash that initiative. The best recent example of government inaction was the continued debate over renewable tax credits. In mid-2008, Congress refused to renew those credits, and they expired at the end of the year. [The credits were finally included in the $700 billion bailout package passed in October 2008.] No company is going to invest with this on-again/off-again policy situation.

Much of our energy structure, and the policies that go along with it, is designed toward what I always call the 19th-century technologies of oil, gas, and coal that we're still using today and we will still be using in the coming years. How do we move into a much more efficient future that both benefits us in a cost-effective way and also, most important, benefits the planet by reducing our carbon dioxide emissions?

At the NRDC, we're very eager to put in place long-term policies to unleash a new energy future that gives predictability to the many people and businesses out there that want to address energy solutions.

>> In recent years, we've seen a sea change in the way that environmental organizations, particularly the NRDC, interact with corporations. I see more collaboration and less combat. Why is that? In particular, how does an organization like the NRDC—one that does a lot of litigation—achieve this balance?

As information on the urgency of global climate change spreads, companies—particularly multinational corporations—recognize the urgency of this issue, and they have begun to enter into the discussion of how to solve this problem. The NRDC is involved with many corporations in that discussion. Some of them are the same companies that might be our adversaries in other places.

So, for example, we're on the U.S. Climate Action Partnership Steering Committee with Shell Oil while we are challenging Shell's leases in the environmentally valuable Chukchi Sea off Alaska's coast, which we think is a very, very important marine environment that needs protection. In this multifaceted world, we have many interests, as do the corporations, and we are able to engage in these multifaceted conversations.

Our aim is to ensure that we get the maximum environmental protection and the policies in place to ensure that. We need to be in conversations with a wide range of interests to accomplish that goal.

>> The NRDC has an office in Beijing. How are your colleagues there dealing with China's rapid industrialization and urbanization? Is China the biggest single environmental challenge on the planet, or is it our own intransigence in the United States?

Well, it's definitely a combination. The U.S. is the largest economy in the world and it had the longest history of being a major greenhouse gas emitter. Until very recently, we were the largest emitter of carbon dioxide in the world. [China took the top spot in 2007.] The U.S. has a huge role to play. We have to take responsibility for what we have done over the past century. If we get moving, the United States will have a tremendous opportunity and advantage.

China, obviously, is of enormous importance. Its economy is growing rapidly. The amount of pollution coming from that economic growth is not only poisoning many millions of people in China, it's also having a global impact as the pollution crosses the Pacific and comes to the United States and—as China's carbon emissions continue to rise—it's escalating global climate change.

Meanwhile, I think there's a real recognition in China among government leaders that they need to address these issues of pollution and global climate change. We've had very good success in exporting some strategies—like California's energy efficiency model of strong standards and energy savings investments, which has kept that state's electricity demand steady for the last 30 years—to energy officials in China who are requesting ap- proaches that they can adopt to reduce their pollution as well as their emissions.

So, China is an enormous challenge that is having an impact globally, there's no ques- tion about it. But we're very enthusiastic about being able to have an office there. It's a growing office focusing on energy efficiency and green building design because China has more new and rapidly growing cities than any other country on the planet. How those cit- ies are designed is going to have a big impact.

China has an opportunity to become a model of efficiency in the 21st century. It has an opportunity to avoid some of our worst 20th-century wasteful practices. Our aim through our Beijing office is to provide the tools and models that the Chinese can use and learn from as they develop their own strategies.

>> The Bush Administration has tried to dismantle environmental programs created over the last four decades. Has the NRDC turned to city and state governments to partner on environmental initiatives?

Increasingly, over the last eight years—as the Bush Administration has tried to move us back in environmental policy rather than forward—we've seen a lot of innovation and new models coming out of cities and states. The NRDC has a history of working at that level as well as at the national level.

We have offices in New York, Chicago, San Francisco, Los Angeles, and Washington, D.C. The mayors in most of these cities, like Mayor Michael Bloomberg in New York and Mayor Richard Daley in Chicago, spearhead a lot of innovation, particularly in green spaces.

Mayor Bloomberg, for example, adopted PlaNYC, which I think will be a real change agent for how New York addresses green issues over the next two decades. They've created a strategy, and it's up to us to ensure that that strategy is implemented. The exciting thing about New York's plan is that it will not only focus on new buildings, but also—because this is a very established, developed city—it focuses on remodeling the old buildings *and* the infrastructure. I think that is something that's going to have to happen all over the country, and New York may provide the model.

>> **Buildings account for 36 percent of the United States' total energy consumption, including 65 percent of its electricity use and 38 percent of its carbon dioxide emissions. How can we make green buildings, which outperform conventional buildings, the rule and not the exception in the United States—or are they already becoming the preferred real estate product?**

We have a long way to go before green buildings are the standard. But I have to say that the rapidity with which green design is getting embraced and adopted is exciting. There are many examples of institutional green commitments. Cities are mandating green. Schools are going green. It's catching on in the commercial and residential sectors. The institutional infrastructure that people notice is going green. That is an educational opportunity. But we have a long way to go.

The only way to make green building become the standard is to create rules, building codes, and zoning requirements that make green the standard. The voluntary approach won't do it.

The spread of green information is key. Demonstrating that green buildings result in real cost savings is a huge plus. So, the more case studies that demonstrate those savings the better.

When people think of green buildings, sometimes they don't realize the full comprehensive approach to making a building truly green. Green isn't only in the building envelope and design, it's what's happening *inside* the building as well—not just the heating and cooling system and the lighting system, but what's happening in the use of electronics, particularly in residential buildings.

The fastest-growing use of electricity is home entertainment electronics, whose energy consumption is equivalent to major home appliances. We really need an educational program so that users understand the role that home entertainment and electronics can play.

>> We're energy addicts. When a flat-screen TV is turned off, it's really not off; it's idling.

Yes. No one really understands that everything is "on" virtually all the time unless you unplug it, whether it's an Xbox, or a flat-screen TV, or a TiVo, or the battery charger for a cell phone. All these things are draining electricity and causing electricity bills to go up all the time. I don't think the efficiency message has gotten out nearly as powerfully as it needs to, especially considering that it's the fastest, cheapest way to reduce our carbon emissions as well as save people money. So, there's a huge educational job that we all have to do, including the NRDC.

>> What is the solution?

Number one is informing people on how much energy their electronics consume and how to use those products in an energy-efficient way. If we show that simple measures—like unplugging electronics when they're not in use—can save money, then all Americans, not just NRDC members, reduce their energy use.

Number two is really improving the design of these electronics. We have, for example, already changed the design of appliances to make them much more energy efficient. Refrigerators use one-third of the energy that they used 20 years ago. That needs to happen in the electronics sector as well. Electronics like flat-screen TVs, battery chargers, and cable boxes on top of TVs need to be redesigned to really reduce energy use. I think that will happen, but that change doesn't happen totally voluntarily or just through education. The Department of Energy [DOE] mandates appliance standards, and we need the DOE to create standards for electronics as well. That's one of the things that the NRDC has made a very high priority.

>> Many people talk about green buildings, but the framework for those buildings—our towns and metropolitan areas—also needs to be developed and redeveloped sustainably.

High gasoline prices are leading people to really think about how we design our communities. Over the last 50 years, our communities have been designed around the car. Now, we are realizing that is not the best strategy and that there are huge costs associated with that choice—pocketbook costs, time costs, energy costs, pollution costs.

Fortunately, we do have a new model of sustainable development. The U.S. Green Building Council's LEED [Leadership in Energy and Environmental Design] for Neighborhood Development program, which the NRDC collaborated on, will bring people closer together, closer to their places of work, which means fewer commutes, easier shopping, and lower transportation costs. I think with the way gas prices are today, that's going to catch on much more rapidly than it has in the past.

It's interesting. I've been in this field for many, many years. In the beginning, we always looked at urban America as the pollution source. Now, we're looking at urban America as sort of the beacon of energy efficiency. People who live in cities use less energy. They don't need to drive cars, because they have public transit. They share the walls in their apartment buildings, so they have built-in insulation and use less energy. They use less of everything.

I think that as our population grows over the next 20 to 30 years, that growth needs to be in urban areas—in already-developed areas. It needs to be infill, and it needs to be around transportation. To me, one of the things we have to really get serious about in this country is providing much better public transit options than we have now.

>> **Almost no one talks about green infrastructure, which is the key to any development and the day-to-day functions of our communities—roads, transit, the electricity grid, stormwater management. How do we make the infrastructure green, more efficient, and lower in cost?**

When the bridge collapsed in Minneapolis, the whole nation was sort of transfixed on "Oh, my gosh, what is the state of our infrastructure right now?" It's sobering. We need to make a very considerable investment in our infrastructure—in our transmission lines that carry energy, in our highways, and in our public transportation.

We have an opportunity coming in the next year—a whole new transportation bill, which comes up regularly in Congress. The question is, will Congress seize the moment and figure out how to make investments in new infrastructure that can move people much more efficiently than the ways we've moved them in the past?

Green infrastructure isn't only transportation, which really does need to be improved, or the electricity grid and investment in renewable energy. It's also in the basics of waste removal, sewage treatment, how to minimize the amount of waste that we're generating.

There's a lot of new thinking going into what green infrastructure is and how you would design it so that you're not dealing with the impact at the end of the pipe—you're ameliorating that impact before it gets into the pipe. I think there's a lot of exciting ideas there, and again, that's where cities and mayors can come in and make a difference because they can really incubate new infrastructure demonstration projects that we can all learn from.

We already spend a tremendous amount of money on infrastructure. We'll be spending $3 trillion just on energy development over the next 20 years. So, it's not necessarily that we need a huge amount of new money; it's more a question of how that money is going to be spent. One of the things that the NRDC is going to be involved in—it will be a very lively debate—is how do we wisely spend on infrastructure?

As the economy weakens, people have grave concerns about what their economic future is, what their job opportunity is, etc. And one of the great things about greening buildings and greening infrastructure is that these are jobs here in the United States, and that job base is growing.

There's a very active green jobs movement going on: Van Jones, Majora Carter, Green for All, and other voices are being raised on this. I think this is a huge opportunity actually. And it's an opportunity in areas where there's a lot of population, where there are a lot of skilled workers. We need to match up that interest and eagerness for jobs with existing skills and opportunities to take those in a new green direction, whether it's putting in insulation and weatherizing buildings or building mass transit or a whole host of other things. There's an opportunity here to make this an economic success story in the United States as well as to get us on a much greener pathway.

>> **This January, a new president will be sitting in the White House. What is your wish list for federal government policies for the next few years?**

The most important thing that the new president must do is to be a global leader on addressing climate change. That translates into many, many different areas.

One is a comprehensive approach to global climate change, which is probably going to come in the form of a cap-and-trade program for greenhouse gas emissions. But the cap-and-trade program alone isn't adequate. We need other policies in other sectors to really get the emission reductions that are necessary.

At the same time, the next president needs to lead with a 21st-century energy policy. Global climate change and energy are very interrelated. That energy policy needs to take us into new technologies and into a much more efficient approach to the way we use energy. And that means that there has to be a very strong policy in the public transportation arena so that we reduce the amount of vehicle-miles traveled, reduce the transportation costs that people are now experiencing, *and* reduce our carbon dioxide emissions. We need a world-class public transportation system.

We need new policies in the building arena so that we do build green, so that we reduce the demands on our power sector—which is the largest source of carbon dioxide emissions—so that when we build new homes, new office buildings, new factories, these are designed green, and that there are incentives to green up our existing buildings, particularly in the cities and areas that aren't growing. Think of the many new jobs, which cannot be outsourced, that could retrofit our existing building stock.

In the metropolitan arenas, we need comprehensive planning policies. We need to figure out how to get beyond the political boundaries more successfully than today so that we can develop green infrastructure and policies for entire regions. We do have metropolitan planning structures, but I think there can be a lot more focus on how to make these regions as efficient and as green as they can possibly be.

The new president must implement all of these measures because global climate change is, I think, the most serious issue facing us, the country, the planet, and future generations.

MINDY S. LUBBER

Mindy S. Lubber is president of Boston-based Ceres, the largest coalition in North America of state pension funds, environmental organizations, and public interest groups. Ceres's goal is to strengthen the environmental, social, and governance practices of corporations. She also is director of the Investor Network on Climate Risk.

"Coastal communities need to be part of our national conversation on climate change. We need strong policies and market-based solutions to reduce their exposure. That means promoting infrastructure investment to adapt to the rise in sea levels. It may also mean limiting or prohibiting development in the most sensitive areas."

In the first flush of the sustainability movement, most corporations focused on green workplaces. Some addressed reducing their pollution and greenhouse gas emissions. Now, companies are beginning to understand that the full breadth of their corporate culture, policies, operations, and business and supplier relationships need to be green, too, if they are going to be truly sustainable and competitive. Lubber works at the trendsetting intersection of business and environmental interests, and her views offer guidance to investors and companies everywhere.

>> How real are most companies' commitments to sustainability? Have those commitments become more genuine, more comprehensive in the past year or two?

Their commitments vary. Generally, companies are very excited about sustainability. A printing company might be using a different ink, paper, and packaging. Another company might be more energy efficient, which saves money and is good for the environment. More often than not today, we're seeing far more interest in, focus on, and execution of sustainability practices. That said, most companies aren't consistent.

That doesn't make them bad. Some companies, for example, are doing well on sustainability as it relates to their packaging, but their fleets might be unsustainable or their buildings might be wasting energy and water. So, we're seeing piecemeal efforts, and our goal is to move companies to a more comprehensive, systemic sustainability program where they're addressing sustainability from the board room to the copy room, and they're holding their CEOs accountable.

There's no question that over the last two years the uptick of interest and actions on the part of corporations as it relates to many different sustainability issues is more intense, more real, more common. It is radically different from even three years ago. There's been a sea change. Sustainability is now more popular, more sensible. Shareholders, employees, customers, and executives want their companies to be more sustainable. Companies that focus on sustainability find that it's easier to hire the best and brightest from top business schools. They're seeing employees who are more excited about going to work and who are more productive.

Now, the drivers for what changed companies and got them thinking about and acting on sustainability are starting to tell companies that they have to be even more sustainable, and because of that, we're seeing substantially more activity.

>> **Incorporating sustainability throughout all aspects of a large, complex multi-national corporation does not happen overnight. How can companies best deal with inconsistencies about sustainability that exist internally?**

Ceres deals with multinational companies with up to 300,000 or 400,000 employees in 40 countries. When we work with each of these companies, our mutual commitment is to push for the necessary systems to help the company become more sustainable throughout its enterprise.

Sustainability has to be systematically imbedded in every business unit of a firm. It can't be seen as a niche issue done at the whim of a CEO. It has to be seen as a core business issue that impacts the bottom line. It has to be analyzed and imbedded in the strategic planning. The board has to discuss it, and the CEO must be held accountable through metrics. That's when things happen.

Companies are not on this planet to save the environment. They're here to make products, provide services, and make money. We have got to show businesses that ignoring the fact of water shortages around the world, for example, is putting their company in peril. If you can't find enough water to manufacture your product in India, you're in trouble.

Many companies haven't been looking at the world in that way. It's our job to define those sustainability issues that impact the bottom line.

A systematized approach makes sustainability issues a fundamental business value proposition for a company. The board has to be looking at the sustainability issues that impact their business in their industry and integrate sustainable thinking into their strategic planning. Sustainability issues become governance issues that are looked at and reviewed at the corporate board level and integrated into the company.

For companies to be more internally consistent on these issues, they have to be systematic, transparent, and they have to measure their sustainability impact. Ceres launched the Global Reporting Initiative [GRI], which asks companies to publicly state their values and goals on sustainability issues, lay out plans for moving sustainability forward, and measure their progress against a defined set of metrics. GRI is now the de facto standard for reporting environmental and social performance used by 1,300 companies worldwide.

If you use GRI, you have to look at where you're having a negative impact, such as in your buildings and workplaces, your products, customers, or supply chains. You have to document your negative impact, document your sustainability actions, and make them transparent. With GRI, you also start capturing the impact of sustainability on your firm, your workers, and on the communities where you're located.

The sheer process of going through the GRI starts changing behaviors. When companies start measuring their impact on the environment—say, their energy consumption or their workplace CO_2 emissions—they start to make some changes.

Until companies build a systematized approach to sustainability throughout the firm, they'll continue to be inconsistent. Ford and GM, for example, have built some good sustainable facilities, but their products, which are 90 percent of their footprint, are not environmentally sustainable. But you have to start somewhere. Set some targets. Measure your success. Up the ante next year.

>> How is Ceres focusing on real estate as a leading cause of energy consumption and climate change pollution? Buildings, for example, are responsible for 38 percent of U.S. greenhouse gas emissions.

Over the years, we've addressed real estate issues as part of our ongoing work. We're now launching a more aggressive program focusing on investors as owners of real estate and of companies. We're working with a variety of investors, including CalPERS [California Public Employees' Retirement System, the largest U.S. pension fund], on reducing energy consumption in their own real estate portfolios by 20 percent within three years.

We're engaging with our companies to promote best practices in their real estate management and forward-thinking about how buildings are designed and constructed. We're educating our companies and investors about all the best real estate practices and encouraging them to take leadership on greening their new and existing buildings.

We're looking at other investment vehicles, like REITs [real estate investment trusts], and moving them to be more focused on investing in real estate that is environmentally sound, and to change their company practices on what they build and how they operate their existing buildings. We're helping companies in the financial sector focus on what properties they are willing to invest in.

>> **How would you evaluate the performance of the real estate industry in the United States in terms of sustainability? Who are the leaders? Who are the laggards?**

The real estate industry is very broad, with many subsectors. Because of that, it provides a wide variety of opportunities to make our built environment more sustainable. Like any other industry, there are companies that have decided to wait to take action until they are forced to do so, either by their customers or by policy makers, and there are forward-thinking companies that early on decided to take the lead in transforming their market. Within the Ceres network alone, there are several excellent examples of leadership when it comes to sustainable real estate.

Bank of America has made a ten-year, $20 billion commitment to promote sustainability in its investments, lending practices, and internal operations, as well as through the creation of new products and services that are geared to promote sustainability. The company is committing $1.4 billion to achieve LEED [Leadership in Energy and Environmental Design] certification in all new construction of office facilities and banking centers. It is investing $100 million in energy conservation measures at all of its company facilities. It is donating $50 million from the Bank of America Charitable Foundation to support non-profit organizations focused on energy conservation, green affordable housing, and other environmentally progressive activities. And it is offering new products, including the Green Mortgage Program that gives homebuyers a reduced interest rate or $1,000 back for each home-purchase mortgage that meets Energy Star specifications.

Jones Lang LaSalle [JLL] is the most recent company to join the Ceres network. JLL's goal is to be the real estate industry leader in environmental sustainability and energy management, both within its own operations and in those of its corporate and investor clients. Earlier this year, the company released its first sustainability report—a relative rarity in the real estate industry. JLL also made a global sustainability commitment that includes adopting best practices for new building construction, improving building energy consumption, increasing employee sustainability training and education, leveraging supply-chain power procurement, and measuring carbon emissions.

Jones Lang LaSalle is establishing the first Sustainability University in the real estate services industry. Employees and clients can learn sustainable strategies, study for professional accreditation such as LEED, and gain specific skills to drive the development, management, and leasing of sustainable and energy-efficient commercial buildings. Founding the Sustainability University is also helping the firm lead the industry by increasing its sustainability-accredited professionals to 200 in 2008 and to 500 in 2009.

This summer, JLL acquired ECD Energy, a provider of environmental consulting ser-vices. This gives JLL and its clients access to ECD's technology platform for assessing the sustainability profile of commercial buildings and for benchmarking across portfolios. The tools assess new building designs, existing building operations, and interior fit-outs in terms of their energy, water, and environmental impact, as well as the health and comfort of building occupants.

AIG [American International Group] has been a leader on sustainability. AIG is a member of the Investor Network on Climate Risk. It is the first U.S.-based insurance company to adopt a public statement on environment and climate change. Its Upgrade to Green insurance product, a first in the industry, enables commercial and residential prop-erty insurance policy holders to rebuild or repair their damaged property to recognized green standards after a covered loss. The Sustain-a-Build Initiative enables customers to receive significant discounts on specific premiums for properties certified under the U.S. Green Building Council's [USGBC] LEED green building rating system.

AIG Global Real Estate has adopted practices that include remediating and redevelop-ing contaminated property, using environmentally sustainable construction materials, and incorporating energy-efficient design and technology into the development of new proj-ects. AIG Global Real Estate also develops and acquires buildings around the world that conform to the USGBC's LEED standards, or equivalent local standards that emphasize cutting-edge efficiency and clean energy technologies.

>> How are homebuilders doing on the sustainability front?

Most homebuilders are lagging in their response to climate change, but some leaders have emerged. KB Home recently issued its first sustainability report, and it announced that by 2010 all of its new homes will be Energy Star certified.

Similarly, Centex announced that it would implement its Energy Advantage program in all new homes beginning in January 2009. The program is expected to make the com-pany's homes up to 22 percent more energy efficient than those built to the most widely used code, the 2006 International Energy Conservation Code. As part of the Centex Energy Advantage Program, all of its homes will be equipped with a power monitor that allows homeowners to track how much energy they use.

Because the residential sector accounts for a large percentage of global greenhouse gas emissions, we need more companies to follow these leaders in building better, more efficient homes.

>> How can companies and investors in the real estate community start adapting to the long-term implications of climate change?

While global climate change is just one of many sustainability changes before us, it has emerged as the most pressing of them all. We are already starting to experience impacts, like more intense storms. Now, every hurricane is not climate change, but storms are more intense because of global warming.

Even if only a portion of Katrina or the hurricanes that we're seeing this year are related to climate change, they're still hitting coastal cities in profoundly deep ways. People are losing homes, jobs, properties, lives. We're seeing insurance companies all over the world *not* insuring coastal homes and communities. Climate change is having a physical and business impact. It's crazy that some people still think that it hasn't started. Already we are seeing responses to it.

A critical question right now is how do we deal with coastal communities—those areas within 40 miles [65 kilometers] of the coast where over half of all Americans live? Do we just abandon them? Many people in Florida can only get insurance through the government; insurance companies won't touch them.

Coastal communities are in danger, and they need to be part of our national conversation on climate change. We need strong policies and market-based solutions to reduce their exposure. That means promoting infrastructure investment to adapt to rising sea levels. It may also mean limiting or prohibiting development in the most sensitive areas.

Closing our ears won't work. Our coastal communities are threatened and we have to act. How do you make sure that coastal cities have the right building and government codes and the right physical protection requirements, like mandating extra-reinforced windows? Ceres is convening a group of people to do just that.

We're bringing together insurers, government, investors, real estate developers, and environmental organizations in our Resilient Coasts Initiative to address climate adaptation using public policy and private market solutions to better protect our coastal communities.

>> What are the best first steps for companies that are new to embracing the benefits of sustainability?

First, they must choose a few sustainability issues that are most near and dear to the business they run. It could be supply chain issues, worker safety, water shortages, or any of hundreds of other challenges. Companies have to take a look at what their impact is on those issues and, conversely, on how those issues impact the company. What happens if there are more violent storms? What happens if the regulations change? What happens if there's a price on carbon?

Next, they must assess their footprint and their vulnerabilities, set goals and benchmarks, and determine how to accomplish those goals. Again, sustainability has got to be dealt with at the highest level. It needs the leadership of the CEO. Sustainability needs a board committee to address it. It needs the entire firm to address it.

Then, companies must pick their opportunity and start addressing sustainability issues one by one: make corporate real estate healthier and more energy efficient; reduce the use of paper; find alternatives to toxic chemicals; change the lighting system. There are unlimited places to get started. The key is to get started.

>> Once companies have captured the low-hanging opportunities of sustainability, what are the most important long-term actions they must take?

They need to look at their impact on the environment and their communities. Then, they need to reduce their impact—use less resources—for their own business interest. A company uses resources to make almost any product. The cost of required commodities is going up overnight; the cost of fuel is going up overnight; water is becoming more scarce. Companies need to look at the easy and the difficult issues and address them.

Executives need to look at their companies in a more sustainable way. They need to shift their perspective from "How do we reduce our pollution in a community?" to "How do we move forward in world of limited resources?" Building a warehouse 50 miles [80 kilometers] out of the city requires more highways, more infrastructure, more driving, more housing, more people moving out of the city, more sprawl—and all of that puts the company at risk.

Sustainability is about making smart comprehensive decisions about your facilities, products, services, operations, and workers.

>> Who are going to be the winners and losers in our age of increasingly limited resources and global climate change? What's going to be the difference between companies that thrive and companies that fail?

The winners will be the ones who get in front of the curve first—the companies that are developing and designing the technologies that produce clean water, green buildings, next-generation hybrid vehicles, and the infrastructure for a 21st-century green economy with millions of new jobs. There is no doubt right now that Congress is going to pass a limit and a cost on carbon dioxide emissions. That will impact everyone, including property owners. Reducing your carbon usage and emissions makes sense now. Companies already doing so are gaining more profits, greater market share, happier employees. Companies that are ignoring these issues do so at their peril.

If I were an electric utility company or a coal company, I'd think long and hard about building five more coal-fired power plants. It will mean more opposition, more regulations to meet, more delays, more cost. I'd be thinking instead about renewable energy.

If I were an automobile company, I don't know how much more handwriting needs to be on the wall. Three Detroit companies didn't change the products they put on the market in the last two years and now they're in significant trouble.

>> How are investors addressing global climate change? What is their role in moving both companies and government to address this and other sustainability challenges?

Investors get involved when the cost is real. They've recognized that sustainability issues, including climate change, have a substantive impact on long-term financial growth.

Investors aren't in business to be environmentalists. Their legal duty is to address risk. Because climate, in particular, and water scarcity create substantial financial risk, we are seeing more and more investment companies, both large and small, weighing in.

They are incorporating stronger valuation practices on climate in their portfolios. They are starting to invest in clean and green technologies. They are telling their money manager to not only do their traditional evaluation of companies when building their portfolio, but to start including climate risk in their analyses. It's investor advocacy through their own investments and who they hire.

>> How can companies best address environmental and social concerns in their supply and value chains?

While a company may not be completely responsible for every person who works for one of their suppliers in Myanmar, it has more clout with the local supplier that hires those workers.

Our companies need to set standards for themselves and then apply those standards to their suppliers. Wal-Mart and Nike will not hire your company if you are using eight-year-old children and paying them 15 cents a day. It is up to large companies with suppliers all over the world to set sustainability standards.

That's hard to do, because they like selling their products for less money than they paid suppliers whose workers earn $1 a week. But that's not acceptable any more.

>> We hear a lot of talk these days about forthcoming federal climate change legislation. How are the companies and investors you work with approaching climate policy? What do you think it will take to achieve meaningful changes to our economy and energy system's reliance on carbon-intensive fuels?

We have finally reached critical mass in understanding that regulating carbon is not only the right environmental, scientific, public health, and national security policy, it is the necessary and right market signal that must be set. More and more companies are saying that if the cost of carbon is real, the right market-driven thing is to put a price on it. When something has value, you think more about it. If it costs companies money to put carbon dioxide into the air, they'll do less of it.

The debate in Congress must reflect the business and financial benefits for companies of regulating carbon, as well as the environmental benefits.

We need the right incentives to jump-start the renewable energy sector and to support many different avenues. If I were a small entrepreneur, I would not be comfortable investing millions in new technologies until I see Congress sending the right market signals to jump-start the technological revolution that we need to have if we are going to reduce our carbon emissions by 80 percent by 2050.

>> What do you consider Ceres's greatest successes in the last three years?

First, imbedding climate change in $7 trillion worth of investors. When CalPERS, the largest pension fund in the U.S., says its investment practice is being affected by climate change, sustainability is no longer a niche consideration.

Second, redefining what constitutes good corporate governance. It used to be that good corporate governance only meant having an audit committee at the board level or separating the positions of the board chair and the CEO. Today, good corporate governance also means examining sustainability and the implications of sustainability. We have redefined good corporate governance to include sustainability, and more and more companies are examining and addressing it at the board level.

Third, making transparency and sustainability reporting common practice for over 150 companies in the U.S. and helping them to produce strong and comprehensive sustainability reports.

>> What do you consider our greatest challenges in achieving a sustainable and prosperous future?

I believe there is some part of human nature that is not prepared to act until it's too late.

There are a lot of people who say they don't believe climate change is real or that nothing they can do will have an impact on climate change. That is simply not the case. The problem with carbon dioxide is that people can't see it, touch it, feel it. They have to take it on faith and on complicated science that they may not understand. People often don't make substantial changes in their own lives unless they're required to do so or if something is so self-evident that it is literally on their doorstep.

Climate change—like all sustainability issues—is a long-term problem, but it has solutions that we must start implementing now.

The worst impacts of climate change won't show up until our sons and daughters are in charge, and by then it will be too late because CO_2 lingers in the atmosphere for 100 years. Even if we were able to cut all carbon emissions today, we would still experience climate change impacts for decades because of this lag effect.

We can—and need to—reduce our carbon dioxide emissions by 80 percent by 2050, but we've got to start yesterday. For our kids' sake, I go to work every day trying to make sure that we do.

VAN JONES

Van Jones is founder and president of Green for All, an Oakland, California-based organization dedicated to providing millions of jobs for Americans through a new green economy. In his new book, *The Green Collar Economy*, Jones explains his solutions to pull the economy out of recession, raise many Americans out of poverty, and protect the environment.

"We have a tremendous opportunity to power ourselves through the recession by fundamentally changing how we provide energy. . . . We need green Keynesian policies—strong fiscal and monetary government policies that fight the recession and go green."

A recipient of Global Green USA's Community Environmental Leadership Award 2008 and named a Time *magazine 2008 Environmental Hero, Jones stands at the cutting edge of transforming a national economy based on petroleum and other nonrenewable natural resources to one rooted in renewable energy, green-collar jobs, and a sustainable built environment. His forthright economic, energy, and development insights are invaluable to a 21st-century real estate industry.*

>> **Looking beyond the collapse of U.S. economic titans like Lehman Brothers, AIG, and Fannie and Freddie Mac, what do you think really caused the current U.S. economic crisis?**

For the large part of 30 years, we have been sold a bill of goods by both political parties, not just by our most recent president, George W. Bush, that we could run the U.S. economy on consumption and not on genuine production; on credit, not on smart savings and thrift like our grandparents; on environmental destruction, not on environmental restoration. So, it was package deal, and most Americans bought it.

By definition, that model is unsustainable. You cannot run the U.S. economy on credit cards, the remains of dead dinosaurs, and the consumption of often-unneeded products that quickly end up in landfills. At some point, you are going to run into trouble—and we have. The house of cards started collapsing last fall, and it's hurting a lot of people.

>> Is the problem only America's spending practices? Aren't other nations following this model or, in some instances, acting as our enablers?

We have a fundamental flaw in the world economy. Today, Americans spend too much and save too little, and the Chinese spend too little and save too much. That creates a huge imbalance in the world economy—where you have mountains of money in China looking for investment, and you have millions of consumers in the U.S. scurrying around the country with credit cards buying things and tapping their homes like ATMs.

I'm not saying that we should stop buying Chinese goods. We want China's and all of Asia's economies to do well. They have millions of people in the most abject poverty, and they need to have better, healthier lives. But the current way of bringing them out of poverty is stupid. These people have to move out of their villages, leave their culture and their families behind, cram themselves into heavily polluted mega-cities, and work long hours at hard and often dangerous jobs to make crap for us.

That's not a good deal for them. And it's horrible for Earth. Chinese air quality is going down, and that pollution floats far from China. Their water quality is going down, and that pollution eventually ends up in the oceans. And they are generating rapidly rising amounts of greenhouse gas emissions.

The entire world economy has been driven by U.S. consumption, not U.S. production or U.S. innovation. The problem for the world economy is that people in the United States cannot afford their consumption binge, and definitely not now.

Unfortunately for the United States and the world, Americans have been pursuing the package deal of economic and environmental recklessness. Our political leadership in both parties has avoided the issue for the past 30 years, and we haven't had any moral leadership to point out the error of our ways.

>> Is there a silver lining in our current economic clouds?

This economic crisis has one advantage: only in dire situations can we talk about new ideas, like shifting our economy back to more innovation and production of the right things—to a *green* economy that turns this economic breakdown into an economic breakthrough.

A green economy recognizes that the only viable economy is environmental, and the only viable environment is economic. The power to make significant change requires both forces. If you try to rev up the economy in ways that don't respect the environment, you will run into speed bumps, like toxic water and air pollution.

Nor can you regulate your way out. You must invent a new way out. You need the raw power of markets and innovations to supply the capital to make the technology and reach the necessary scale to create real, lasting, and profitable change, and you need the government to guide the process.

That's not easy, and it's not overnight. The shift to a green economy requires that we stop borrowing and start building again—that we stop relying on credit from overseas and rely instead on U.S. creativity to power the economy.

>> Where should we start this "new way out?"

The place to start is energy. We have a tremendous opportunity to power ourselves through the recession by fundamentally changing how we provide energy—not only switching to alternative energy, but how we distribute that energy. We need green Keynesian policies—strong fiscal and monetary government policies that fight the recession and go green. We need a real stimulus, not a silly stimulus. Last year, everybody got their government checks, went to Wal-Mart and bought flat-screen TVs, and powered the economy in China. We must stimulate *our* economy.

Suppose we focus on energy conservation as one key green economy policy. We weatherize and retrofit a few million buildings, so we are going to save money and we are going to cut carbon dioxide emissions. We double pane the window glass, we blow safe insulation into the walls, we replace the old and inefficient boilers, and we add some solar panels if it makes sense. What do we get? A few million energy-efficient buildings.

And we can pay for those retrofits with energy savings in three years, according to an interview with Amory Lovins in a recent *McKinsey Quarterly* [July 2008, "Using Energy More Efficiently: An Interview with Rocky Mountain Institute's Amory Lovins"]. Energy savings are quick, so are reduced carbon emissions, and people get work at once. That's a key component—new green jobs for millions of Americans that want to work and cannot find a job, much less a decent job.

If the federal government created a revolving loan fund, it would help cities retrofit their buildings. Those cities would pay back the loan fund from their energy savings over time, so the fund would be revenue neutral.

Right now, our energy strategy is to send billions and trillions of dollars to the Pentagon to protect our oil supplies around the world so that we can send billions and trillions of dollars to other countries to buy that oil. I'd take 10 percent of the Pentagon budget, retrofit millions of buildings, reduce our energy use and loss of billions of dollars to oil suppliers, build thousands of wind and solar farms, produce a bunch of electric vehicles, and be done with it.

Let's call the program Retrofit America. It has incredible cobenefits—cheaper energy, cleaner air, jobs for people, less entanglement overseas in various resource wars. From my point of view, it's a great set of opportunities and it's all part of a package. You build the alternative-energy equipment here. Each wind tower is 20 tons of steel; each wind turbine has 8,000 parts. You could put Detroit back to work—not making SUVs that will destroy the world, but manufacturing wind turbines that will help save the world and strengthen America.

The logo for Retrofit America should not be a hybrid car or a polar bear on an ice floe, but a modern version of World War II's Rosie the Riveter making solar panels and wind turbines. Let's turn the middle of country, the Plains states, into a Saudi Arabia of wind. Our Plains states are a tremendous national resource.

>> What good is all this new energy if it's generated hundreds of miles from the nation's biggest cities and economic centers?

We must construct a highly efficient smart energy grid to major population centers. Yes, that's expensive, and it takes a lot of work, which will create jobs. It will also require a breakthrough in transmission lines and storage. You have to invent that. If we can direct our best minds and R&D money to that challenge, rather than to less beneficial tasks like extracting oil from tar sands and oil shale—the nastiest power carbons we can find—we can create the strongest economy in the world without wrecking large swathes of Canada and pouring out huge quantities of greenhouse gases in the process. When I hear the phrase "Drill, baby, drill," I think of "Spill, baby, spill."

We face a stark choice: we can create an oil-independent superpower for decades into the future, or we can keep sending billions of dollars to oil producers and fighting other countries for oil.

>> Does America have the political will to pull this off?

I think so. We've done it before. In the 1950s, we had a bunch of old rural dirt roads in much of the nation. We were a country, but we couldn't drive across it. So, we created an interstate highway system for national security—to move troops and materials around the nation, if need be—and to connect American business and Americans with each other.

Yes, it was expensive, but we recognized that we couldn't afford *not* to do it. And once people could get around the U.S. easily, our economy went through the roof. More recently, think of the Internet superhighway, which moves data and information, not people and cars. That cost lots of money, and it created in turn a major transformation in our economy and in our lives.

Now, we must build the smart energy grid that will give us a comprehensive, highly efficient national energy grid to move alternative energy around, not the current antiquated and inefficient patchwork grid. With this American invention, we beat the global warming beast, we supercharge the world economy, and we make the United States the global leader in one of the key technologies and products of our age, which we can sell to or share with the rest of the world. That's the next ten-year agenda.

>> Won't long-powerful interests resist alternative energy sources and a smart energy grid?

Yes, of course. We must fight against legacy polluters like coal and oil companies. They must realize that the carbon age is over and that this is the dawn of the renewable energy age.

Some companies will rigidly and openly oppose the shift to the new age. Others will become the "dirty green" companies—the ones who say all the right things while clinging to their traditional ways of doing things. The energy industry is already offering three dirty green strategies for energy: so-called clean coal, which is just as suspicious as "healthy" cigarettes; powering our cars with biofuel unicorns; and lighting our houses with the nuclear tooth fairy.

But once legacy polluters *really* get it—and they start losing their sway in Congress and their ad campaigns no longer convince the American people—they will jump the fence and help make renewable energy and the smart energy grid a reality.

>> You're talking about a complete transformation of how we think about, generate, distribute, and use energy. Isn't that too radical a leap for most Americans?

You don't have to be a flaming radical to pull this off. You follow Adam Smith. You cut energy demand, and you expand renewable energy supply. That is how you cut energy prices. It's better fuel standards for cars. It's investing in mass transit, so you cut the demand for gasoline and diesel fuel by half. Once you have the smart energy grid, you plug the car in at night.

It took today's financial breakdown for people to finally say, "This economy is not working. What can we do?" The smart energy grid is a great answer. Put Americans to work; rely on American ingenuity and American technology.

And while you figure out how to build the smart energy grid, go get the caulk guns and the new windows and retrofit millions of homes and buildings across America to reduce energy use and save money. Spend that retrofit money in America and give Americans jobs; don't keep sending unnecessarily large amounts of money—and jobs—overseas.

>> Won't cutting energy demand mean a reduction in jobs?

Cutting energy demand—amazingly—increases jobs. The Center for American Progress, a Washington, D.C.–based think tank, estimates that investment in clean energy generates *four times* as many jobs as similar investment in the oil industry. By cutting energy demand in a recession, you can put four people to work instead of just one person. When you cut demand, you bring down prices. When you increase jobs, you expand supply with solar and wind power, and geothermal.

My hope is for a much better future on the other side of today's economic breakdown than anybody is anticipating.

>> How will the green economy affect real estate development and investment?

Denser, more walkable communities will be more desirable because transportation costs are going to be higher in the future. The current slump in oil prices is only temporary. Big houses with very few people and lots of rooms that you must heat and cool at high cost won't be attractive. You can do a lot with passive solar and geothermal; you can do a lot with smart engineering. But at the end of day, people may want less square footage from a cost point of view.

We may see a cultural return to more modest, better-designed homes, a more social life, and the idea of thrifty not being seen as cheap or uptight, but as a reflection of wisdom and sanity, which will affect all buildings. Smart growth will win out, not at the pace its proponents hope for, but in a way that *will* affect development.

The way that people choose to consume may change. The big-box stores—which are essentially showplace warehouses for crap from overseas—may not be a good bet going forward, particularly if you are wiping out productive farmland to build them. But that thought is more of a prayer than a prediction.

>> Do you foresee companies scaling back on their sustainability programs to save money?

I see a danger of cutbacks happening, mostly at those companies that were doing sustainability for the wrong reasons like the green PR, or doing it the wrong way so that it wasn't paying off. Those companies are already cutting back.

>> So, what's the answer?

We need government action. Companies are going to go back and forth on sustainability based on short-term market signals. We need a government response based on a long-term economic strategy for the nation. Energy prices go up or go down, but if the government says, "We are going to become energy efficient, and companies must make genuine plans and then carry them out," we'll see real change. The federal government must put a price on carbon. That's unpopular now, but it's necessary.

And government must make it easier for people to do smart energy. Right now, it's hard for people to do the right thing. It's still expensive to retrofit, so we need some incentives. And the building codes are tough. We need green scissors to cut through the red tape.

My hope is that the case for a job-generating clean-energy revolution and green economy will be so compelling to the new president and new Congress that they will embark on it. Once they have started, I think we can create so many winners that politicians will be lining up to support these programs because these programs will create a growing constituency for clean and green versus dirty and dumb.

We stand at the end of the carbon age and at the dawn of the solar age—the dawn of the second industrial age. The earlier Industrial Revolution hurt people and it hurt the planet. The new one must help people and help heal the planet. That's the mission statement for the new century, and it's infinitely doable.

EARL BLUMENAUER

U.S. Representative Earl Blumenauer, an Oregon Democrat, began his public
service career in 1972 at the age of 23 in the Oregon House of Representatives. In
1978, he became a Multnomah County commissioner in Portland. Starting in 1986,
he served as commissioner of public works on the Portland City Council. He has
served since 1996 in the U.S. House, where he has been an
advocate for livable, sustainable communities.

*"With the bursting of the real estate bubble, people are
looking at value. Communities that are more compact
and have choices about movement are actually better
values. If you check the areas that have been brutalized
in declining home values, Portland's not one of them."*

*Having worked at the city, county, and state levels, Blumenauer now works at the national
level as a member of the House Ways and Means Committee, the Budget Committee, and
the Select Committee on Energy Independence and Climate Change. Because he participated
in some of Portland's innovative growth and environmental initiatives several decades ago
and now has considerable experience at the federal level, Blumenauer provides a unique
perspective on sustainability and the built environment.*

>> **Why is Portland such a successful testing ground for smart growth and environ-
mental policies, from the urban growth boundary adopted in 1979 to its green
building policies today? Is it the size of the city? Its political structure? Its citizens' values?**

Portland offers a unique combination of a community with a strong planning tradition going back to its turn-of-the-20th-century parks, and the blessings of a
spectacular natural setting, interesting topography, and rivers. Our history has
also contributed to our success. Our New England founders established a very
small street grid with 200-foot [61-meter] blocks—each block is just an acre [0.4
hectare]—which established a pattern that was very human scale. So, the combina-

tion of planning, natural landscape, and the small street grid really gave Portland a terrific foundation.

Forty years ago, a new generation of business, political, and civic leadership built on that foundation in equal measures. Some fascinating corporate leaders were sympathetic to commonsense planning. We had a generation of political and civic leaders— mostly young Oregonians who had gone off to school somewhere else and then came home—who became involved in community affairs. Finally, in the 1970s, we had quite a progressive array of political leadership, from 12 years of visionary governors who were supportive of land use policies, to a young mayor named Neil Goldschmidt, and many members of the legislature. It was a truly intoxicating stew.

The scale of the city has also contributed to our success. Portland is large enough to have scale and significance, but we are not so large that people get lost, and we're not so large that it ever became difficult to manage. Scale and perspective are two of the fundamental building blocks of a good city. When you look at New York, Los Angeles, Chicago—the scale is daunting. You don't know where to begin and the costs are great, so, it's harder to show results quickly.

>> **The urban growth boundary has always received considerable attention. What other smart growth and environmental policies have really made a difference in Portland?**

The urban growth boundary's media coverage is appropriate because it's a key organizing principle, concentrating growth and development where it is most appropriate.

But what most people don't know is that the boundary was enacted within the framework of a comprehensive *statewide* planning process in 1973. The state legislature's Senate Bill 100 required every square inch of the state to be mapped and zoned to establish growth goals and guidelines. Every municipality had to have an urban growth boundary.

You cannot just drop this planning framework onto a city in the midst of a state and pretend that the city is an island. An urban growth boundary must be coordinated so that other communities play by the same rules. I don't mean that they should have an identical plan, but they should also have boundaries to protect farms and forests, and to provide for different types of housing, recreation, and economic development. With everybody playing by the same rules, you have diversity and balance with no one gaining a competitive advantage by slacking off from those rules.

At the same time, we abolished the State Highway Commission and established the Oregon Transportation Commission, which was a significant shift in perception and action. That legislation—I must say with all due modesty that I was the main sponsor—

mandated 20 years before ISTEA [the Intermodal Surface Transportation Efficiency Act of 1991] a comprehensive, multimodal statewide transportation plan.

So, we had statewide land use and transit plans mapped out. Then Portland became the first city in the U.S. to enact a comprehensive energy policy—it was our response to the energy crises of the 1970s—that emphasized conservation from the city government on down. The late professor Arthur Nelson analyzed the difference between Portland and Atlanta in per-capita energy use over ten or 15 years, and it was striking that Atlanta's per-capita energy expanded dramatically and Portland's actually shrank slightly.

One other government policy also had a significant impact. In the 1970s, the city of Portland created a downtown plan before the state land use legislation kicked in. We thought through the role of retail, emphasized downtown housing, laid the foundation for public transit, and we limited the number of downtown parking spaces to 43,000. Again, this plan put everybody on the same footing because developers were not competing to have the most parking possible for each project. So, it was a truce in the parking space race, and it was to everybody's benefit because parking is so expensive and limiting it strengthened our transit profile. We have dramatically higher utilization of transit today than other similar-sized cities. In fact, it's one of the highest rates in the country. Nearly half of downtown Portland commuters today are arriving by transit.

>> **Are other cities learning from Portland? Can you identify any specific policies and projects in the U.S. and worldwide?**

We have been linking land use and transportation to fight sprawl for 30 years, and I have been preaching light rail and land use to various communities for years. Now, all major cities, including Denver, Salt Lake City, Houston, and others, have light rail, and they are asking hard questions about land use. Even Phoenix, which used to be the largest city without regularly scheduled transit, opened the Valley Metro transit system in December 2008, and it has $6.5 billion in development planned along those lines.

We have also seen communities emulating our first modern streetcar lines, including Little Rock, Seattle, and Kenosha, Wisconsin. Some 80 cities in the U.S. are at some stage of analysis or development of a streetcar line.

Cycling is also taking off. We're seeing a much greater appreciation of this most-efficient form of urban transportation. Chicago, for example, is moving forward very aggressively on bike lanes.

>> **You have worked hard to make alternative energy solutions a key strategy in Oregon. Where does Oregon stand in its development of renewable energy resources? How have these solutions affected its real estate and the economy?**

Oregon made the decision not to wait for the federal government. It is one of a grow-ing number of states with its own renewable energy standards. Our standard provides a floor—a base market—for our renewable energy programs.

Oregon requires our utility companies to start switching over to renewable energy. Ore-gon's Renewable Portfolio Standard mandates that the state's three largest utility companies provide 5 percent of their retail sales of electricity from clean, renewable sources of energy by 2011, 15 percent by 2015, 20 percent by 2020, and 25 percent by 2025. Smaller utilities and electricity service suppliers must meet less-rigorous targets. Portland General Electric already has one of the highest per-capita rates in the country of customers using green power. Customers voluntarily pay more for power from renewable energy sources.

Oregon has also used tax credits to encourage the development of renewable energy resources in the state. Since 1980, Oregon businesses that have invested in renewable en-ergy projects and building owners who generate alternative energy have been eligible for a business energy tax credit equal to 35 percent of the cost of the project, with a cap of $10 million. In 2007, the legislature increased the credit to 50 percent of the project cost taken over five years—10 percent per year. Tax-exempt entities like universities that install renew-able energy systems or work on renewable energy projects can use a pass-through partner like a taxable business to receive discounted lump-sum payments instead of the five-year tax credit. By 2007, more than 13,000 energy tax credits had been awarded in the state.

Oregon also gives a residential energy tax credit of up to $1,500 to homeowners and renters who pay state income taxes and buy [energy produced from] renewable energy technologies—solar, wind, geothermal—or energy-efficient appliances and technologies.

We are sending a genuine signal to our utility companies and alternative energy de-velopers that renewable energy will be a fundamental part of our energy mix. Oregon already produces 1,200 megawatts of wind energy—that's enough to power more than 300,000 homes—and we should expand to as much as 5,000 megawatts by 2015.

Some international renewable energy companies have their American headquarters in Portland, plus we have many related consultants and smaller businesses. Vestas Wind Systems, a Danish company, for example, has its U.S. headquarters in Portland, where it employs more than 300 workers. Several organizations here are involved in the develop-ment of wind energy. It's exciting. Portland is competing with Houston and Denver to be the wind energy capital of the U.S. It's a good competition to have among cities.

Nationally, the importance of the shift to renewable energy is almost as great as the one happening in transportation. Wind and solar are vital technologies, but the most im-portant strategy is energy conservation. We cannot continue to waste more energy than any other country in the world.

>> How have all of these efforts affected Oregon's real estate industry?

Even though Oregon's land use, transportation, and renewable energy solutions are a work in progress, they have clearly impacted real estate and the economy. They have certainly changed the direction of our commercial and residential real estate markets.

Some of Portland's most desirable and cutting-edge new properties are energy and water efficient and were constructed with healthy building materials. We are seeing that these green properties are commanding a premium for rents and sales, and it gives them a market differentiation. With the national economic problems, our Portland real estate market has held up better than most communities. Everybody that I talk to tells me that because of the lower operating costs and health benefits of green buildings, the premium is likely to continue.

The creative, thoughtful developer will reap significant savings by looking at a massive development and thinking about how much energy can be squeezed out of it. Developers are already trying to construct buildings that generate more energy than they use. Oregon has a renewable portfolio standard. We have tax incentives for alternative energy.

As the opportunities for alternative energy like solar, small-scale wind power, and hyper-efficient construction expand, we will see a return to the earlier steam-powered heating and cooling city districts that provided energy to buildings in downtowns. Building owners and developers will be bidding to provide heating and cooling services to adjacent buildings.

Many cities and developers can utilize the geothermal exchange with underground water to generate energy, and you don't have to be a large-scale developer or city to do it. A restaurant in Portland uses water below the building for heat exchange to power its cooling and refrigeration.

>> Automobile-dependent suburban sprawl is one reason for our costly reliance on foreign oil and our growing greenhouse gas emissions. How can we shift new development from our current *all*-sprawl policies to alternatives like compact, mixed-use, transit-oriented development? Are Americans even ready for an alternative?

Part of what's going on is that events are catching up to us. With the recent spike in energy prices and the current economic crisis, people are rethinking the value of personal vehicles, where they live, and where they work. That's already caused shifts in travel patterns and real estate investment.

With the bursting of the real estate bubble, people are looking at value. Communities that are more compact and have choices about movement are actually better values. If you check the areas that have been brutalized in declining home values, Portland's not one of them.

Also bursting is the demographic bubble. The baby boomers grew up in Ozzie-and-Harriet communities. Now, we have more single-person households than families—singles, not couples. Single-person households will outnumber families with children in 2030. So, who's going to live in all of the suburban single-family houses we've built?

A baby boomer turns 60 every eight seconds. As these baby boomers turn 65, we will see a shift from detached to attached housing, from owning to renting, and less reliance on cars. The cost of a car is approximately $10,000 per year; Portland residents drove 20 percent less than the average American household. That translated into a $2,500 savings a year. That money can go toward health care, food, housing, retirement savings.

If everybody in the community is investing that $10,000 in their cars, where does it go? Most of that car money goes elsewhere, not into the local economy. It's hard to think of an investment, an expenditure that people make, that has less direct dollar-for-dollar benefits for themselves or their community than a car, because 70 percent to 80 percent of that money goes to other cities or overseas.

All of these catalysts are changing Americans' perceptions about sprawl, housing, workplaces, transportation, and communities, and they are beginning to drive compact, mixed-use, transit-oriented development. We are already seeing a slow-motion, very profound realignment of development patterns that will be taking place over the next 25 to 30 years that is superimposed on renewable energy and this movement toward value.

>> How can we retrofit existing sprawling metropolitan areas across the United States to make them more sustainable? Where will the money come from? Where's the political will? Won't major corporate forces—like the automobile industry, oil companies, and highway construction companies—fight any change in the current development pattern?

Part of the problem is that people in the development business have cut their teeth doing the same thing over and over. They have a template for a cookie-cutter subdivision, or generic office buildings, or an office park, or an enclosed mall, and all of these formulas have always been tilted toward suburban sprawl development. Financial institutions know what they like to finance, which are the buildings and projects with which they are familiar.

Getting the broader development community and associated professions—engineers, architects, real estate agents, and bankers—to be a little bolder, you must overcome internal forces. They know how to do the formula, and often clients think that's the only available model. We have to spread the word about the other, more sustainable models.

Another part of the problem is that sometimes you have to pay more for land and development in an infill location—one that's closer to utilities, transportation, and attractions, with environmental benefits. That's a black mark. And there's more. Infill locations usually require more adaptations to be made, more design reviews, and the planning requirements are a little more complex than most suburban jurisdictions. You aren't dealing with an empty, flat piece of land. You have to knit the new development into the surrounding community fabric and environment; you can't just plop it onto a site. All of that can cost more money compared to standard greenfield sprawl development.

Now, we face an additional complication for more sustainable, more contextual development. The financial community has fallen into such turmoil that banks are contracting; they are taking on less risk. If a developer has a new idea, like sustainable development, that new idea is seen as a risk and it is going to be put at the bottom of the pile. It's a tough sell.

The current economic crisis and the banking industry's reluctance to finance anything new are also impacting important strategies and technologies that could curb sprawl and help us make our metropolitan areas more sustainable.

We are trying, for example, to turn Portland into the streetcar capital of the U.S. We have completed work with Oregon Ironworks, a local manufacturing firm, on the prototype of a modern U.S. streetcar. For the first time in 60 years, we will be manufacturing streetcars in the U.S.

Oregon Ironworks has immediate sales opportunities in Portland and Tucson. Those cities are ready to place their orders. Now, this is a company that has been operating for half a century. It does complicated things like boats for the Israeli navy, the doors of missile silos, and big equipment for dams and nuclear power plants. Oregon Ironworks has an established line of credit; it has a relationship with its lender; it has never missed a payment. But, as of a week ago [November 2008], when it wanted to exercise a portion of its line of credit to fund its streetcar construction, its lender was unwilling to extend part of its approved line of credit because the manufacture of highly efficient, attractive streetcars is an unfamiliar investment.

The lender actually asked, "What's the market?"

Hello! We have it in Portland. And another 80 cities in the country are exploring or already constructing light-rail systems—Birmingham, Boise, Honolulu, Las Vegas, Little Rock, Minneapolis–St. Paul, Orlando, Seattle. Last week, a group from Cincinnati came to Portland, we had a dinner, and we were talking about Portland's streetcars, and they want to build a system in Cincinnati. Build it in America!

In Phoenix, $6 billion of development is actually being constructed along the new Valley Metro lines. It's stunning. Twenty years ago when I talked about light rail in Phoenix, people scoffed. Phoenix was one of the largest U.S. cities with no Sunday bus service. It was the second most automobile-dependent city in America, and it was resisting light rail even just a few years ago. Now look at it.

There's the market. Oregon Ironworks is an example of an established American company doing everything right. It is a great and profitable firm, but because the product is unfamiliar to the lender, the bank is getting nervous about giving it access to its line of credit to manufacture the streetcars cities across the country want.

But there is good news: we can use the forces of change that I've already discussed, plus the obsolescence of our existing building stock—so much of the commercial inventory has a very short life cycle—coupled with the pressures of growth to plan and make the right infrastructure and development decisions.

We are going to add between 100 million to 200 million new Americans by midcentury. [The official U.S. Census Bureau population estimate for 2008 is 303 million, and the official projection for 2050 is 420 million.] Where are they going to live? We need national policies. I'm on a personal mission to have us think about building a new America. Water, transportation, energy: we need to make significant investment and changes. If we have the appropriate vision, and if the federal government partners with communities, as it has done historically by providing incentives and other support, we don't have to grow further into greenfields. We have a lot of land, like rights-of-way along suburban arterials, that can be reclaimed and reused. We can take some of our massive land banks, like shopping malls, and retrofit and expand them with new uses, like housing and offices, and connect it all with light rail.

We are also looking at some significant changes in retail activity. Wandering the aisles of the Costcos of the world to buy vats of peanut butter eventually loses its charm for many people. I suspect that people will concentrate on turning the time and energy they spend on shopping, browsing, and parking back into things that make a difference, like the farmers' market, which keeps money in the community.

As we change our policies on everything from transportation to agriculture, we are going to see that local money circulating, and people will feel better spending more because they get to know the farmer and they are getting this spectacular experience. And farmers' markets also protect land around the urban fringe.

I think we'll also be seeing more personal forms of agriculture, like rooftop kitchen gardens on top of our flat-roofed urban buildings. At the Rocket Restaurant in Portland, for example, the chef has rooftop raised gardening beds. He is growing some amazing fruits and vegetables that he serves at his restaurant below, including some exotic vegetables that are too delicate to transport. A rooftop salad. He's giving his customers the freshest ingredients while saving money on buying and transporting produce.

>> President Obama has made a lot of promises about expanding renewable energy, reducing greenhouse gas emissions nationwide, and accelerating the development of green buildings, among many other sustainability plans. Will the current economic crisis limit or even kill such initiatives?

Yes and no. The current economic crisis will make the task more complicated, but in a perverse way it may be just what we need. Temporarily, Congress is relaxing some of the strict budget-balancing requirements. The very definition of economic stimulus is that it's deficit finance.

Once we cross that bridge, we have an excellent chance of including in the economic stimulus package significant energy-efficient infrastructure, and targeting technologies and development strategies that reduce the carbon footprint and enhance our communities.

One of my chief interests is strengthening the partnership between utility companies and environmental organizations to accelerate the retrofit of our power grid and embed renewable energy in the utilities.

>> We have discussed some daunting problems and costly, difficult solutions. Are you hopeful, pessimistic, or somewhere in between about the nation's ability to recognize these problems and take the necessary measures?

From my vantage point, we have a once-in-a-generation opportunity—maybe a once-in-a-century opportunity—created by the convergence of the challenges that we face and the path to sustainability. They match up perfectly. That convergence is going to lead to the next generation of technology and renewable energy and green building. Everything that we have talked about in our conversation actually saves money and makes money and offers hope. They provide a wider range of opportunities for people who work in blue-collar and white-collar and green-collar industries. They create opportunities to bring people together at a time of economic anxiety and concern about the future of the country and the planet, and chart a new and more hopeful course.

With a potentially transformational president and this convergence of events, we have a chance in a remarkably short period of time—no more than a decade—to implement the changes I've discussed and actually see the results.

Americans are moving from fright and apprehension to an understanding of this opportunity. I see the shift in attitude everywhere. I'm more encouraged now than at any other time in my public career.

MICHAEL GAINER

Michael Gainer is a political organizer, teacher, contractor, and the founder and executive director of the not-for-profit Buffalo ReUse Inc., which deconstructs buildings and recycles, salvages, and reuses their construction materials. Gainer and Buffalo ReUse also provide green job training and employment for young adults.

"In most of the country, even if people want to do the right thing, they are not going to pay two or three times more for something because it's green, or cool, or 'in.' Anything green, including deconstruction, must make sense financially."

Every year, tens of thousands of U.S. houses are demolished, sending tons of recyclable building materials to landfills. Still more mountains of recyclable materials come from buildings and homes undergoing extensive renovations. Standing in front of the demolition bulldozers is Gainer. His "green deconstruction" insights extend far beyond housing to any kind of structure—factory, warehouse, office building, retail center—and to more sustainable community land use and development patterns.

>> How did you start Buffalo ReUse?

I attended a building reuse conference in Atlanta and I knew I had finally found my call-ing, my role. I saw a better way to both help the urban infrastructure and provide young adult-training job programs for kids who were out of school and out of work.

To start, a consultant and I put together some presentations about building deconstruc-tion and reuse. With a working group of 15 to 20 people, I prepared our mission and vision statements, talked to people in the community, and talked to the city's political leaders.

About six months later, I approached Empire State Development [ESD, the lead eco-nomic development entity for New York state] to get some funding to do a research and development pilot program on building deconstruction in Buffalo. We got unofficial ap-proval in April 2007, so we got to work. We deconstructed our first house that month.

We salvaged over six tons of reusable lumber, as well as doors, windows, foundation stone, bricks, and fixtures. We recycled metals, clean waste wood, and concrete. Two weeks later, we deconstructed our second house.

In the summer of 2007, we began organizing Buffalo ReUse to operate on a full-time basis and to get more funding. In September 2007, we started working full-time with a crew of five employees. We got official approval from ESD in November 2007. Our first check from the state arrived in April 2008. Thus far, from government and private sources, we've received nearly $250,000 in seed funding.

Our goal is for the city of Buffalo to invest $150 million to $250 million in deconstructing unwanted structures, most of which would otherwise be dumped in landfills.

>> What work has Buffalo ReUse undertaken in Buffalo, and why?

A two-story house will yield about 45 tons of rubble when conventional demolition contractors crunch up the house and haul it away in dumpsters. Buffalo ReUse Services, however, deconstructs residential structures, and then salvages and recycles the majority of materials from those buildings. We also remove appliances, cabinetry, fixtures, and other materials from buildings about to undergo a renovation.

We resell the materials that we salvage in our ReSource store to the community for use in repairs and improvements to existing buildings. Many of these materials can be used in new ways. We can, for example, take old-growth wood like floor joists, wall studs, and rafters to a lumber mill where it gets turned into three or four different products for baseboards, paneling, and flooring.

We just don't go into a neighborhood, deconstruct a house, and leave. A critical part of our work includes job training and leadership development for young men and women 18 to 24 years old. That's key.

The organization was born out of the current housing crisis in the city. We have 10,000 to 15,000 abandoned houses, most of them on the east side of Buffalo. We are also seeing an increase in abandonment in inner suburbs like Tonawanda, Cheektowaga, and Lackawanna.

The city of Buffalo peaked in 1950 with just under 600,000 people. We have a population now of 270,000 people, so it's half of what it used to be, and we are left with an infrastructure that's twice the size of what we need. Although the housing stock has aged and in many cases has not been maintained, there is still a tremendous amount of high-quality materials of significance and character that have survived a hundred years or more and will outlast many contemporary building materials if they can be diverted from the wrecking ball and the landfill.

Right now, the city employs the usual cookie-cutter solution that you'll find across the country: just tear down anything that's abandoned. It's a political win every time they take down a house, because neighborhoods want empty blighted houses removed, particularly if they pose a threat like a fire hazard or criminal activity. The city has tentatively planned the demolition of 1,000 homes annually for the next ten years at huge cost—$200 million–plus—through Restore New York, a federal grant designed for development, not solely demolition.

Unfortunately, the city is demolishing houses that could be reused and have value later. We are also throwing away tons of reusable materials. Yes, we have a declining population and the city is larger than its current needs, but we must find a middle ground between what's currently being done and what should be done.

If states such as Washington and Colorado can mandate that demolition contractors must recycle up to 40 percent of a building, why can't Buffalo? If it were required that every demolition contractor recycle even 25 percent of a building, it would create an infrastructure for more deconstruction efforts. Demolition contractors would then call *us* to salvage the properties they're demolishing and we could divert thousands of tons of reusable material from the landfill and make those materials accessible to low-income residents and property owners.

Buffalo ReUse and other nonprofit groups in Buffalo that advocate for low-income property owners and job development programs are rallying to convince the mayor that some of the Restore New York funding could go toward spearheading a more sustainable model for our community.

Our cities need to identify neighborhoods where houses should be preserved. That moves us out of the demolition-as-usual mindset and into a lot more strategic planning. Much of the materials from deconstructed houses in severely depressed neighborhoods can be used to repair and improve houses in viable neighborhoods that need to be supported.

>> In what ways has the city of Buffalo, its developers, and its citizens supported—or not supported—the work of Buffalo ReUse?

The city has been very helpful. It crafted RFPs [requests for proposals] for deconstruction. City officials have met with us to work on job training and neighborhood development.

We have a contract from the city to take down ten buildings, which is enough, hopefully, to take care of our costs—$9,000 to $12,000 depending on the size of the house. That's competitive with traditional demolition. That's our goal for our R&D grant: we want to demonstrate that building deconstruction can be a competitive option over the wholesale demolition and dumping of buildings.

We have a strong network of support that includes many volunteers, community organizations, and positive press attention.

>> Why would a city, or a developer, or other property owner invest in building deconstruction? What's in it for them?

In most of the country, even if people want to do the right thing, they are not going to pay two or three times more for something because it's green, or cool, or "in." Anything green, including deconstruction, must make sense financially.

We are a not-for-profit organization. We recently received our 501(c)(3) approval. We can offer tax deductions to a property owner—homeowner or developer or the city—based on the resale value of the materials that we salvage, as verified by a third-party appraiser. The amount usually varies from $8,000 to $12,000 for a middle-class house in Buffalo, although it can be higher based on the value of the materials. That also helps us be competitive with standard demolition, even if our labor costs are slightly higher.

>> How much material are you recycling from demolished houses?

That depends on whether or not the building has a foundation. Our goal is to recycle more than 50 percent in tons of a fully built house. When we can reuse the stone from the foundation, we get a higher diversion ratio. If the house doesn't have a foundation, we might only be able to recycle 30 percent.

The reality is that most houses have a lot of heavy materials that are not recyclable, like plaster walls and often four or five layers of asphalt shingles, which have contamination challenges.

Our goal is to deconstruct a house as quickly and efficiently as possible so we can get to the really salvageable materials—foundation stones, beams, two-by-eights and two-by-tens, tongue-and-groove subfloors, finished floors, windows, doors, cabinets, hardware.

We want to take down a building in a time-efficient and cost-effective manner so we can get to more houses and divert more total material from the landfill. So we are conducting cost/benefit analyses. Does it make sense to carefully remove paneling, plaster, and lath just to get to some two-by-fours? Or is it better to lose some recyclable wood to move faster and do more houses?

We're learning as we go. For example, we're now using a new technique called hybrid deconstruction that combines human labor with the use of a telescopic forklift. We used to take down the buildings in a very traditional manner: we started with the roof, then we'd take off the siding, take out the floors, and slowly hand down the roof rafters. It took us five to six weeks to deconstruct one structure.

With our new technique, we can deconstruct a house in six to eight days, not six to eight weeks. Maybe we divert 45 percent of the material, rather than 55 percent, but we can do so many more houses. At the end of the month, we have diverted tons and tons more material, although it's fewer tons per house.

>> Isn't your hybrid deconstruction technique applicable to areas that are actually growing, where houses are being demolished to make way for new development?

Yes. Even in our city, half of our projects have been part of redevelopment programs—mostly private development. We just completed a project for Mercy Hospital. We have done three projects for one developer here who is putting up condominiums. Hybrid deconstruction is a tool that can be used anywhere.

Green deconstruction overall has great promise because it is more efficient, which increases its competitiveness. We also offer tax deductions, which helps make green deconstruction more financially viable.

We are also finding a growing consciousness among builders. They want to tap into the credits of green building programs. With green deconstruction, they can get LEED [Leadership in Energy and Environmental Design] points for recycling, reclaiming, and reusing building materials from a demolished structure.

>> Do Buffalo and other cities run the risk of demolishing houses that could be desirable in the future?

Sad to say, cities like Buffalo are doing this every day. Two buildings that I would deem as highly desirable came down on Northampton Street recently. They could have been saved; they could have been rehabilitated; they could have been assets for the neighborhood, and now they are gone.

Older buildings that could be rehabilitated and become valuable assets to a neighborhood are being replaced with new buildings made with the cheapest materials, composite materials, vinyl siding. They don't fit with the architectural quality and integrity of the rest of the neighborhood.

We don't have enough hours in the day or the resources to save and rehabilitate these wonderful older houses. Our cities and communities need to develop an interim strategy for how we can save these buildings now, mothball them for the future, and make them useful and valuable assets later. That tool has not been taken out of the toolbox yet.

We are starting to pilot test different creative strategies, like the Community Peace Mural Project, which was a collaboration between our organization and 30 schools. The students created works of art on four-by-eight sheets of plywood that we then attached to vacant housing near the schools. The project addressed the community concerns that vacant houses are ugly and dangerous by beautifying those houses and making them more secure so that people cannot easily enter them.

We want residents and schools invested in their neighborhoods again—try to get them to envision new things for their neighborhoods. In another project, we are working with a neighborhood school to plant 150 trees in the neighborhood. The project is getting students to come out with their parents and get involved.

>> **Is there some cutoff date when a house that lacks high-quality materials can no longer be saved and reused? For example, is there anything of real value in cheaply built post–World War II tract houses?**

Yes, there is. As with all houses, it really depends on water and fire damage and how much it has been stripped. We can always recycle something. Even if we cannot reuse the lumber, we can recycle it so it doesn't go to the landfill. It gets ground up into mulch used in a community garden, or a park, or someone's front yard.

Of course, whatever the age of the house, we have to be cautious about toxins. We don't recycle painted wood of any era; no post–World War II plywood with glue. Prewar houses have higher-quality materials, but you still must be careful.

>> **Can entire blocks be cleared—with the utilities turned off to save money—and stockpiled for possible future development demand? Buffalo, for example, is located on Lake Erie, which could make the city a highly valuable and desirable location in the future if the United States starts running out of water.**

I have thought about that idea. It's a challenging situation. Buffalo has very few completely abandoned streets with nobody living on them, so it's tricky about relocating people, particularly ones who have spent their entire lives there.

But look at the Genesee County Land Bank near Flint, Michigan. They have land banked and removed structures and put land away for future use. That's a successful model that can be duplicated in Buffalo and elsewhere.

We need to right-size Buffalo. We need to stabilize neighborhoods close to jobs and community assets like libraries and schools and create vibrant community districts with mass transit. That's applicable to any city with a declining population.

>> **On November 16 to 18, 2008, Buffalo ReUse Services cosponsored the first Great Lakes Deconstruction Conference, which offered creative solutions and innovative practices to address many of the issues we've discussed. What was the best thing to come out of that conference?**

We had 150 people show up, from practitioners like contractors and architects to government policy people. They came from Detroit, Cleveland, Pittsburgh, Rochester, Syracuse, Albany, the entire Great Lakes region, plus Pennsylvania, Massachusetts, even Ontario.

The best thing was the transfer of knowledge, the tremendous sharing of information at the conference. Youngstown, Ohio's Mayor Jay Williams, for example, shared his ideas about right-sizing and giving tax incentives to folks to bring people closer to the city center and reduce costs.

The most reassuring thing about the conference was the intention of those 150 people to use their money and resources to be more creative in both development and redevelopment. They were trying to turn one problem—abandoned buildings—into multiple opportunities. Many activities overlap, from demolition and redevelopment to recycling, revitalizing downtowns and neighborhoods, creating more urban open space, redirecting development patterns, and job training for young people.

>> What lessons does Buffalo ReUse offer other cities—including those that are demolishing homes or other buildings for site or district redevelopment?

First of all, I feel like there's a lot to share, but we also have a lot to learn. We hosted the Great Lakes Deconstruction Conference not because we have all the answers, but to bring people to the table who can share best practices and provide inspiration and energy and focus on how to initiate similar efforts in cities struggling with similar issues.

One of the biggest lessons Buffalo ReUse offers is how to leave the neighborhood in a better place following deconstruction. With conventional demolition practices, the building is knocked down and that's it. The street and the neighborhood have an ugly empty gash. Grass isn't even planted.

At Buffalo ReUse, we want to enhance spaces and create new assets like pocket parks, and community gardens, outdoor performance space for the high school, and athletics fields so kids don't have to play soccer or baseball in the street. Even just planting trees and installing short fence lines increase the property value of the vacant lot and demonstrates to the public that someone cares about the space and is watching over it.

We want communities to take ownership and decide what *they* want to do with the space we have created.

Another lesson is that we must evaluate which houses can be deconstructed and which houses should be demolished. Maybe the roof has leaked so much that the interior is unsalvageable. Maybe the house was fire bombed. Those kinds of structures may require more time and money for deconstruction than they are worth. At the same time, they do have a foundation, water, sewer, electrical. That infrastructure is a good framework for reconstruction.

We must, as I pointed out before, identify the healthier neighborhoods that should be preserved, not pockmarked by the loss of a few bad houses.

>> If you could wave a magic wand and get anything you wanted, what would it be?
I am an idealist grounded in practicality. You have to be. It's not enough for something to be a good idea; you have to implement it in a cost-effective manner.

So, the biggest thing I would want is that we start as a community making decisions that have a long-term impact on our collective future, whether it's how we deal with materials and use or how we educate our children.

A lot of people consider these abandoned houses to be liabilities. We see them as assets, both as homes and materials.

We want to provide a home and jobs for young adults who are out of school and out of work. Our community doesn't have a lot of respect for these young adults. You can identify a community's commitment by how they spend their money. Not one dollar in Buffalo has been allocated for 16- to 20-year-olds. But we *are* paying for them—with police, with criminal justice. We are not thinking long term on how best to solve problems and important issues. Our goal is to connect the dots.

With my wand, I'd put young people to work improving the quality of life in our neighborhoods and empowering them with marketable skills and knowledge and experience that enable them to develop a strong sense of self-worth and direction for their lives.

So, you have a community development tool, an education tool, and you improve the quality of life for people living in your community—a win-win-win.

CÉSAR ULISES TREVIÑO

César Ulises Treviño founded the Mexico Green Building Council (Consejo Mexicano de Edificación Sustentable, or Mexico GBC) in 2005 and is its current president. He is a committee member of the International Initiative for a Sustainable Built Environment and he has been secretary general and treasurer of the World Green Building Council (WGBC).

"Being the first nonprofit creating advanced green building practices, we were facing every single challenge possible. We were the first to hand the green building award out, so we were required to solve every issue: educational, technical, market driven. There was nothing else around. . . . We were like a green building midwife."

After an initial delay, Latin America is now embracing the green building movement. Mexico has been joined as a WGBC member by Brazil and most recently by Argentina. Other nearby nations are forming green building councils. Latin America can learn from European and U.S. best practices and occasional missteps to reap the cost and health benefits of green buildings. It also can show Europe and the United States how to use simple, moderate-cost strategies from its own longstanding building practices to achieve green building advantages. Treviño provides invaluable insights into these issues, and many more.

>> When was the Mexico Green Building Council founded?

The council was conceived in 2003 and relaunched in 2005.

>> When did the Mexico Green Building Council become an official full member of the World Green Building Council?

Mexico GBC was a founding member of the WGBC in 2003.

>> How many members does the Mexico GBC currently have?

We don't offer individual memberships. We want to keep the organization to corporate memberships, from small to large companies. Like the USGBC membership structure, our corporate affiliates come from similar types of businesses: manufacturing, design and engineering, financial institutions, and other NGOs [nongovernment organizations]. It's all goodwill where we work together—positive synergy. We have over 60 corporate memberships, including Cemex, Colliers, Carrier, Holcim, HSBC, Loreto Bay, Milliken, and Trane.

>> When will the Mexico GBC launch SICES [Sistema de Calificación para Edificaciones Sustentables], its new green building rating tool?

Of course, as any green building council does, one of our first tasks was to assess what opportunities we had to create our own market transformation tool—our own green building rating system. We stopped the development of the new system very early because we ran the preliminary analysis to determine if we had in Mexico enough regulations and building codes to create something equivalent to CASBEE [Comprehensive Assessment System for Building Environmental Efficiency, Japan]; LEED [Leadership in Energy and Environmental Design, United States]; Green Star [Australia]; and BREEAM [Building Research Establishment Environmental Assessment Method, United Kingdom].

We reviewed different areas like indoor air quality, resource management, water conservation, and we had to put SICES on standby because we found that we didn't have enough relevant regulations that could go into a green building rating system, and because third-party certifying and regulating bodies must be overseen by several public organizations. Hence, creating our own system would imply the development of new codes and even reshaping legal frameworks. We found out that it wasn't realistic to create and deploy a national system in less than three to five years.

We are working on ground preparation activities. We particularly want to encourage more commitment from the Mexico GBC members. We need more critical mass, and a broader representation from the industry. Soon, we will have reached the point when we will have more voices, more affiliates and partners, and they will have input in such an initiative. This effort will resume in a few years.

Meanwhile, we have gotten closer to the USGBC [U.S. Green Building Council]. We have devised a collaborative scheme. Knowing the power of LEED in Mexico and in Canada, and being part of NAFTA [North America Free Trade Agreement], if we wanted to make an immediate impact, we knew we would be better off using a rating system that has international recognition and can be adapted to the Mexican market.

So, we decided to set our view and eyes closer to the USGBC. We have a license agreement with the USGBC for Mexico. We are specifically partners in educational programs. We will be the entity in our country that will offer official LEED workshops and reference guides. We have started to promote LEED in workshops and seminars.

>> How many buildings in Mexico have earned LEED certification?

Still only two. The first building was the International Business Center [Centro Interna-cional de Negocios, or CIN] in Ciudad Juárez, Chihuahua, opposite El Paso, Texas. It is a 50,000-square-foot (4,600-square-meter) office building that earned a basic LEED certi-fied rating in 2006. The 32-story, 855,000-square-foot (80,000-square-meter) HSBC Corporate Tower in Mexico City earned a LEED Gold rating in 2007.

>> Why have so few Mexican buildings earned LEED ratings?

Earning LEED certification is a rigorous, time-consuming, and pricey process. The develop-ers and investors have been waiting to see if it was actually possible to achieve a LEED building. We had no experience in Mexico until recently. We are where the United States was five or six years ago.

During the course of the HSBC Tower project, most people remained skeptical. They were waiting for the five-year design, construction, and certification process to end.

The HSBC Corporate Tower got much more publicity than the Juárez office building because it was a much larger high-rise tower and because it was located in a prominent Mexico City location. People then realized that it was possible to construct a LEED build-ing in Mexico with domestic resources. As soon as we achieved the LEED Gold certifica-tion in late 2007, it was possible to feel the renewed interest in registering projects for LEED certification. We now have over 60 registered buildings countrywide.

Out of those buildings, a few started with great interest, but they were not well-guided and they have dropped off. Many other projects are using LEED as a guideline for their design and best practices, but some have decided not to pursue actual certification. So, LEED is having an impact far beyond those 60 registered projects.

Some developers say, "I want to be conservative. I don't want to take risks on my success formula. I will try to be green and I will use LEED, but I don't want to go into the formal certification process because the market is just waking up." But some forward thinkers realize that their decisions today will be effective in several years, when the mar-ket will be very different. They will be reaping the benefits of having LEED certification in the building image, in rents, and in true building value.

The companies and developers who complete or start green buildings now will have a real advantage. As tenants start to demand green buildings, which happened in many U.S. cities in 2007 and 2008, they will have those properties to rent out. If people wait four or five years before they start a green building, when they finally complete the project, they will be competing against many other properties whose owners also waited four or five years just to be certain that green was really coming to Mexico.

>> **LEED is a highly respected and increasingly influential system. Yet, many American real estate owners, developers, architects, engineers, and other professionals complain that it is complicated and expensive. What is your experience with LEED in Mexico?**

Right now, using LEED is a burden in some respects. First, is the actual cost of the registration and certification process. Second, we must translate from U.S. measurement systems [inches, feet, and gallons] to metric units. Third, we must register and document projects in English language. Fourth, one of the main challenges is that we are to follow foreign codes and regulations that most Mexican practitioners are not acquainted with.

Fifth—the big challenge—is that we must work on education. In my point of view, LEED is coming quickly to the Mexican market. Until recently, there was very little awareness for sustainability in general, and now the first green issue developers know is LEED.

It is a challenge when you go from zero to high-performance so fast. It's a big step. The market sees that LEED is a very effective transformation tool, but it is composed of different codes and new players and environmental indicators like indoor air quality plans, commissioning agents, green product labels, full energy modeling, etc., that are not part of the conventional design and building practice in Mexico.

The challenge in many firms is their capability to deploy according to LEED standards, to be flexible enough, and to be willing to adapt quickly. The companies are facing new challenges, and new requirements, new procedures, new calculations. Many leading companies are capable of adapting quickly; they just need more green building guidance and field experience. The firms that are heading those current 60 LEED-registered projects are adapting the most quickly.

I frequently tell the investors, owners, and fellow professionals, "You want world-class certification in environmental performance and energy efficiency, but are *you* changing enough?" Some want the certification without making a profound commitment and transformation. "If you don't put in enough commitment and enough knowledge into what you are getting into," I say, "you won't gain all the tangible and intangible benefits of your green actions."

In Mexico, we see a lot of misinformation, and naturally, the market gets confused. In the U.S., there are different green building rating systems. Here, we don't have that issue. Our issue is a lack of information, so people misinterpret what LEED is all about.

Some people are very optimistic, and they see everything in a rosy pink color and think LEED certification is a piece of cake. They soon realize that it's tough and demanding. Other people drop out of LEED certification early because they think that it would be too complicated or expensive. There's only gossip and that misinformation spreads out.

>> What is one of the most widespread pieces of misinformation?

The most common misinformation is the alleged extra cost of green design and construction. Some contractors or professionals claim that it is 20 percent. That's wrong and unsubstantiated. That's a curious claim when they haven't done any green buildings or sustainable developments at all.

We are showing people that the truth is a much lower cost premium—even no extra cost, or even less cost than a conventional building, and operations savings. We are documenting those case studies. We have number-filled studies from other countries.

The incremental cost for the LEED Gold HSBC Corporate Tower was 5 percent. That is below the U.S. cost premium of a few years ago for a LEED Gold high rise.

>> Mexico, like many countries trying to adopt sustainability practices, struggles with poverty, pollution, and governmental challenges. How can the Mexico GBC surmount these challenges to really make green buildings and broader sustainability efforts a vital part of Mexico's built environment, government policies, and business practices?

The Mexico GBC is supporting green building at local and national levels for all kinds of buildings, commercial and institutional. We are spreading the word of good practices and success stories. We are approaching the municipal governments to explain the benefits from green building and infrastructure for the government—how it benefits them.

The Mexican government is taking some real actions to bring green to the entire population. The National Environmental Ministry, for example, is concerned about climate change. Mexico wants to pioneer one of the first large [green residential] projects as a candidate for its clean development mechanism—create a protocol for large housing developments that would be recognized as energy efficient and CO_2 friendly. They would trade their saved carbon, which is another financial incentive. The protocol is far advanced. By the end of this year, it will be submitted to the U.N.'s Climate Change Initiative. It is a very complex process to create the protocol and have it be accepted. The payoff won't make up for the time, but if we create a model, it can be reused on other projects.

Right now, we are working together with some governmental organizations that are responsible for housing development, particularly low income. They are looking for expertise to help them to develop their own green expertise for buildings and neighborhood development.

The lead agency, Conavi [Comisión Nacional de Vivienda, the Mexican government's National Housing Commission], is responsible for the promotion and development of housing in the country. In Mexico, we have the challenge of constructing 700,000 residential units a year to accommodate the rising population, and most of the housing is low income. The government wants some part of that new stock to be designed and built in a greener fashion, so this agency is creating new standards for green design and construction, with a focus on energy efficiency, water conservation, and better use of construction materials. The standards are being developed now; they are not done.

In the near future, the program will include healthier building materials. Not right now. You can only do so much at the start. Otherwise, you are too ambitious.

The private sector will build the housing with financial support from the government, and the government will offer low-interest loans to the homebuyers. The government launched [in 2008] a green mortgage program where the developer is allowed about $1,000 extra money to put into green technologies for the housing—specifically, thermal solar systems for domestic hot water, energy-efficient appliances and lighting, better insulation, and water-saving toilets and showers.

At the end of the day, with the green mortgage the final user can buy a house that includes green or sustainable technologies and that saves money.

>> Will the new low-income green housing be certified?

This initiative is planned to turn into an assessment and rating system for low-income housing and development. Eventually, we want to propose a certification scheme. At this point, we don't know if it will be voluntary or compulsory; it's still in the planning stages.

Once the low-income green homes rating system is finalized, we expect more subsidy money for low-income green housing. We think that this sector will grow quickly in the future.

>> How important is green infrastructure to Mexico?

Very important. The legal framework for the development of infrastructure—roads, utilities, sewers, harbors—has very little environmental protection. We are sending out the message by developing green projects near environmentally sensitive areas that there is a better opportunity long term where conservation is a key. Many eco-tourism programs are being successfully reported where people previously used to devastate an area. Now, they realize in protecting those natural settings that they make immediate money, create a more sustainable community, and create long-term value for the development. When [they're] 25 or 30 years old, the buildings will be worth upgrading because of their protected setting.

>> Are companies in Mexico supporting the market shift to green buildings?

Corporations want their own facilities to have green certification because it aligns with their corporate social responsibility [CSR] objectives. Big companies want to start their environmental commitment. They first look at their offices and production facilities. They want to lower operational and maintenance costs. They see how they can construct new facilities with a green certification. We see that some of the principal clients for LEED Core and Shell [a ratings system for base building elements such as structure, envelope, and heating and cooling] are these companies. They want to rent a place or occupy an owned facility that demonstrates its ability to reduce its environmental impact.

>> Are these Mexican companies, or international companies in Mexico?

Both, now. Two years ago, it was transnational companies located in Mexico. Now, CSR policies have gained terrain in small and large companies in Mexico. So, the interest is all over. They want to commit to sustainability in a tangible, real form. The LEED certification is the believable proof, not a press release.

>> What are the major roadblocks to moving green buildings into the Mexican mainstream?

Of course, the green costs that we talked about. That's a problem in so many nations.

We do have one real cost problem—getting reasonably priced green building products that are not readily available in Mexico right now. We don't have formal Mexican manufacturers for zero-VOC [volatile organic compound] paints and sealants. We have some low-VOC manufacturers, but that's not those products' main selling point. We cannot find high-performance kitchen appliances and air conditioners in our stores. If you want high-performance products, they must be specially ordered.

If you ask stores about high-performance items, they don't want to be bothered. They want to make the easiest sales pitch. They don't want to bother making the harder sales of these high-performance technologies. They want to keep the same level.

Often, manufacturers and stores say that there is not enough demand in Mexico. Yes, the market needs to grow up to create the demand for these products. We just need to be able to purchase the products.

The U.S. had the same problem five or six years ago. Most green products and technologies were more expensive than conventional ones, or they were hard to find. Now, of course, plenty of reasonably priced, easy-to-find green products and technologies are available in the U.S. Eventually, demand for these products in Mexico will grow, and the market will solve the cost and availability problem.

Do you want to know what really bothers me? Some high-performance products are being manufactured here for export and we never get to see them. If we want them, you must pay for the import [from the countries where the manufacturers sell these products], shipping, and taxes. High-quality photovoltaics are being manufactured in Tijuana, but those products are for export only. That's pitiful.

We know that Mexican factories manufacture air-conditioning units that are higher efficiency than the ones being sold in the domestic marketplace, and we don't get to see that line of products offered in the country.

The next roadblock is the availability of technical and professional resources. Right now, we really need professional education for every party engaged—architects, engineers, and builders. Many professionals love to talk about *green* or *sustainable*, but how does that really translate into facts or simple actions? How much do they really know? Green sells—it's the right thing to do for building and construction—but who can show you the way? Who can advise you so that you don't get discouraged or illogically happy about issues without knowing the commitment required? Every nation needs this professional body of knowledge.

LEED is great, but the education must be part of greater green practices in Mexico. When people go from nothing to one high-performance green system, you see some very curious results when they interpret green in their own way. If you don't have the education and information to understand the intent of the credits, people get confused and they make decisions for projects which are not really effective. Or you overdesign or overtechnify a green building and create an overly complex solution that is expensive for the value of the benefits and hard to maintain over time.

So, having the concept of integrated design as a part of green building development is key. We need to get our 101, our first lessons, right. We are going to make important progress very quickly. I wouldn't be surprised if the number of projects grows exponentially when it happens, just as it has done in the U.S. over the past five years. Are we ready? Are there enough professionals? Is there enough knowledge sharing and networking?

We have other challenges. At one point, two or three years ago, being the first nonprofit creating advanced green building practices, we [the Mexico GBC] were facing every single challenge possible. We were the first to hand the green building award out, so we were required to solve every issue: educational, technical, market driven. There was nothing else around, so we had the challenge to solve every single item on the request list. We were like a green building midwife.

>> **Are building codes and standards a problem for green buildings in Mexico? Do they block or discourage many green features as they have done in many nations, including the U.S.?**

Yes, it is a problem. We have building codes, of course, about the type of building that can be constructed in a location and its density. But in terms of more advanced codes, there are not enough. And Mexico does not have enough building regulations to cover green buildings. We have regulations for energy efficiency, something related to sustainable management of the site, and hazardous waste. But if you are talking about advanced ideas, about indoor air quality, or life-cycle analysis, or green building products, we are not there yet. There are few regulations, and the ones that we do have, like energy efficiency for commercial buildings, they are not followed by the developers. So, that's a frightening thing.

The government was also concerned about foreign building standards coming into Mexico—that people would follow them, but they wouldn't follow or even know about equivalent Mexican regulations. I understand the authorities' concern. They told us, if you want support, we need to see how we can include our own regulations into this LEED rating system and include equivalent criteria in our building codes, because otherwise the government sees that the market or building professionals are prioritizing foreign codes instead of national codes.

>> How will the current global recession affect green buildings in Mexico? Are green buildings at risk in today's economy?

At this point in time, I can tell you something different: we are seeing that green buildings are becoming a market differentiation opportunity for many developers. Yes, many projects are being halted or not started, but we see that the ones going forward are using better green practices.

And here's something interesting: developers are now recognizing the value of green. I often get the telephone calls: "We just finished this project. Is there anything that I can do, any retrofits, to increase the operations savings for condo purchasers?" Green building is becoming a very attractive option during these difficult times.

Developers are reassessing how they create and develop buildings, and they are looking for innovative ways to offer good products. And the users are becoming more aware of environmental issues. If buildings include genuine green elements, they can overcome the constrained market.

>> Many other nations like Argentina, Poland, and Vietnam that now want to have green buildings and make sustainability more important for their nations are "emerging" members of the World Green Building Council. What advice can you offer these nations?

Right now, the Mexico GBC is in the very early stages of assisting Costa Rica, Colombia, and several other countries.

For Mexico, one of the most important recommendations is focus on the assessment regulations, roles, and responsibilities of public and private organizations so the GBC can identify as soon as possible what roles it could play and how it can include itself in the overall construction in their country.

Become educators; develop new regulations. You should promote new projects, focus on gaining greater support from corporations.

These new GBCs will find challenges on every front. In our case, we had to understand how to focus our efforts, where we should put our energy, how to collaborate with other organization that could be partners in the larger context of green building so we could be more effective.

The Mexico GBC has a very important message to deliver: if the government is taking the lead on low-income green housing, why try to do it? Be one of the supporting organizations to that government program. Take the lead on something else that the government is not doing.

Focus on a few issues. You cannot do everything. Focus your time and energy on what really matters.

S. RICHARD FEDRIZZI

In 1993, S. Richard Fedrizzi became the founding chairman of the U.S. Green Building Council (USGBC), and in 2004 was appointed president and chief executive officer. He also was one of the founders of the World Green Building Council (WGBC) in 2002.

"This economic firestorm we've been through has been a wakeup call at many levels. When it comes to what the building industry can affect, we've learned that using less saves more than money, that quality endures, that it's not enough to do the same thing better. We need to do different things. And we are."

In the past five years, Fedrizzi has helped triple USGBC's membership and significantly expand its national and international leadership on sustainability and green building issues. In the nearly two years since his last interview, he has overseen the Leadership in Energy and Environmental Design (LEED) program's ongoing evolution and helped guide the USGBC through a global recession. He discusses the impact of the economic crisis on the USGBC, green buildings, and the sustainability movement.

>> Do you think the global economic crisis will stall—or even kill—green buildings?

Sustainability issues—issues such as climate change and fossil-fuel dependence, clean drinking water, and food safety—are some of the most pressing issues of our time, and the economic times in which we find ourselves don't change that fact. But as I keep telling people, if there ever were a catalyst for the green revolution, it should be the outrageous financial mess that we currently find ourselves in.

By the numbers, green development continues to experience a powerful trajectory precisely because green buildings create jobs that can save energy, water, and money—and drive innovation and global competitiveness in the process. That's a straightforward business solution to a financial problem, and it can provide immediate returns.

By their nature, green buildings are in lockstep with the imperatives of today's realities: doing more with less, doing the simple now, reusing and repurposing not just materials, but also people and their skills, and engaging them in the rewards and responsibilities of the low-carbon future as participants, not bystanders.

While some of the 30,000-plus LEED projects in the pipeline will undoubtedly come on line somewhat slower than originally envisioned, there's little evidence that green building practices are experiencing any sort of downturn. In fact, we're finding anecdotally that interest in greening existing buildings is *increasing* because of the amount of money it saves, whether you're a family in the suburbs, a global corporation with a huge building portfolio, a school, a hospital, or a big-box retailer.

And many of the means to accomplish these savings are small, fast-payback investments. On the energy front, there are weather stripping and insulation, energy-efficient appliances, smart controls that monitor energy use and shut off lights and other systems automatically, green roofs, better use of daylight, individual temperature controls in workstation areas rather than across entire floors. On the water front, there are low-flow plumbing fixtures, dual-flush toilets, and rainwater-capture and graywater systems that save precious potable water for drinking and funnel the rest to landscaping and toilet uses. Some of this will pick up because of the new stimulus dollars, and some of it was already being driven by municipal and state rebates and tax incentives.

The world has changed, and people are beginning to change their habits and mindsets. Sustainability is our future—if our intent is to have one.

>> How has the economic crisis affected the USGBC? Are fewer new members joining?

We have more than 19,000 organizational members of USGBC. We had 2,400 new members sign up in the first quarter of 2009—that's an *increase* in our growth rate—including Boston University, Carter Real Estate, city of Cincinnati, city of Napa [California], Hearst Corporation, and Orkin Commercial Services, among others. Other recent members include Chevron, Procter & Gamble, Wells Real Estate Funds, the North Face, MetLife, and Microsoft.

More interesting, retention is about 76 percent. That's a little down from 2007's 79 percent, but we think we'll be back there by the end of the quarter.

But the numbers matter far less than the hands-on active engagement of our members in everything we do. USGBC is a hybrid organization. We're more social entrepreneurship than trade association, especially in how we engage our stakeholders as true partners in developing and advancing our mission. We find that our members join us precisely for this reason—they want to participate in shaping our new green economy, and we need every one of them to continue our success.

>> How has the economic crisis affected your LEED program? Have you registered fewer green buildings for certification since October 2008?

From October 2007 to October 2008, we registered 2,850 projects, about 600 million square feet [55.7 million square meters]. From October 2008 to March 2009, we registered about 4,650 projects, just under 1 billion square feet [93 million square meters] in six months. That's impressive. With the credit situation being what it is, of course, all building is slowed, but we're hearing from virtually every market sector that the commitment to LEED continues to grow.

What's really exciting is the explosive growth in registrations for existing buildings. We registered four times as many projects from 2007 to 2008, and in the first two months of 2009 we registered more projects than we did in all of 2008. This is huge, because it is in our existing building stock where we will make the biggest strides in tackling climate change.

Against this backdrop, we're also rolling out LEED 2009, which is the biggest update to the rating system yet. It includes a number of significant changes across every aspect of the certification program.

The most significant technical change to the rating system was the reweighting of all existing credits and aligning them to a 100-point scale across all the commercial rating systems. Because climate change and energy efficiency continue to be the highest priorities, the highest weightings are given to those credits whose achievement helps address these pressing concerns. We've also established regionally specific environmental priorities with a new credit category that allows projects to earn up to six extra points for credits that are especially important in a given region.

>> Will the recession limit the market for the new LEED programs for retail space and schools?

Twenty percent of America goes to K-12 schools daily. More than a quarter of those students, teachers, and staffs are in buildings that are considered substandard or dangerous to occupant health. We developed LEED for Schools to be a practical rating tool for green schools design, construction, and operations. Green schools have measurable impact on all the dimensions of sustainability, including health, and they also provide economic benefits to cash-strapped school districts. The typical green school saves on average $100,000 a year in direct operating expenses.

The ultimate measure of success is the number of green schools that are built, renovated, and retrofitted for our children. In February 2009, 49 school projects registered and six new school projects became LEED certified. That's twice the recent average for certified projects in one month and the most in one month since August 2008. This brings the total to 1,160 registered and 147 certified school projects through the end of February 2009. There is at least one registered school project in all 50 states, Washington, D.C., and Puerto Rico.

As for retail, we have retailers lined up to participate in the program as soon as it is launched this summer.

The LEED for Retail rating systems—one for new construction and one for commercial interiors—were designed to recognize the unique nature of the retail environment and to address the different types of spaces that retailers need.

And retailers have very different needs. Customer traffic and water use can vary greatly from office buildings, and the lighting needs in particular are very different. Retail also comes with equipment that is unique to restaurants and grocery stores, and that equipment can contribute to process energy loads in ways that hadn't been considered in LEED before. Retail also frequently builds out several identical stores from one prototype. We've included a volume certification process for those projects.

More than 80 project teams have participated in the pilot and they represented all types of retail in all kinds of settings. To date, we have 145 certified projects and 739 registered projects. We expect this to be a very popular rating system going forward.

>> **Many of the USGBC's members develop and manufacture green building materials, products, and technologies. What impact is the recession having on these companies and on the future of green innovations?**

Specifiers in both residential and nonresidential construction predict increased use of green products in the next five years. In fact, nearly the entire industry reports that they are incorporating some kind of green building product into their projects.

In keeping with the push for greater energy efficiency, the highest rates of specification are occurring in the electrical category, followed closely by mechanical, thermal, and moisture protection. Most expect that automation controls will join that leader group rapidly. As retrofits continue to accelerate versus new construction, which is slowing with the economy, the emphasis on products that contribute to energy efficiency will grow, and those sectors will continue to push innovative solutions into the market.

Innovation is a tricky business. The vast majority of innovation in our country has been on incrementals—things that slightly improve upon something that already exists or shaves cost from an existing process. One real game-changing innovation can cause a cascade of new materials, products, and technologies to be created. Green building has been that kind of innovation, and across the board whole categories of the building industry have responded. That might slow down a bit here in the short term, but we're never going back.

>> Has the USGBC worked directly with the Obama Administration on any of its current or future programs?

USGBC is engaging closely with the Obama Administration to demonstrate that immediate and long-term investments in green building and in the green economy are the down-payment needed to restore America's economic leadership.

As federal, state, and local governments work together to rebuild and reenergize our economy through the economic recovery package, the U.S. Green Building Council is focused on supporting the implementation of the federal investment in green and energy-efficient building. Green building is among the cornerstones of a clean-energy economy. The building industry makes up 14.7 percent of U.S. GDP [gross domestic product] and uses 40 percent of our nation's energy. Greening our existing buildings would result in an estimated savings of $160 billion in energy costs while creating green jobs that can't be exported. And that's good news for our nation's economy, state and local government budgets, business bottom lines, and the financial well-being of American families.

USGBC was front and center in advocating for an unprecedented commitment to green solutions in the economic stimulus package. Today, we are working with our members as they help their states and local communities realize the full economic and environmental benefit of the American Recovery and Reinvestment Act of 2009.

We all have a stake in the new green economy, and professionals in every sector of the green building industry are well-positioned to play a part in the implementation of the federal stimulus plan. Some $9 billion is designated to address public safety and other government services, which may include school modernization, renovation, and repair consistent with a recognized green building rating system. For homes professionals, the act provides $5 billion for the federal Weatherization Assistance Program, which provides assistance to low-income families in weatherizing and improving the energy efficiency of their homes. It allocates another $4 billion for the Public Housing Capital Fund, which provides funds to public housing agencies nationwide for the development, funding, and modernization of public housing developments.

Firms and professionals working with commercial and institutional buildings can look to become involved with projects covered under the $5.55 billion granted to the federal General Services Administration [GSA] for federal buildings, including $4.5 billion for measures to make GSA facilities high-performance green buildings, as defined by the 2007 energy law. In additional, the state energy programs received $3.1 billion, and the energy efficiency and conservation block grant received $3.2 billion.

All these things add up to a powerful linkage between green buildings, energy efficiency, and green jobs at a time when all are critically important.

We continue to meet directly with the Administration on its economic recovery plan, providing strategic advice to senior energy and environmental officials on transforming the country's built environment, or presenting bold new ideas on expanding the green economy. And we continue to believe that green building is a central plank to rebuilding a healthy and sustained economy while putting Americans back to work.

>> Has the global recession negatively affected the scope and work of the USGBC's partnership with the Clinton Climate Initiative [CCI].

Absolutely not. In fact, we've recently signed an expanded partnership agreement to work toward radically reducing CO_2 and other greenhouse gas emissions from the built environment on a global scale, with an initial focus on accelerating efforts to drive efficiency in existing buildings.

Retrofitting buildings represents an immediate and measurable opportunity to cut greenhouse gas emissions and improve our economy, and it fits in with CCI's priority to retrofit projects around the world. To date, the Clinton Climate Initiative's Energy Efficiency Building Retrofit Program has helped partners to initiate more than 250 retrofit projects encompassing over 500 million square feet [46 million square meters] of real estate in more than 30 global cities. These include retrofit projects across the municipal, private, commercial, education, and housing sectors.

Clean energy and alternative energy are important but will take time to bring to scale. Energy efficiency is something we can do now.

>> What green building trends will emerge—and really make a difference—in the coming decade?

The innovation that is occurring in the building industry is phenomenal. The work Autodesk is doing that they showed us at Greenbuild [2008] is a step change in the industry's evolution, much like desktop CAD [computer-aided design] was. This change in architectural practice will compress the period of time true integrated design can take hold in the industry. And this is one of dozens of innovations in everything from building materials to systems controls that is reshaping our industry and our environment.

Building green schools is another huge trend. In green schools, the building and how it interacts with its environment becomes curriculum, and that will allow us to raise a whole generation of "sustainability natives." With that embedded knowledge and perspective, those students will dramatically reshape our culture, our political landscape, and our built environment.

Extending the benefits of green building beyond the structural footprint and into the neighborhoods and communities these buildings occupy will be another significant trend. LEED for Neighborhood Development, which will be out this summer [2009], will go a long way toward accelerating smart growth principles and driving a more holistic approach to how we build our communities.

>> Before the economic crisis, what were the greatest roadblocks to green buildings in the United States?

The biggest roadblock was the lack of knowledge people had about green building practice and the misinformation out there that's part and parcel of any significant change to the status quo. When we finally began having enough data to lay out the business case for green building, we were able to make rapid strides. Once people got their foot in the door, the obvious practical benefits became overwhelmingly apparent and virtually every corner of the industry leaped in with both feet. As that happened, knowledge went up, costs went down, and the question ceased to be "should we build green?" and became "how fast can we build green?"

>> Today, what are the greatest impediments to green buildings created by the global recession?

Fear, uncertainty, and doubt—not about green building specifically, but about every aspect of our life. It causes people who should know better to cling more tightly to the status quo that we can't afford. The status quo was to do the least we could to make the most we could. It rewarded cheap and disposable. It encouraged bigger for the sake of bigger.

This economic firestorm we've been through has been a wake-up call at many levels. When it comes to what the building industry can affect, we've learned that using less saves more than money, that quality endures, that it's not enough to do the same thing better. We need to do different things. And we are.